Topics in
Cognitive Development

Volume 1
Equilibration: Theory, Research,
and Application

Topics in Cognitive Development

Marilyn H. Appel, Editor-in-chief
Medical College of Pennsylvania, Philadelphia

Volume 1 **EQUILIBRATION: THEORY, RESEARCH, AND APPLICATION**
Edited by
Marilyn H. Appel, *Medical College of Pennsylvania*
Lois S. Goldberg, *Glassboro State College*

A Continuation Order Plan is available for this series. A continuation order will bring delivery of each new volume immediately upon publication. Volumes are billed only upon actual shipment. For further information please contact the publisher.

A Publication of the Jean Piaget Society

Topics in Cognitive Development

Volume 1
Equilibration: Theory, Research, and Application

Edited by

Marilyn H. Appel
Medical College of Pennsylvania
Philadelphia, Pennsylvania

and

Lois S. Goldberg
Glassboro State College
Glassboro, New Jersey

Plenum Press · New York and London

Library of Congress Cataloging in Publication Data

Main entry under title:

Equilibration.

(Topics in cognitive development; v. 1)
"A publication of the Jean Piaget Society."
The majority of the papers in this collection represent the combined proceedings of the first and second annual symposia of the Society, 1971 and 1972, with revisions and extensions of some papers.
Includes index.
1. Cognition in children—Congresses. 2. Piaget, Jean, 1896-   —Congresses. I. Appel, Marilyn H. II. Goldberg, Lois S. III. Jean Piaget Society. IV. Series. [DNLM: 1. Child psychology—Congresses. 2. Child development—Congresses. 3. Cognition—Congresses. 4. Psychology, Educational—Congresses. W1 TO539LI v. 1 1971-72 [WS105 E66 1971-72]
BF723.C5E64   155.4'13   77-5010
ISBN 0-306-33001-6

© 1977 Plenum Press, New York
A Division of Plenum Publishing Corporation
227 West 17th Street, New York, N.Y. 10011

Printed in the United States of America

Contributors

Marilyn H. Appel   Medical College of Pennsylvania, Philadelphia, Pennsylvania

Hans Furth   Catholic University, Washington, D. C.

Jeanette McCarthy Gallagher   Temple University, Philadelphia, Pennsylvania

Henry Gleitman   University of Pennsylvania, Philadelphia, Pennsylvania

Lila R. Gleitman   University of Pennsylvania, Philadelphia, Pennsylvania

J. McVicker Hunt   University of Illinois, Urbana, Illinois

Bärbel Inhelder   University of Geneva, Geneva, Switzerland

Jonas Langer   University of California, Berkeley, California

Celia Stendler Lavatelli   Late of the University of Illinois, Urbana, Illinois

Lois P. Macomber   Temple University, Philadelphia, Pennsylvania

Jean Piaget   University of Geneva, Geneva, Switzerland

Barbara Z. Presseisen   Research for Better Schools, Philadelphia, Pennsylvania

Elizabeth F. Shipley   University of Pennsylvania, Philadelphia, Pennsylvania

Beth Stephens   University of Texas, Richardson, Texas

Ina C. Uzgiris   Clark University, Worcester, Massachusetts

Preface

Professor Piaget, who at this writing is in his eightieth year, has dedicated his life to the exploration and explanation of the genesis of knowledge. The Piagetian model rests on both a philosophical and a biological foundation, with psychology as the link between these two disciplines.

This volume, the first in a series that will record the official Symposium Proceedings of the Jean Piaget Society, is unique in that it encompasses theoretical, empirical, and applied aspects of Piaget's epistemology. The majority of papers in this collection represent the combined proceedings of the first and second annual symposia of the society. Professor Piaget's address, presented at the First Annual Symposium of the Jean Piaget Society in May, 1971, highlights the papers within this volume. This paper is outstanding in the clarity with which the concept of equilibration is explicated.

It is the intention of the society, through this volume and subsequent ones, to extend the monumental body of knowledge provided by Piaget. The editors hope to implement transmission of the concepts within these selected papers so that they may serve as an impetus for future investigations. We are indebted to those who provided us with the invaluable editorial and secretarial assistance necessary for such an undertaking.

In addition to Professor Piaget's paper, those by Bärbel Inhelder, Hans Furth, and Jeanette Gallagher were presented at the First Annual Symposium of the Society. These were subsequently edited by Calvin Nodine, Rhymes Humphreys, and Jeanette Gallagher and published by the Society in 1972. Revisions and extensions of the original papers are found in the present publication.

Lois S. Goldberg
Marilyn H. Appel

Contents

PART III: APPLICATION

Introduction

The four papers that comprise the first section of this collection are devoted to theoretical considerations within cognitive development. Sequentially, the first three papers are intended to provide a logical structure within which an analysis of the Piagetian concept of equilibration is undertaken. Piaget's own presentation, "Problems of Equilibration," is therefore followed by Hans Furth's commentary, which was given immediately following Piaget's address. Gallagher's explication of the concept of equilibration follows, exploring the biological, logical, and cybernetic antecedents of this construct. The final paper within the first section, by J. McVicker Hunt, considers the implications of Piaget's epigenetic view of intelligence as it relates to sensorimotor development.

In Piaget's paper, "Problems of Equilibration," the three classical factors necessary for cognitive development are delineated. In essence, these factors are the physical environment; innateness or hereditary programming; and social influences. It is Piaget's thesis that in addition a fourth factor, equilibration, must be considered in order to provide for coordination between and among the three classical factors, as well as to suggest the notion of the self-regulations that are necessary at all levels of cognition. Three types of equilibration are suggested: the relationship between assimilation and accommodation; the coordination or conflict among subsystems; and the differentiation and integration of part to whole knowledge.

Furth, in reacting to Piaget's discussion of equilibration, raises three questions. The first asks if, indeed, the concept of equilibration is not more closely related to the classical factor of maturation and hereditary programming than it is to physical or social experience. The second question involves Piaget's use of the term *equilibration.* Furth asks for clarification, noting that *equilibration* refers not only to a process but also to a state. The final question touches upon the issue of whether or not there is an affective or humanistic aspect in intelligence and, further, if this humanistic aspect carries with it some motivational qualities. A brief reply by Piaget then follows Furth's commentary.

Gallagher's paper, "Piaget's Concept of Equilibration: Biological, Logical and Cybernetic Roots," presents an intensive examination of the concept of equilibration. Her paper suggests that Piaget's view of this concept is drawn largely from three interrelated sources. One major source discussed is the influence of the "neobiologists," such as Waddington. Piaget is said to draw analogies between biological and cognitive aspects of self-regulatory mechanisms and Waddington's concepts of "competence," "induction," and "homeorhesis." A second source explored is the influence of the concept of logical necessity, which is said to be reached through a series of progressive equilibrations, explaining not only the transitions from stage but also the transitions between substages. The final source of influence, cybernetics, suggests that through mechanisms such as feedback or precorrection, equilibration can be seen as a stable exchange system that controls the relationship between the organism and his environment.

Finally, in "Sequential Order and Plasticity in Early Psychological Development," J. McVicker Hunt explores some issues that he suggests are raised by Piaget's epigenetic view of intelligence. The first issue concerns the selection of criteria in the determining of levels, structures within stages, and the stages themselves. The process for defining the Hunt–Uzgiris scales of sensorimotor development that follows is illustrative of the concern for the determination of levels or landmarks within stages. The second issue examines ordering within stages, necessitating validation of the sequential organization of intellectual development hypothesized by Piaget. The third issue raised is that of the nature of transition or transformation within or between stages. Hunt suggests that these transitions are implied by changes in behavioral organization based upon coordination of systems, motivational qualities, and generalizations. The final issue relates to the processes or causes that underly these transitions and is investigated by means of the assessment of object construction in five samples under varying learning conditions. The reported results suggest that environmental circumstances substantially influence the rate of sensorimotor development.

Piagetian-inspired research has proliferated both within the United States and abroad. Outstanding among contributors to the extant body of research has been Bärbel Inhelder, Piaget's long-time collaborator. Her paper opens the second section, which presents five research papers notable for their investigation of a wide variety of topics with varying populations, in diverse geographic locations.

With "Information-Processing Tendencies in Recent Experiments in Cognitive Learning," Inhelder summarizes research findings that attack the problem of examining transitions between substages through conservation and class inclusion experiments. Four successive steps are labeled: juxtaposition, opposition, compromise, and integration. Inhelder suggests that these results demonstrate that development cannot be considered as a branching process of refined differentiations, but rather as the interaction of different subsystems. These interactions, as they lead to conflict situations, are said to require reciprocal assimilation between varying subsystems in order to approach a higher order of structuration.

Using the Hunt–Uzgiris scales, Uzgiris longitudinally examines infant development within the sensorimotor period for consistency of structural organization across various domains. General concepts extracted from these results are reported in her paper, "Some Observations on Early Cognitive Development." Three levels of organization within the sensorimotor stage are delineated: the utilization of subcomponents in actions; the regulation or modification of actions by outcomes; and the implicit or nonovert adaptation of actions equivalent to thought. Uzgiris cautions that these findings are not meant to be conclusive. It is therefore suggested that these structurations be examined in future investigations under varying circumstances.

Jonas Langer has approached Piaget's equilibration thesis through a wide variety of research hypotheses. In "Cognitive Development During and After the Preconceptual Period," Langer describes ongoing research that investigates the development of transductive preoperations during the representational stage, from approximately 2–5 years, and its manifestations in physical, social, and personal preconcepts. Children were questioned regarding a series of four family portraits, spanning approximately 15 years, and were asked to make judgments on the relations between pictures as well as between the individuals portrayed. Langer also presents some considerations of developmental filiations between operative and figurative thought along with some comments on the question of the interactive aspects of cognitive development.

In "The Emergence of the Child as Grammarian," Gleitman, Gleitman, and Shipley present demonstrations of some young children's awareness of syntactic and semantic properties of language. Rudiments of such "metalinguistic" functioning are shown in 2-year-olds, who gave judgments of grammaticalness in a role-modeling situation. The growth of these abilities is documented for a group of 5- to 8-year-old children who were asked explicitly to give judgments of deviant sentences. Adultlike behavior in these talented subjects was found to emerge in the period from 5 to 8 years. Possible relations of metalinguistic functioning to other "metacognitive" processes are suggested.

After a brief review of the structuralist position, Lavatelli reports in "Environment, Experience, and Equilibration" her findings based on an examination of logical development among the Houk-Lo boat people of Hong Kong. She suggests that the rate of logical development is not a function of socioeconomic status itself but of the opportunities within an environment that provide the interactions necessary for logicomathematical thought. Teaching techniques and specific activities that foster the transition to logical thinking are presented for incorporation within the preschool curriculum.

Attempting to integrate Piagetian research into classroom practices, which is essentially what Lavatelli has done in the previous paper, Stephens, in her paper "Application of Piagetian Theory to Remediation of Reasoning," suggests three guidelines: present activities that are motivating but not frustrating at the child's level of development; emphasize experiences that are activity-oriented; and provide a teacher with a knowledge of Piagetian theory and the ability to assess reasoning as defined by the Geneva school. With these guidelines, two remediation projects were undertaken, one with congenitally blind subjects and the other with mentally retarded, socially maladjusted subjects. With factors determined in previous research, a modular approach that provides sequential activities based on a common factor or basic cognitive ability was developed. The modules include systems and variables, reproductory imagery, and cooking. The goal of this research was to utilize these modular systems as an intervention technique for a period of at least 15 months in order to determine if a significant change in cognitive development was effected.

Implications derived from the Piagetian model and its related research are applied to curricula within the three papers that comprise the final section. Both Barbara Presseisen and Marilyn Appel present innovative Piagetian-based curricula in the areas of social studies and science, respectively. Lois Macomber's paper, which opens this section, is not related to a particular curricular area but instead offers a detailed description of the preoperational child's thought and its implications for education.

Macomber's paper, entitled "Some Implications of Jean Piaget's Theory for the Education of Young Children," delineates four modes of thinking that characterize children in the preoperational stage. They are transductive thought, egocentric thought, magical thought, and animistic thought. She discusses the inability to conserve, to use reversibility of thought, and to display perceptual constancy during this prelogical stage of development. Changes in curriculum and instruction consistent with an understanding of the preoperational child are proposed. Suggestions for modification of the physical classroom and its equipment are made, along with a redefinition of the teacher's role in such an educational environment.

Presseisen's paper, entitled "Piaget's Theory Applied to a Social Studies Curriculum," suggests that the application of Piaget's theory to curriculum can be seen through an examination of the changes in the development of curriculum. Key elements in curriculum design are suggested: content, process, instructional design, management plan, and evaluation. Presseisen suggests that these elements must be taken into account if Piaget's theory is to be examined more effectively as a basis for curriculum development in the social sciences. She continues with a consideration of Piaget's thoughts on social education. Finally, she describes an actual social studies program under development that applies Piaget's theory to its curricular organization. Included is a description of how the application has been made, what constraints were placed upon the testing of the program, and what were some tentative results of the testing.

In her paper, "The Application of Piagetian Learning Theory to a Science Curriculum Project," Appel describes an individualized program that has evolved from the process of curriculum development in science over the last 50 years. Three stages in science curriculum development are discussed: fact-centered (Stage I); process–structure focus (Stage II); and individualized and interdisciplinary (Stage III). Appel goes on to describe and compare the three major programs that have had the greatest impact on science teaching in the past 15 years. These include the Elementary Science Study (ESS), Science–A Process Approach (SAPA), and the Science Curriculum Improvement Study (SCIS). A program entitled "Personalized Approach to Science Education" (PASE) is discussed in terms of a theoretical model of curriculum design and its relationship to the Piagetian model of development and learning.

PART I:
THEORY

CHAPTER 1

Problems of Equilibration [*]

Jean Piaget

University of Geneva, Geneva, Switzerland

The title "Equilibration" refers to one factor that I think is essential in cognitive development. In order to understand the role of this factor, we must relate it to the classical factors that have always been understood to be pertinent in cognitive development. There are three such classical factors: the influences of the physical environment, the external experience of objects; innateness, the hereditary program; and social transmission, the effects of social influences. It is clear that all three are important in cognitive development. I will begin by discussing them separately. But as we discuss them, I think we will see that no one of the three is sufficient in itself. Each one of them implies a fundamental factor of equilibration, upon which I shall place special emphasis.

I will start by discussing the role of physical experience. It is clear that this is indispensable in cognitive development. There can be no development without contact with physical objects, that is, contact with the physical environment. In terms of classical empiricism, the role of acquired experience simply amounts to perceptions that we draw from objects and associations among perceptions. As I see it, there never can be pure association in the classical sense in which the empiricists mean it. The manner of linkage that always intervenes in the whirlpool of associations is in reality an assimilation in the biological sense of the term, an integration of external data into the structures of the subject.

Any action on the part of a subject gives rise to schemes of assimilation. That is, an object can be taken into certain schemes through the actions that are carried out on it; each of these schemes of assimilation goes hand in hand and with an aspect of accommodation of the schemes to the situation. Thus, when a subject takes cognizance of or relates to an object, there is a pair of processes

*Translation by Eleanor Duckworth

going on. It is not just straight association. There is a bipolarity, in which the subject is assimilating the object into his schemes and at the same time accommodating his schemes to the special characteristics of the object. And in this bipolarity and sharing of processes, there is already a factor of equilibration between assimilation and accommodation.

Assimilation is a form of integration. It presupposes an instrument by which the data can be assimilated into the structures of the subject. An excellent example of assimilation as integration is the notion of horizontality of the level of water. Children see water in various forms every day. They see water in glasses from which they drink; they see water in bottles that they tip. Moreover, they see water running in bathtubs and lakes and rivers. In all cases, the water is horizontal. So the notion that water is horizontal should be a basic permanent notion. It even seems to assert itself in a more primitive manner as the child's own body is bound to positions where horizontality or verticality intervene. He can tell whether he is standing up or whether he is lying down; he is aware of the sensoritonic attitudes. You would expect this postural awareness to give him the understanding necessary to realize that water is always horizontal.

In some research we did many years ago, we asked the child to predict what would happen to the water inside a bottle if we tipped it. The child was unable to see the water inside the bottle because it was covered. He was asked to draw a picture of the water inside the bottle when it was tipped. The average age at which children could answer this correctly and draw a horizontal line was about 9 years of age. I say average age because, of course, some children advance more rapidly than others. Moreover, the populations we studied were from an impoverished area of Geneva, and it is possible that in more highly civilized regions the age is younger. However, in Geneva the average child is 9–10 years of age before he can predict where the water will be in the covered container when it is tipped. Before that, he always draws the line parallel to the bottom of the bottle as it is when the bottle is upright. Then there are various intermediary stages between drawing a parallel and drawing a horizontal line. This seems to be quite strong evidence of the fact that seeing is not enough, because children have been seeing this phenomenon all their lives. But within the experiment, we even gave the children a chance to see by taking the cover off the bottle. If the child had drawn the water parallel to the bottom of the bottle, when we uncovered and tipped the bottle and the child compared the bottle with his drawing, he would say, "Yes, that's just the way I drew it. Just like my drawing." He doesn't even seem to be able to see that the line is horizontal.

Why is the child unable to see that the line of water is horizontal? The reason for this is that he does not possess the necessary instruments of assimilation. He hasn't yet developed the system of coordinates that will enable him to put the water into a frame of reference with points outside the bottle, such as the table top or the floor. As adults, we operate with a coordinate spatial system of verticality and horizontality at all times. The child doesn't have the framework that enables him to make the extrafigural comparison needed to go outside the framework of the bottle. He reasons only by an intrafigural frame of reference until about the age of 9, when these systems of coordinates are being built. He remains inside the framework of the bottle; his only points of reference are the base of the bottle, which results in his drawing the water parallel to the base or sometimes to the corners of the bottle. He may draw a line from one corner to another that is slightly tipped, but it is still not considered horizontal. His frame of reference remains the bottle itself.

This seems to me a very striking example of the complexity of the act of assimilation, which always supposes instruments of integration. A well-developed structure within the subject is needed in order for him to take in the data that are outside. Assimilation is clearly not a matter of passively registering what is going on around us. This leads to the critical examination of the famous stimulus–response scheme, the classical model of behaviorism.

It is true, of course, that stimuli give rise to responses. However, this only raises much more basic, more preliminary questions. Why does a given stimulus give rise to a certain response? When is an organism sensitive to a particular stimulus? The very same organism may at one time not be sensitive to a particular stimulus and not give any response to it and then later be sensitive to the stimulus and respond to certain stimuli, whereas other organisms may not. Therefore, the fundamental question is: What makes an organism respond to a certain stimulus?

The organism is sensitive to a given stimulus only when it possesses a certain competence. I am borrowing this word from embryology in the sense in which Waddington has used it. He has referred to the influence of an inductor. Waddington has shown that an inductor that modifies the structure of the embryo does not act in the same way at all levels of development. If the inductor is present before the embryo has the competence to respond to it, the inductor has no effect at all; thus, it does not modify the structure. The embryo must be at a point of being competent to respond to the inductor before the inductor can have its effect.

The phenomenon is the same in cognition. Stimulus–response is not a one-way road, a unilateral scheme. A subject is sensitive to a stimulus only when he possesses a scheme that permits the capacity for response, and this capacity for response supposes a scheme of assimilation. We again have to create an equilibrium between assimilation, on the one hand, and accommodation to a given or an external stimulus, on the other hand. The stimulus–response scheme must be understood as reciprocal. The stimulus unleashes the response, and the possibility of the response is necessary for the sensitivity to the stimulus. The relationship can also be described as circular, which again poses the problem of equilibrium, an equilibrium between external information serving as the stimulus and the subject's schemes or the internal structure of his activities.

I would like to make two final points concerning the role of the physical environment. I will first discuss the development of the notion of conservation. As you know, if one transforms a ball of clay into a sausage shape, the young child will tell you that there is more clay in the sausage than in the ball because the sausage is longer. Second, even though no clay was added and no clay was taken away, the child believes that the sausage shape and the ball will weigh differently. The child will also say that one would displace more water in a vessel than the other, indicating different volumes in the ball and the sausage shapes. These notions of conservation are acquired in a certain order: first, the conservation of the substance, that is the quantity of material; next, with quite a notable time-lag, the conservation of weight; finally, the conservation of volume, in the sense one can evaluate volume by the displacement of the level of water. What strikes me as very interesting is that the conservation of the amount of clay—the conservation of the substance—is the first concept of conservation that a child attains. But it is clear that conservation of substance—that is, the amount of clay—is not observable. The child can observe the size of the clay, perceive its volume, and lift it to sense its weight, yet he believes they have changed. And yet somehow he believes that the amount of clay has remained the same even though it is not observable or clearly measurable.

It is, it seems to me, very important that conservation of substance can only be the product of reasoning. It is not a product of perception. The child has simply become aware that something must be conserved when things are transformed in order to make the process of rational thought at all possible. So the scheme of the conservation of the amount of clay imposes itself on the child for rational rather than for perceptual reasons.

Finally, I would like to distinguish between two kinds or experience in connection with the factor of external experience. Classical empiricists assume there is only physical experience. In physical experience, information is drawn from the objects themselves. For example, you can have various objects and see that they differ in weight. But there is a different kind of experience that plays a necessary role at the preoperational level. I will call this *logicomathematical experience.* In logicomathematical experience, the information is drawn not from the object but from the subject's actions and from the subject's coordination of his own actions, that is, the operations that the subject effects on the objects.

There is a very banal example of logicomathematical experience that I have often quoted. One of my friends who is a great mathematician described to me an experience that he had as a child. While counting some pebbles, he arranged them in a line, counted them from left to right, and found that there were ten. He then decided to count them from right to left and found there were still ten. He was surprised and delighted, so he changed the shape again. He put them in a circle, counted around the circle, and found there were still ten. With mounting enthusiasm, he counted around from the other direction and there were still ten. It was a great intellectual experience for him. He had discovered that the sum ten is independent of the order of counting. But unlike their weight, neither the sum nor the order is a property of the pebbles. The sum and the order come from the actions of the subject himself. It was he who introduced the order and it was he who did the counting. So logicomathematical experience is experience in which the information comes from the subject's own actions and from the coordinations among his actions. This coordination of actions naturally poses a problem of equilibrium much more than a problem of action from external experience.

Finally, as for the role of experience, it is clear that there is an undeniable role played by experience in cognitive development; however, the influence of experience has not resulted in a conception of knowledge as a simple copy of outside reality. In external experience, knowledge is always the product of the interaction between assimilation and accommodation, that is, an equilibrium between the subject and the objects on which the knowledge rests.

The second factor I would like to discuss is that of the innateness or hereditary programming of development. It is, of course, obvious that the factor of innateness plays as fundamental a role as the maturation of the nervous system and is a condition of cognitive development. But it is a condition that only opens up possibilities. The problem is how these possibilities are realized, that is, how they are actualized. In sensorimotor development, it is easier to see how hereditary transmissions play a central role. For instance, at the sensorimotor level, the coordination between grasping and vision seems to be clearly the result of the myelinization of certain new nerve paths in the pyramidal tract, as physiologists have shown. This myelinization seems to be the result of hereditary programming. However, in the domain of higher, representative, and especially operational cognitive structures, these structures are not innate. Logical transitivity, for example, imposes a necessity on the subject with an obviousness internal to the subject. Yet this necessity is not a proof of innateness.

We have conducted a very simple experiment to test the notion of transitivity. We asked children first to compare the length of two pencils. Children see that A is smaller than B. We then hide A and show B and C; C is very obviously longer than B. We then ask the child, "Do you think that C is longer than the first one you saw, smaller than the first one you saw, or about the same length?" The little children will say, "I can't tell. I didn't see them together." The child does not make the inference we would make from the information that allows for transitivity. It seems to impose itself on us with a feeling of necessity that C must be longer than A. But small children do not have that same feeling of necessity. This feeling of necessity is tied to the operational structure I have been calling *seriation* or *serial ordering*.

As you know, if children are asked to put ten sticks in order or length from shortest to longest, their ability to do so develops through very varied stages, in which they experience some laborious trial and error. Small children are likely to make pairs of short and long sticks but fail to coordinate the pairs among themselves. They have recognized that some sticks are short and some are long, but not much more than that. Older children make trios—the repetition of a pattern of short, medium, and long—but do not coordinate the trios among themselves. Slightly older children are able to produce an incomplete empirical series, that is, with errors, gropings, and corrections. Finally, at about 7 years of age, children have developed a method, a method that I call *operational*. They first look for the shortest of all the elements and place it on the table, then look for the smallest of those remaining and place it next to the shortest, and then look for the next shortest and place it. I refer to this method as *operational* because it implies a certain reversibility. It implies the comprehension of the fact that any element—say, element *E*—is at once bigger than all those preceding it and smaller than those that remain. There is a coordination that permits a construction of the seriation without errors. When this system is followed, once you know that objects *A, B,* and *C* were the shortest on the table, it is not necessary to compare object *D* with objects *A, B,* and *C.* You know that it must be longer than them and that it must be shorter than the others.

The notion of transitivity is, thus, tied to the operational structuration of the series. Transitivity feels necessary to us and imposes itself upon us because of the nature of the closed operational structure; it is a result of the closing of this structure. And this, of course, means equilibrium. The structure, until it is closed, is not in a state of equilibrium. Once it is closed, we again find equilibrium to be an important factor.

The notion of the influence of innate factors in development is gaining new acceptance these days. Two of its leading proponents are Chomsky, the linguist, and Lorenz, the ethologist. Chomsky, of course, has done very great work in his development of the notion of transformational grammar, work that I admire greatly. He has hypothesized that from the beginning of these transformations, there is a fixed innate core that contains the most general forms of language, for example, the relationship between subject and predicate. This innate core contains both the possibility of construction of language and a rational structure, which consequently would be innate.

It seems to me that this hypothesis is not necessary. As we all know, language develops during the second year of childhood and not from birth. As we also know, it develops at the end of the period of sensorimotor development, with all the numerous stages of construction involved in this form of intelligence. It seems to me that sensorimotor intelligence, once achieved, contains all that is necessary to furnish Chomsky's innate fixed core without having need to appeal to a hereditary structure.

Konrad Lorenz, the great ethologist, agrees with Kant: the important forms of our thinking, the important categories, are present in us before any experience; that is, they are innate. He goes as far as to say that the general ideas of the mind are preformed in the embryo before the individual has the need for them, just as the horses' hooves or fishes' fins are preformed in the embryo before they are needed by the adult. However, Lorenz, as a biologist, recognizes the limitations of such an explanation. Each animal species has its own heredity. Then, if one brings the ideas of intelligence or reason back to innate structures, that means that heredity can vary from one species to another following the hereditary patrimony of the species. Realizing this difficulty, Lorenz follows through very logically by concluding that these innate notions are not necessary, as they might be if the hereditary programs were constant across all species. Since hereditary programs vary from species to species and there is nothing necessary about them, these innate ideas must be only innate working hypotheses. Thus, this means that innate ideas have lost their aspect of necessity. This does not mean that essential categories are not *a priori* and cannot exist before any experience, but it does mean that they cannot be accounted for by their intrinsic necessity.

I would conclude in discussing the role of biology as a factor of development that what is important for us to take from biology is not the notion of hereditary programming, since it is variable and it cannot lead to the kind of necessity that we feel. We should take the much more general notion of self-regulating mechanisms. Self-regulating mechanisms are important throughout every level of biological development. One finds regulation at the level of the genome, where self-regulatory mechanisms are an essential condition of functioning. There are regulations in the course of embryological development that Waddington calls *homeorhesis*. At the physiological level, homeostasis is a self-regulating mechanism; similarly, in the nervous system, the reflex arc is a homeostat. On the level of human conduct and even at the level of logical operational thinking, there are similar self-regulatory mechanisms. It seems to me that this notion of self-regulation, which consequently is one of equilibration, is much more fundamental and much more general than the more narrow notion of variable hereditary programming. It is, then, self-regulation that is the important idea for us to take from biology.

I now come to the third classical factor of development: the social factor, the role of education and language in development. I will try to be very brief so that I can get on to equilibration. The role of education and language is clearly fundamental, but once again it is subordinated to assimilation. There can be no effect of social or linguistic experience unless the child is ready to assimilate and integrate this experience into his own structures.

The special problem of the relationship between language and logic is one that I would like to discuss at some greater length. Many people are of the opinion that an individual's grasp of logic is dependent upon the syntax and the logical relationships embedded in the language in which people are speaking to him. Logic develops out of the language. This is the position of the logical positivists.

In Geneva, one of our colleagues, Hermine Sinclair, has done some work on the problem of the relationship between logic and language. Sinclair was a linguist before she came to Geneva to go into experimental psychology. In her research, she first identified two groups of children. One group were nonconservers, in the sense that they thought that a change in shape would entail a change in the amount of substance. The other group were conservers, in that they knew that the change of shape did not alter the amount of the substance. Then, she looked at the language of these two groups of children in different situations. For example, the children were asked to compare short, long, fat, and thin pencils. She found that the children who were nonconservers did not use comparative terms in describing the pencils and did not contrast two dimensions. They would just say that one pencil is big and that one pencil is fat. The children who were conservers, however, used comparisons. They talked in sentences that contrasted variables, such as saying that one is fatter but shorter, the other thinner but longer.

Sinclair then trained the nonconservers to learn the verbal expressions of the other, more advanced group. This language training was not easy, but it was possible. After the nonconservers had mastered the language expressions of the conservers, she readministered the conservation experiment to see whether the training increased their ability to conserve.

Progress was only minimal; nine-tenths of the children made no progress toward conservation, although they had mastered the more sophisticated language. One-tenth of the children made very slight progress. This would lead us to believe they would have made this progress normally in that period of time. We have been pursuing other research in Geneva since Sinclair's study; it all supports the general conclusion that linguistic progress is not responsible for logical or operational progress. It is rather the other way around. The logical or operational level is likely to be responsible for a more sophisticated language level.

I am now discussing the role of equilibration, that is, the fourth factor in psychological and cognitive development. It seems to me that there are two reasons for having to call in this fourth factor. The first is that since we already have three other factors, there must be some coordination among them. This coordination is a kind of equilibration. Secondly, in the construction of any operational or preoperational structure, a subject goes through much trial and error and many regulations that in a large part involve self-regulations. Self-regulations are the very nature of equilibration. These self-regulations come into play at all levels of cognition, including the very lowest level of perception.

I will begin with an example at the level of perception. We have studied a number of optical illusions, by asking subjects to make perceptual judgments of an optical illusion. For example, we have often used the Müller–Lyer illusion, an illusion of the diagonal of the lozenge, which is always underestimated. One can present the subject with a successive series of judgments to make between the standard and the variable. The variable varies between presentation but the standard is a constant. The subject has to judge whether the variable is shorter than, longer than, or equal to the standard. I have always admired the patience of children under 7 years of age who will sit through 20 or 30 or 40 presentations at a time.

In children under 7 years of age, we find no notable transformations, that is, at the end of 30 or 40 trials, they make the same errors that they did at the beginning. With adults, on the contrary, the repetition of the judgment results in a very clear diminishing of the illusion. Some are able to eliminate the effect of the illusion altogether. Among children from 7 years (the beginning of cognitive operations) to adulthood, one can observe a progressive diminishing of errors. It is important to note that the subject does not know the results of his judgments. There was no external reinforcement, yet the perceptual mechanism seems to have its own regulations, so that after 20 or 30 or 40 trials, an adult subject can eliminate the effect of the illusion altogether.

At the representational level, in both preoperational and operational structures, we can distinguish three kinds of equilibrium. The first one is the relationship between assimilation and accommodation, of which I previously spoke. There is an equilibrium between the structures of the subject and the objects; its structures accommodate to the new object being presented and the object is assimilated into the structures. It is this first fundamental form of equilibration that was exemplified by the horizontality of water and the notion of conservation. I will not repeat these examples here.

The second kind of equilibrium is an equilibrium among the subsystems of the subject's schemes. In reality, the schemes of assimilation are coordinated into partial systems, referred to as *subsystems* in relation to the totality of the subject's knowledge. These subsystems can present conflicts themselves. In general terms, I will say that, for example, it is possible to have conflicts between a subsystem dealing with logicomathematical operations (such as classifications, seriation, and number construction) and another subsystem dealing with spatial operations (such as length and area). For example, when a child is judging the quantity of a number of sticks, there may be in one collection a small number of long sticks laid out. In another collection, a larger number of shorter sticks may be laid out. If he is basing his judgment on number, he would make one judgment of quantity. If he is basing his judgment on length, he would make a different judgment of quantity. These two systems can evolve at different speeds. Of course, as they evolve, there is a constant need for coordination of the two, that is, an equilibration of subsystems.

The third kind of equilibrium in cognitive development appears to be fundamental. Little by little, there has to be a constant equilibrium established between the parts of the subject's knowledge and the totality of his knowledge at any given moment. There is a constant differentiation of the totality of knowledge into the parts and an integration of the parts back into the whole. This equilibrium between differentiation and integration plays a fundamental biological role.

At the level of cognitive functions, there is a fundamental form of equilibrium because integration, as a function of differentiation, poses new problems. These new problems lead to the construction of new actions upon the previous actions, or new operations upon the previous operations. The construction of operations upon operations is probably the secret of development and of the transition from one stage to the next.

I would like to point out that the notion of operation itself involves self-regulatory mechanisms. They are—in Ashby's sense, in his cybernetic terminology—the perfect regulations in that the outcome is anticipated before the act is actually carried out. The feedback, which at lower levels has incomplete reversibility, now becomes a feedback with perfect reversibility in the sense of inversion or reciprocity. This is an example of perfect compensation—otherwise said, attained equilibrium.

I would like to explain the reasons for the role of equilibrium. All operational subject structures, on the one hand, and all causal structures in the domain of physical experience, on the other hand, suppose a combination of production and conservation. There is always some production—that is, some kind of transformation—taking place. Similarly, there is always some conservation, something that remains unchanged throughout the transformation. These two are absolutely inseparable. Without any transformation, we have only static identity. The world becomes rigid and unchanging in the sense that Parmenides (c. 539 B.C.) conceived it. Without any conservation, we have only constant transformation. There is total change; the world is always new and it becomes unintelligible. It becomes like the world of Heraclitis with its river in which one was never able to bathe twice. In reality, there are always both conservation and production.

Conservation demands compensations and, consequently, equilibration. If something is changed, something else must change to compensate for it, so that a conservation results. Even in physics, all the transformations that take place involve compensations that lead to a conservation. These compensations are organized in group structures, in the mathematical sense of the term. Furthermore, there is no conservation without production, and production with conservation results in a constant demand for new construction.

Where I speak of equilibrium, it is not at all in the sense of a definitive state that cognitive functioning would be able to attain. Attained equilibrium is limited and restrained, and there is a tendency to go beyond it to a better equilibrium. I would speak of the law of optimalization, if this term did not have technical meanings too precise for its psychological use. So, simply stated, there is a continual search for a better equilibrium. In other words, equilibration is the search for a better and better equilibrium in the sense of an extended field, in the sense of an increase in the number of possible compositions, and in the sense of a growth in coherence.

I would now like to point out the fundamental difference between biological or cognitive equilibrium and physical equilibrium. In physics, equilibrium is a question of a balance of forces. Take, for example, a balance with two weights, one on each side. Between the two are the level and the fulcrum, which are only organs of transmission. They are passive mediators permitting the action from one side to the other.

In another example, the Le Châtelier–Braun experiment, a piston presses down on a container that is full of gas. The gas is compressed while the force of the piston increases the pressure. The force of the piston heats the gas, making it agitate. This makes the gas hit back with pressure on the sides of the container and eventually back onto the piston. It compensates for the initial force that was pressing down on the piston and presses the piston back up again. Le Châtelier referred to this as the moderation of the original cause. Here again, the container plays the role of the transmitter, a passive mediator that receives and sends back the shocks.

In biological or cognitive equilibrium, on the other hand, we have a system in which all parts are interdependent. It is a system that should be represented in the form of a cycle. A has its influence on B, which has its influence on C, which has its influence on D, which again influences A. It is a cycle of interactions among the different elements. It also has a special feature of being open to influences from the outside. Each of the elements can interact with external objects. For instance, the cycle can take in A′ and B′.

In the case of biological or cognitive equilibrium, the links are not passive; they are the very sources of action. The totality presents a cohesive force that is specific and that is precisely the source of the assimilation of new elements of which we have been speaking since the beginning of this talk. The system forms a totality in order to assimilate the outside elements. This equilibrium between the integration and the differentiation of the parts in the whole has no equivalent in physics. It is found only in biological and cognitive equilibrium.

In closing, I would just like to cite two references on the matter of the cohesive force of the totality, the source of equilibrium in biological and cognitive structures. The first is from Paul Weiss, the great biologist, who in his work on cells pointed out that the structure of the totality of the cell is more stable than the activity of its elements. Inside the cell the elements are in constant activity, but the total structure of the cell itself has a much more continuing stability.

My second reference is in the cognitive domain. I would like to speak of the works of Presburger, cited by Tarski, which point out the existence of systems that as totalities are closed on themselves and are completely coherent. All aspects are decidable, in the logical sense of the term, within the total system, while the subsystems are not so closed and every aspect is not entirely decidable. This seems to me a very fine example of the kind of equilibrium about which I am talking; the totality has its own cohesion and equilibrium by integrating and differentiating the parts at the same time.

CHAPTER 2

Comments on the Problems of Equilibration

Hans Furth

Catholic University, Washington, D.C.

Piaget has made a very succinct and convincing statement of the factor of equilibration; if you are too willing to accept it, it may be that you do not sense the revolutionary note contained in Piaget's theory, in particular his notion of an internal equilibration. Summarized below are some of the main points discussed as well as two or three questions that Piaget may wish to consider further to clarify the notion of equilibration.

This notion is a difficult one for most students of Piaget, and at the moment Piaget is very much concerned with elaborating this concept. He is fleshing in, as it were, the concept of internal equilibration to make it more real and amenable to psychological investigation. Perhaps an anecdote would help us here. Piaget spent 2 or 3 days in Washington last year and we were driving over some bumpy roads. I told Piaget to hold fast because a particular stretch of the road was very bumpy indeed. To this he replied, "Well, as long as I can hold my pipe in equilibration in front of me I feel safe that nothing will happen to me." So I often wonder about the influence of this pipe on Piaget's theory.

In general, you must have noticed that Piaget's theory is full of what can be called dialectical terms: assimilation versus accommodation, organism versus environment, operative versus figurative, and so on. Because of this bipolarity, the equilibration concept seems natural and almost necessary. Piaget's first illustration is the concept of accommodation. Many people may misunderstand *accommodation* as referring to a process that takes place only when something new is acquired. Whereas if you were asked, for instance, the sum of 5 + 3, there would merely be assimilation on your part with no corresponding accommodation, since the answer is quite familiar to you. Piaget has made it clear that this is not the case—that accommodation is simply the counterpart of assimilation. Wherever you have assimilation you also have accommodation. This state of affairs presents, therefore, an equilibration in itself: an equilibrating between the taking in of data and the structuring and the adaptation of the subjective structures to the given data.

Piaget's next point was that there is always a coordination and therefore the need for equilibration between a figurative content and the operative framework within which this content is being assimilated: Piaget gave the example of the perception of horizontality. The third point that Piaget made seems to be the most crucial and should perhaps have been the first point. It concerns the organism and the environment. We have been accustomed, if not brainwashed, to look at an organism as one entity and the environment as another, separate entity, and then we ask how these two things get together. However, from a biological viewpoint, these two things have never been separated at all. Quite the opposite. An organism can exist only insofar as it is related to or corresponds to the environment. Given this organism—environment matrix or polarity, the notion of equilibration expresses that this polarity is being coordinated. In this connection, Piaget first distinguishes two kinds of experiences of the person's world, namely, an experience that he calls physical or simple and another type of experience that is really an experience of our own action on the environment and is called logical, or logicomathematical. Here again, there is a need to coordinate these two kinds of experiences. These experiences do not happen separately. In differing degrees, they are always present as mutual components in any kind of experience, and it is important that these two components be coordinated.

Piaget then went on to refer to innateness, and here is the first question. It must be clear to everyone that Piaget is not an empiricist in the strict sense. For him, the environment is not the total and chief determining factor of development. On the other hand, the newness of Piaget's conception is precisely that he refuses to posit the mental structures to be developed as innate, and therefore, he uses the concept of equilibration to explain this development. Piaget mentions three traditional factors operating in development: (1) maturation or the physiological growth of the hereditary organic structures; (2) physical experience; and (3) social experience. He says that there is a need for a fourth factor to equilibrate or coordinate these three different factors. Piaget treats the three factors as if they were on the same level, and then he adds internal equilibration as a fourth factor dominating the three. It would seem that there must be a much closer relationship between maturation of the hereditarily given and the factor of equilibration than between equilibration and the other two factors, namely, physical and social experience. Would Piaget agree?

Piaget then focused on the biological self-regulations that are present in any organism. When people wonder how one can speak of internal self-regulations and not consider them innate, Piaget's answer would be that some biological self-regulations are indeed innate. No organism can exist without some such regulatory mechanisms. Indeed, these mechanisms constitute the organism as a biological entity. Piaget would differentiate the innate self-regulations from the specific program and the qualitatively different specific structures into which these self-regulations develop in the course of the individual's life.

A final point was made and perhaps was not stressed enough, namely, the difference between learning, in the strict sense, and development. Piaget mentioned language and education; he pointed out that education can take place only within the framework of structures to which a particular learning and a particular language have been assimilated. And here again, we have two poles within a common matrix, learning and development—two poles that are never separate. Some development is always a part of learning and some learning is a part of development. This, of course, explains the difficulty of understanding the distinction between development and learning. These are not two things that are neatly divided. Piaget pointed out that once these two aspects are postulated, a concept of equilibration is required to coordinate them.

The second question deals with the use of the term *equilibration*. Equilibration, in addition to other external factors, explains development. Thus is it a motivating, coordinating process. On the other hand, the structures themselves can be called *equilibria*. The developmental products of equilibration also are structures of equilibration. And so the word *equilibration* is sometimes taken in one sense, as a process, and sometimes in the sense of a state. When a word is used in two different perspectives, it is always difficult for one to be quite clear about its precise use. Would Piaget like to comment on the use of the term *equilibration?*

An additional comment is related to the foregoing. Piaget has not stressed it much, but it is quite clear that the fact of equilibration constitutes the most basic motivational factor of development. Piaget is working on this concept and he is attempting to give it a firmer empirical and theoretical base. He discussed competing or contradicting subschemes that have to be coordinated. This sounds much more familiar than the equilibration of assimilation and accommodation and other simiar conceptual distinctions. It makes sense to postulate that a child develops because he finds contradiction in his experience. The child encounters one viewpoint implied in one situation and a seemingly contrary viewpoint in another situation; therefore, he has to coordinate these two views and, in so doing, grows mentally. Piaget has always tried to differentiate between the intellectual cognitive factor and the affect or motivating factor. There are many occasions on which he has stated that he does not concern himself with affective or motivating factors. Yet it is quite clear that the concept of equilibration provides a motivating factor within intelligence. Development is not something simply added to an infant's knowledge. Development and human intelligence are correlative. Piaget has not explicitly mentioned this very important internal motivating factor within the knowing intelligence, but it is obviously an integral part of his theory.

In conclusion, it is interesting to note that there is concern for the subject of epistemology and a theory of knowledge. Perhaps it has not occurred since the time of Kant that so many students from all parts of the world have come to listen to a scholar whose chosen topic is both philosophical and difficult. Further, to focus on the concept of equilibration is singling out the most difficult aspect of this subject area. I would like to venture to speculate on the reason for the interest in Piaget's theory. Kant was the philosopher who explicitly affirmed, and in this sense liberated, the thinking subject. He was the person who first made it clear that we, the subjects, are imposing structures on the environment, that knowledge can never be a thing that is simply a copy of a reality, ready made by nature or by God. And here is Piaget 180 years later. Piaget considers himself a Kantian, but he wants to go beyond Kant. The way in which he goes beyond Kant is very significant. Kant postulated an innate *a priori* that ultimately determined man's intelligence. Piaget accepts the message of an internal *a priori,* but he puts it at the end and not the beginning of human development. Through his concept of equilibration he brings the *a priori* down to earth and connects it with the internal self-regulations present in all biological systems.

Kantian philosophy freed the way for the spread of physical science and its concomitant technology, and we have inherited and enjoy the blessings—and we can freely admit—suffer all the indirect curses of science and technology. What we need now is not primarily more science and technology but to become full human beings so that we can learn to live with what science and technology have helped us to achieve. Piaget's conception of intelligence may be the kind of theory that answers the need of our society more than any other theory of intelligence proposed by today's scholars. Let me conclude with three final points on this humanistic aspect of intelligence.

First, Piaget's view of intelligence is biologically and humanly relevant. Students all over the world are clamoring for relevancy. Many students of psychology are unhappy about the methods and the content of current psychology courses. They claim, not without justification, that they have never encountered a child who is learning paired associates except in the laboratories of psychology departments. However, when Piaget talks about the child and his way of learning, one feels that he is describing real-life situations and real children. In this sense, his is a very humane and relevant psychology. Second, even though Piaget stresses internal factors as being paramount, he does not disregard the influence of the environment. The environment is the thing that internal factors feed on. The internal factors cannot function without the environment. Therefore, there is no need to go to the extreme of saying either that intelligence is innately determined or that intelligence can be made to function by means of clever programs of external situations. We can work full time in improving the environment with the knowledge that providing a better environment means healthier food on which intelligence can grow. The reader may know that I am very much involved in education. My aim is not merely to change the curriculum of elementary schools but to put a different philosophy in the place of the traditional emphasis on reading and specific learning skills. In short, for this young age level, I want to see a school primarily for thinking and not a school for reading. To teach it, the teacher must know what thinking is. Piaget provides a practical and meaningful conception that can guide the teacher in evaluating whether or not a school activity is conducive to thinking on the part of the child.

Finally, Piaget's theory provides an internal motivation for intelligence, and motivation is just about the most basic factor in the learning process. Any teacher knows that successful learning is chiefly related to motivation. Intuitively, the popular concept of reinforcement behind all learning makes much sense. However, Piaget appeals to an internal reinforcement, that is, to an intelligence that carries within itself its own reinforcing motivation. This then is a very positive theory, not in the sense of an empiricist—positivist philosophy, but in the sense of an optimistic, humanistic, practical, and revolutionary theory of intelligence.

Piaget's Reply

Piaget replied to Furth in the following way:

I will be very brief because the hour is rather late. I am very interested in these questions that have been raised, at least insofar as I have understood the general sense of the questions.

The first question is: Isn't the notion of equilibration as a general factor really much closer to maturation and hereditary programming than it is to the other two factors? Isn't it a mistake to consider maturation and experience—physical experience and social experience—on the same plane because maturation seems closer to equilibration?

Yes, of course equilibration is very closely related to biological equilibration. There is a good deal that is programmed in the mechanism, but the important thing is that content is not programmed. Equilibration does resemble biological equilibration, but it goes much beyond it. For instance, if you take a leg off a crab, the total organism reorganies itself to establish a new equilibrium that was certainly not foreseen in the hereditary programming. This is the kind of equilibration that takes place in content that is really distinct from what is actually programmed hereditarily. So equilibration is similar to—is close to—maturation at the point of departure, but it goes very much further.

The second question is my use of the term *equilibration*, which refers sometimes to a process and sometimes to a state. I should have been clearer in my use of this term. For me, it refers above all to a process. But, in some cases, there can be states that are in equilibrium. However, the equilibrium is conserved even when it becomes incorporated into a further search for better equilibria.

For instance, take the operational idea of the series of whole numbers. This is quite firm and stable, stably equilibrated even when we go beyond it into fractional numbers negative numbers and unreal numbers—imaginary numbers. Bur the original notion of a series of ordered whole numbers retains its equilibrium. So one must keep in mind that even when there are certain stages of equilibria, there is always the additional process of equilibration. There is always virtual possible work. Development is the process of always adding to temporary and limited states of equilibria. This is why I would like to insist on the difference between the equilibration, which is the search for a better equilibrium, and the state of equilibrium.

The third question is: Isn't there already an affective aspect in intelligence? I am in total agreement with this; there certainly is an affective aspect. Each scheme provides its own need to be fed and to act. The scheme seeks to reproduce; to repeat itself and to incorporate all sorts of new things into itself. So the very existence of a scheme has its motivational aspect, which is at one with its structural aspect. I am in complete agreement with Dr. Furth on this.

I'd like to thank Dr. Furth for these questions, which I find very interesting. I responded to them very schematically now because of the time and because I understood them only schematically. I hope to have time to go into them in more detail with him.

CHAPTER 3

Piaget's Concept of Equilibration: Biological, Logical, and Cybernetic Roots

Jeanette McCarthy Gallagher

Temple University, Philadelphia, Pennsylvania

American scholars have expressed their dissatisfaction with the concept of equilibration in various ways. Bruner (1959) labeled it "useless"; Almy (1966), "frustrating." Mischel (1971) called the concept a "misleading metaphor," and Flavell (1971), perhaps speaking for many of his colleagues, stated, "If you've ever had the experience of trying to explain exactly what Piaget means by 'equilibration' to a class of students, you know that the concept is far from clear" (p. 191).

Furth posed a vital question in response to Piaget's paper "Equilibration,"[1] when he requested a clarification of the concept as a process or as a state. Undoubtedly, this is the issue responsible for the confusion surrounding the total concept of equilibration.[2] However, in Piaget's answer to Furth, equilibration clearly emerged as a process: the *search* for a better state of equilibrium. Therefore, Piaget (1971a, pp. 36–37) can discuss at the same time "mobile equilibrium" and "highly stabilized equilibrium forms," both produced by the self-regulatory or equilibration process. It is important to clarify here that the understanding of equilibration includes, but reaches beyond, that of equilibrium.

Further, to comprehend equilibration as *the* coordinating factor of cognitive development, it is necessary to relate it to the following: experience of the physical environment, maturation or hereditary programming, and the action of

---

[1] In this essay, "Piaget's paper on equilibration" refers to his address on that topic delivered to the first meeting of the Jean Piaget Society, printed in this book.

[2] Crabtree (1969) attempted to outline the history of the concept of equilibration but failed because he used a physical model for the framework. His explication of the inadequate uses of the term *equilibration* is, however, helpful.

the social environment, including cultural and educational aspects.[3] As Piaget explained each of these classical factors, he incorporated equilibration into the comprehension of each. If equilibration is the coordinating factor of self-regulation, it is impossible for it to act only as a complicating fourth factor. Equilibration is the core of Piaget's theory of cognitive development; to gloss over the concept is to distort the theory.[4]

The purpose of this essay, therefore, is to guide scholars, especially new students of Piaget, to some of the sources from which the concept of equilibration springs. Three themes emerge from Piaget's paper on equilibration:

1. The use of concepts from contemporary biologists, such as Waddington, to clarify equilibration.
2. The importance of logical necessity or compensation systems to an understanding of progressive equilibration and the inherent connections to Inhelder's research.
3. The incorporation of a cybernetic model into cognitive functions as equilibration organs regulating behavior.

Although each of these themes is discussed separately, it becomes obvious that many interrelationships exist.

The emphasis upon equilibration as self-regulation or autoregulation results from Piaget's concentration on the analogy between biological and cognitive adaptation, both of which require the two poles of assimilation and accommodation tending toward harmony through successive equilibrations (Piaget, 1970b, 1971a; Piaget & Inhelder, 1969). This search for biological analogies is not new to Piaget. However, it seems as if Piaget turns frequently to modern biologists such as Paul Weiss and C. H. Waddington to explain more fully the mechanisms of self-regulation.

This neobiological influence is the core of one of Piaget's most important books: *Biologie et connaissance: Essai sur les relations entre les régulations organiques et les processus cognitifs.*[5] Therein, Piaget posed this hypothesis: "Cognitive processes seem, then, to be at one and the same time the outcome of organic auto-regulation, reflecting its essential mechanisms, and the most highly differentiated organs of this regulation at the core of interactions with the environment" (1971a, p. 26). The importance of equilibration as the self-regulator of interactions is highlighted throughout Piaget's book, and particularly in this explication of the basic hypothesis: "knowledge is not a copy of the

---

[3] For a more complete treatment, see Piaget (1970b) and Piaget and Inhelder (1963).
[4] The depth of the discussion on equilibration in introductory texts and articles on Piagetian theory provides instructors and students with a guide for evaluation.
[5] Available in translation as *Biology and Knowledge: An Essay on the Relations Between Organic Regulations and Cognitive Processes.* Chicago: University of Chicago Press, 1971. Some of the basic concepts in *Biologie et connaissance* are reiterated in Piaget's (1970b) summary of his theory and also in Piaget (1967a).

environment, but a system of real interactions reflecting the auto-regulatory organization of life just as much as the things themselves do" (p. 27).

Piaget turned to Waddington, professor of genetics at the University of Edinburgh, for a clarification of the interaction referred to in the foregoing hypothesis. Piaget acknowledged the striking parallels between the organic embryogenesis studied by Waddington and the kind of "mental embryology" Piaget proposed in his theory of the development of intelligence.

The assimilation–accommodation interaction model also is more clearly understood in the light of Waddington's concept of competence. In the embryological sense, competence is similar to a reactive—rather than a passive—"optimal readiness-to-respond" notion (Waddington, 1961, p. 63). Piaget (1970b) utilized this notion of competence to stress the inadequacy of the stimulus–response theory: "It is obvious that a stimulus can elicit a response only if the organism is first sensitized to this stimulus (or possesses the necessary reactive 'competence' as Waddington characterizes genetic sensitization to specific inducers)" (p. 707).[6] Waddington (1966) added the idea that embryonic induction is a phenomenon that supposes that one part of the egg induces or influences neighboring parts to develop in conformity with itself (p. 16). Such phenomena as embryonic induction and competence are *self-regulating* features of interacting embryonic cell populations (Goodwin, 1969): Piaget (1971a) clearly views self-regulation or equilibration as a central problem ofcontemporary biology.

By analogy, the self-regulatory processes of biological functioning operate at all levels of cognitive functioning:

1. Perceptual: trial-and-error learning processes (groping) "as when a man learning to ride a bicycle takes evasive action against a probable fall, before it happens, by holding himself steady while the wobbling diminishes" (Piaget, 1971a, p. 11).
2. Thought operations: especially logicomathematical thought such as conservation of substance and transitivity. (These examples were presented in Piaget's paper on equilibration.)

The characteristic of logicomathematical thought most important to its functioning as a "vast auto-regulatory system" is its ability to be reversible (Piaget, 1971a, p. 12). We will revisit this concept.

For now, it is important that if cognitive functioning on any level is possible, its regulation must be understood in terms of interactions. To know is not to copy reality but to react to it. To react, it is necessary to have the competence or capacity to do so. For both Piaget and Waddington, self-regulations or progressive equilibrations exclude preformation in the sense of innate structures, as well as responses caused entirely by the environment. Environmentally caused

---

[6] See Piaget and Inhelder (1969) for a critique of stimulus–response theory; the critique is based in part on several Waddington concepts.

responses disregard the competence of the subject (Piaget, 1971*a*; Waddington, 1966, 1969). Therefore, development can be understood only as an assimilation −accommodation interaction that leads to stable equilibriums; the complete process is equilibration.

In addition to competence and induction as regulatory mechanisms, Waddington's concept of homeorhesis, a kinetic equilibration, is discussed by Piaget (1971*a*). Waddington (1969) has compared *homeostasis* and *homeorhesis*:

> homeostasis is used in connection with systems which keep some variable as a stable value as time passes. . . . We use the word homeorhesis when what is stabilized is not a constant value but is a particular course of change in time. If something happens to alter a homeorhetic system the control mechanisms do not bring it back to where it would normally have got to at some later time. The "rhesis" part of the word is derived from the Greek word *Rheo,* to flow, and one can think of a homeorhetic system as rather like a stream running down the bottom of a valley, if a landslide occurs and pushes the stream off the valley bottom, it does not come back to the stream bed at the place where the diversion occurred, but some way farther down the slope. (p. 366)

In this light, homeostasis becomes "stabilized parts" and homeorhesis, "stabilized paths" (Waddington, 1969).

Piaget utilizes both of these concepts, homeostasis and homeorhesis. The latter, however, as a regulatory mechanism, connotes a dynamic equilibrium in contrast to the more static homeostasis. As Waddington's analogy of the stream and the homeorhetic system suggests, such a system is like a force returning development to its normal course; that is, it acts as a self-regulator. The homeorhetic system and the necessary channels or "creodes" controlled by it have been likened by Piaget (1971*c*) to his theory of stages.[7]

In conclusion, then, Waddington's concepts of competence, induction, and homeorhesis are some of the regulatory mechanisms incorporated into Piaget's exposition of equilibration. But because regulatory mechanisms are *inherent* in the functioning of living organisms, these mechanisms are central to an understanding of the interactions with the environment at all levels of the knowing subject. As Piaget (1971*a*) has stressed, all life is essentially self-regulatory (p. 26).

Next, the theme of *logical necessity* becomes clear in Piaget's discussion of equilibration. When equilibrium is reached, the child realizes that a certain amount of clay is conserved even when the shape of the clay is transformed. Piaget stresses that a correct conservation judgment of the amount of clay "imposes itself" on the child; that is, this judgment is an unavoidable, logical, or intrinsic necessity. The child's logical conclusion is attained through progressive

---

[7] The links between homeostasis and homeorhesis have not been forged fully, according to Piaget (1971*a*). Piaget (1971*b*) noted that cross-cultural studies may modify his earlier use of terms borrowed from embryological development (see especially pp. 46–62).

equilibrations: "Once one knows, one knows forever and ever" (child to In-helder, cited by Piaget, 1971c, p. 5).

In an earlier essay on logic and equilibrium Piaget stressed progressive equilibrium as a result of changes in probability or increasing sequential prob-ability.[8] For example, to reach the final equilibrium point of conservation of an amount of clay, a child progresses through four strategies (see Piaget, 1957, pp. 49–52):

1. Judgment of nonconservation or centration on the length of the distended ball rather than on its width or thinness (the most primitive strategy).
2. Centration on width ignored in strategy 1, but without coordination of actions, that is, continued failure to reconcile the two dimensions.
3. Hesitation or oscillation because of incomplete coordination of action result-ing from lack of complete reversibility, that is, empirical reversibility or *renversabilité*.
4. Acceptance of conservation as a necessity, a result of *compensatory coordi-nation* of the opposing dimensions of distension and thinness.

In the fourth strategy, the child may argue: "You haven't added anything or taken anything away." "You have changed the shape, but you could put it all back the way it was." The child also might argue: "You gain here [pointing to length] what you lose there [pointing to width]." Each of the arguments is one of *logical necessity*.

For the third strategy there are momentary forms of equilibrium, but these are not stable. In terms of the game theory, the complete reversibility of the fourth strategy leads to a more stable and productive, although more costly, equilibrium. The logical necessity of the fourth strategy can be understood as an intrinsic form of causality or lawfulness (Furth, 1969, p. 207). These strategies or stages of progressive equilibration are regulated, however, by cyclic rather than linear causality, because the model was borrowed from cybernetics with its notions of circular or feedback systems (Ashby, 1956; Piaget, 1970c). The equilibrium reached in the fourth strategy is fully reversible, allowing for precorrection of errors or perfect regulation in the cybernetic sense (Piaget, 1970b, p. 274, and next section). Further, the actions of the previous strategies become coordinated at the fourth strategy. The coordination of actions tends to balance itself by self-regulation (Piaget, 1970c; 1972).[9]

To understand equilibration, then, it is necessary to conceive it as a process, that is, progressive equilibrations leading to greater and greater probability that

---

[8] Piaget was influenced by Ashby's (1956) scheme of self-organizing systems related to interactions of the nervous system and the environment.

[9] The passage from action to operation (formation of thought) and the necessity of reversibility are clarified in a new essay by Piaget, "The Role of Action in the Formation of Thought," 1972.

equilibrium will be reached. In its final movement toward stability, the equilibrium is assured by logical necessity (Piaget, 1957). Furth (1969) has summarized logical necessity:

> He [Piaget] related equilibration to implication as an intrinsic form of causality within a total organization and to the lawfulness peculiar to dynamic systems as they are studied in cybernetics. Piaget likes to draw a parallel between probability laws of equilibration and the transition from unpredictable or less predictable and ultimately logically necessary responses of strict implication. In this light the development of intelligence appears to an observer as a coordinated sequence of behavior such that a present stage of development is most likely, considering the immediately previous one, even though the intrinsic probability of its occurrence, considered from levels far removed, appears only small. For Piaget, the concept of equilibration makes comprehensible why, in retrospect, alternatives or degrees of freedom for further evolution or development are progressively reduced with succeeding stages. (pp. 207–208)

Piaget's theory of stages (1971c) is based on his previous notion of logical necessity:

> The transition from one stage to another is therefore an equilibration in the most classical sense of the word. But since these displacements of the system are activities of the subject, and since each of these activities consist of correcting the one immediately preceding it, equilibration becomes a sequence of self-regulations whose retroactive processes finally result in operational reversibility. The latter then goes beyond simple probability to attain logical necessity. (Piaget, 1970b, p. 725)

The structures or systems of operations of the stages *become* necessary; they are not so in the beginning. For example, the formal structures become necessary after the concrete operations are complete (Piaget, 1971c, p. 9).

Further, the concept of progressive equilibration elucidates the internal development of transitions from one substage to another, as well as transitions from one stage to another. Inhelder's unique experiments were designed to link the concept of progressive equilibration to a dynamic model of transition mechanisms.[10] Inhelder selected children who manifested, for example, conservation of numerical quantity but not conservation of length. Initially, the children were in the fourth stage of logical necessity for conservation of length. Those who profited most from the operational exercises were, in all probability, at the third stage, or oscillation between dimensions in attaining conservation of length. Inhelder's research probed for learning actitivies that reveal the understanding of the child's transition to more difficult conservation concepts once an

---

[10] The dynamics of the effects of partial structures' conflicting with equilibrated structures may be the fluid type of intellectual activity that Stephens's factor-analytic studies may be tapping (Stephens, this volume; 1972).

equilibrium has been reached in, for example, conservation of numerical quantity (Inhelder, 1976).

Explication of conflict situations resulting from interactions of subsystems is the most important facet of Inhelder's study. Because the child is unable to cope with the number and length of the matches concurrently, he experiences a disturbance of a previously attained equilibrium; equal numbers mean equal lengths (Inhelder, Bovet, & Sinclair, 1967). (These conflict situations are analogous to inducers or influencers in the Waddington sense.) The process of coping with these conflicts, disturbances, or imbalances is the self-regulatory process of equilibration (Furth, 1969; Gallagher, 1972).

When, however, through progressive equilibrations, the child functions by means of reversible structures, he has attained *mobile* equilibrium, characterized by *mobile* compensations or active responses. Therefore, Inhelder found that the child adds an extra number of his short matches to compensate for the longer lengths of the experimenter's matches. This occurs when the child has reached conservation of length. As soon as the correct judgment of conservation, with operational reversibility as its source, imposes itself on the child, this judgment becomes the result of a compensating transformation or regulation (Piaget, 1959b, 1967b).

Inhelder's learning studies indicated that the child's possession of logico-mathematical thinking in one area may lead, after a disturbance, to a recombination of already existing capacities, resulting in an advanced level of functioning in another area.[11] Inhelder's paper, therefore, complements Piaget's (1971a) emphasis on progressive equilibration:

> If equilibrium in action is defined as an active compensation set up by the subject against exterior disturbances whether experienced or anticipated, this equilibration will explain, among other things, the more general character of logico-mathematical operations—that is, their reversibility (to every direction operation there corresponds an inverse one which cancels it out . . .). (pp. 11–12)[12]

To summarize, the logical necessity is tied to a logicomathematical structure consisting of a system of compensations assured by reversible operations. It then

---

[11] The notion of disturbance follows from its cybernetic meaning: "A disturbance is simply that which displaces, that which moves a system from one state to another" (Ashby, 1956, p. 77).

[12] The disturbance or conflict aspect of equilibration has been used in the noting of the educational implications of Piagetian theory (Gallagher, 1972; Langer, 1969; Palmer, 1968; Presseisen, 1972). Unless this aspect is kept within a "reversibility compensation" framework, however, the concept of logical necessity (cyclic causality linked to an organic model) becomes confused with an overstress on "need" and tension reduction (linear causality linked to a physical model). Perhaps Mischel's (1971) analysis of cognitive conflict overstressed the need apart from *need for necessity* (Piaget, 1969b, 1971a).

follows that operations of thought may be considered a vast self-regulatory or equilibrated system.

Finally, Piaget chose to elaborate on the fundamental equilibrium established between parts and the totality of the subject's knowledge at any given moment. This part—whole equilibrium, a recurring theme in Piagetian writing, is the focus of several sections of *Biology and Knowledge* (1971a). At the 1956 World Health Organization meeting, scholars struggled with the necessity for a clearer exposition of the equilibration factor as a regulating mechanism ensuring coherence of the new construction, that is, parts—whole equilibrium. Then Piaget (1960) stated the problem:

> In the field of the cognitive functions in particular, the problem is to understand how new learning, discovery and creation may not only be reconciled with but take place at the same time as control and verification in such a way that the new remains in harmony with the acquired. This is once more a problem of equilibration. (p. 77)

In other words, when we study knowledge acquisition, how can we assure continuity of structures (systems of operations) and simultaneous integration of new elements into these structures? Is it possible to have a synthesis of structuralism and development within the totality of knowledge? Actually, this is the same problem: the coexistence of change with continuity or stability.

Piaget has rejected structuralism without genesis or development (like Kant's *a priori* synthesis forms) as a solution to the parts—whole equilibrium question. On the other hand, the empiricist's genesis without structuralism is equally inadequate because knowledge acquisition is viewed as accumulation, rather than assimilation into structures (Piaget, 1969, 1971a).

If all development is a kind of organization, than as biologists like Paul Weiss frequently have stressed, organisms are hierarchically ordered systems. Weiss's (1963) formulation of the "many body" problem in physics weakens the accumulation answer of empiricism:

> If a is indispensable for both b and $c;$ b for both a and $c;$ and c for both a and $b,$ no pair of them could exist without the third member of the group, hence any attempt to build up such a system by consecutive additions would break down right at the first step. In other words, a system of this kind can exist only as an entity or not at all. (p. 192; see also Weiss, 1968, 1969)

For both Weiss and Piaget, then, development is impossible without organization or regulatory mechanisms.

Cybernetics, probably the most influential of all disciplines in affecting interdisciplinary currents, provides Piaget with a model to clarify how the whole is conserved throughout a series of regulated transformations.[13] This discipline is a theory of guiding, communication, "and explanation of how one mechanism

---

[13] Ashby's (1956) account of cybernetics written for workers in the biological sciences is often cited by both Piaget and Waddington.

can direct others, or itself, by means of transmissions and the retroactive or anticipatory effects of information given" (Piaget, 1971a, p. 61). Cybernetic models are important to an understanding of cognitive mechanisms because knowledge acquisition is viewed in its dynamic aspects of organization regulation (an assimilatory model rather than a copy model). It was stressed earlier that equilibration is the self-regulating factor of the development of knowledge. Because cybernetic models incorporate self-controlling systems directed toward adaptation, such models help clarify the many possible analogies between biological and cognitive functioning (Piaget, 1971a, see especially Chapters 3 and 4).

The final words of Piaget's address on equilibration are essentially a re-emphasis of the necessity for regulatory mechanisms. Regulation, according to Piaget (1971a), is a retroactive control maintaining the equilibrium of an organized structure. Further, this equilibrium is reached on the cognitive level when compensations are assured by reversible operations, that is, logical neces-sity reached by progressive equilibration.

Therefore, equilibration, as a coordinating factor of cognitive development, is something more than the mere construct of equilibrium. It is not a cumber-some fourth factor but *the* regulator or prime instrument without which knowl-edge acquisition is impossible. Without self-regulation, such mechanisms as organization, conservation, and adaptation (the interaction model of assimila-tion–accommodation) would lose identity and continuity. Information accumu-lation without regulation would lead to a confusion of changes without self-conservation, and therefore without "life" (Piaget, 1971a, pp. 202–203; also see Pinard & Laurendeau, 1969).

Living organisms are open systems in the cybernetic sense because they exchange information with their environments. However, if an organism is too open—if information accumulation exists without organization—the system dis-integrates. The question becomes: How is it possible to combine the stability of a closed system, one without exchanges, with that of an open system? We have returned full circle to the original query: How is it possible to have both continuity or stability and change?

The answer to this essential question lies in the positing of an equilibrating system as a cybernetic synthesis involving circuits or feedback loops of in-creasing complexity between the organism and the environment (Piaget, 1967a). The essential aspect of such a cybernetic synthesis is progressive closure, which simultaneously permits unlimited exchange or extension of the environment. This is possible only when cognitive mechanisms function as specialized regu-latory organs controlling exchanges with the environment (Piaget, 1971a, p. 354).

In the evolution of knowledge, the logicomathematical structures and emerg-ing operations allow both stability and exchange. The stability or closed-system aspect is maintained by the achievement of equilibrium, which infers reversibility and consequent conservation of the system. Operations, as self-regulatory mechanisms, become perfect regulators. The achieved equilibrium includes compensation and consequent precorrection or avoidance of error, that is, control. In addition, logical stability is a perfect regulator.[14] It allows the equilibrated system to act as an exchange or open system. Therefore, a previous structure can be assimilated into a new one without the elimination of the old. Viewed in this way, Piaget's equilibrated or exchange system incorporates Bertalanffy's concept of equilibrium as a stable state in an open system. The equilibrium is characterized by mobility and activity, with both a stable and an open form of a continual flux of exchanges (Piaget, 1967a; see also discussions between Piaget and Bertalanffy, 1960).

Cognitive functions, then, are specialized factors of self-regulation controlling the exchanges underlying all behavior or the entire system of action schemes. The relation between behavior and environment cannot be studied without the incorporation of the concept of control through equilibraton. Behavior, like all organization, involves regulations. Skinner's (1971) proposal that we can neglect mediating states of mind betrays a lack of understanding of modern biology, which, of necessity, emphasizes the role of self-regulation. It is the factor of self-regulation, incorporating organization and function that distinguishes life from nonlife (Longuet-Higgins, 1969). Cognitive functions are part of life. Therefore, equilibration, as the self-regulatory mechanism of cognitive development, is central to Piaget's theory.

References

Almy, M. *Young children's thinking.* New York: Teachers College Press, Columbia University, 1966.
Ashby, W. R. *An introduction to cybernetics.* London: Chapman & Hall, 1956.
Bruner, J. S. Inhelder and Piaget's "The growth of logical thinking." I. A psychologist's viewpoint. *British Journal of Psychology,* 1959, *50,* 363–370.
Crabtree, W. B. Piaget's concept of equilibration in educational thought. Doctoral dissertation, Indiand University. University Microfilms, Inc., Ann Arbor, Michigan, 1969.
Flavell, S. H. Comments on Beilin's paper. In D. R. Green, M. P. Ford, and G. B. Flamer (Eds.), *Measurement and Piaget.* New York: McGraw-Hill, 1971.
Furth, H. G. *Piaget and knowledge: Theoretical foundations.* Englewood Cliffs, N.J.: Prentice-Hall, 1969.
Gallagher, J. M. Cognitive development and learning in the adolescent. In J. Adams (Ed.), *Understanding adolescence* (2nd ed.). New York: Allyn & Bacon, 1972. (In 3rd ed. with I. C. Noppe, 1976.)

---

[14] See Piaget's essay on structuralism (1970c) for the meaning of a logical or mathematical operation that is a "perfect" regulation from the cybernetic point of view. Because every operation is reversible, Piaget states that "an 'erroneous result' is simply not an element of the system (if $+n - n \neq 0$, then $n \neq n$)" (p. 15).

Goodwin, B. C. A statistical mechanics of temporal organisation in cells. In C. H. Waddington (Ed.), *Towards a theoretical biology.* Chicago: Aldine, 1969.

Inhelder, B. Information processing tendencies in recent experiments in cognitive learning, in press.

Inhelder, B., Bovet, M., & Sinclair, H. Développement et apprentissage. *Revue suisse de psychologie,* 1967, *26*(1), 1–23.

Langer, J. Disequilibrium as a source of development. In P. H. Mussen, J. Langer, and M. Covington (Eds.), *Trends and issues in developmental psychology.* New York: Holt, Rinehart, & Winston, 1969.

Longuet-Higgins, C. What biology is about. In C. H. Waddington (Ed.), *Towards a theoretical biology.* Chicago: Aldine, 1969.

Mischel, T. Piaget: Cognitive conflict and the motivation of thought. In T. Mischel (Ed.), *Cognitive development and epistemology.* New York: Academic Press, 1971.

Palmer, E. L. The equilibration process: Some implications for instructional research and practice. Paper presented at the American Educational Research Association meeting, February 1968. Reprinted in I. J. Athey & D. O. Rubadeau (Eds.), *Educational implications of Piaget's theory.* Waltham Mass.: Ginn-Blaisdell, 1970.

Piaget, J. Logique et équilibre dans les comportements de sujet. In L. Apostel, B. Mandelbrot, & J. Piaget, *Études d'épistémologie génétique,* Vol. 2; *Logique et équilibre.* Paris: Presses Universitaires de France, 1957.

Piaget, J. Apprentissage et connaissance (première partie). In P. Greco & J. Piaget (Eds.), *Études d'épistémologie génétique.* Vol. 7, *Apprentissage et connaissance.* Paris: Presses Universitaires de France, 1959. (*a*)

Piaget, J. Apprentissage et connaissance (seconde partie). In M. Goustard, P. Greco, B. Matalon, & J. Piaget (Eds.), *Études d'épistémologie génétique,* Vol. 10, *La logique des apprentissages.* Paris: Presses Universitaires de France, 1959. (*b*)

Piaget, J. The general problems of the psychobiological development of the child. In J. M. Tanner & B. Inhelder (Eds.), *Discussions on child development,* Vol. 4. New York: International Universities Press, 1960.

Piaget, J. Intelligence et adaptation biologique. In F. Bresson (Ed.), *Les processus d'adaptation.* Paris: Presses Universitaires de France, 1967. (*a*)

Piaget, J. *Six psychological studies* (ed. by D. Elkind). New York: Random House, 1967. (*b*)

Piaget, J. *The mechanisms of perception.* New York: Basic Books, 1969.

Piaget, J. [*Genetic epistemology*] (E. Duckworth, trans.). New York: Columbia University Press, 1970 (*a*)

Piaget, J. Piaget's theory. In P. H. Mussen (Ed.), *Carmichael's manual of child psychology,* Vol. 1. New York: Wiley, 1970. (*b*)

Piaget, J. *Structuralism.* New York: Basic Books, 1970. (*c*)

Piaget, J. *Biology and knowledge.* Chicago: University of Chicago Press, 1971. (Originally published, 1967, as *Biologie et connaissance: Essai sur les relations entre les régulations organiques et les processus cognitifs.*) (*a*)

Piaget, J. *Psychology and epistemology.* New York: Grossman, 1971 (*b*)

Piaget, J. The theory of stages in cognitive development. In D. R. Green, M. P. Ford and G. B. Flamer (Eds.), *Measurement and Piaget.* New York: McGraw-Hill, 1971. (*c*)

Piaget, J. The role of action in the formation of thought, 1972. (Reprinted in W. Overton & J. Gallagher (Eds.), *Knowledge and development,* Vol. 1, *Advances in research and theory.* New York: Plenum, 1977.)

Piaget, J., & Inhelder, B. Les opérations intellectuelles et leurs développement. In P. Oleron, J. Piaget, B. Inhelder, & P. Greco (Eds.), *Traité de psychologie expérimentale,* Vol. 7, *L'Intelligence.* Paris: Presses Universitaires de France, 1963.

Piaget, J., & Inhelder, B. The gaps in empiricism. In A. Koestler (Ed.), *Beyond reductionism: The Alpbach Symposium, 1968. New perspectives in the life sciences.* London: Hutchinson, 1969.

Pinard, A., & Laurendeau, M. "Stage" in Piaget's cognitive-developmental theory: Exegisis of a concept. In D. Elkind & J. H. Flavell (Eds.), *Studies in cognitive development: Essays in honor of Jean Piaget.* New York: Oxford University Press, 1969.

Presseisen, B. Z. Piaget's conception of structure: Implication for curriculum. Unpublished doctoral dissertation. Temple University, Philadelphia, 1971.

Skinner, B. F. *Beyond freedom and dignity.* New York: Knopf, 1971.

Stephens, B., McLaughlin, J., Miller, C., & Glass, G. Factorial structure of selected psycho-educational measures and Piagetian reasoning assessment. *Developmental Psychology,* 1972, *6,* 343–348.

Tanner, J. M., & Inhelder, B. (Eds.). *Discussion on child development,* Vol. 4. The fourth meeting (1956) of the World Health Organization Study Group on the Psychobiological Development of the Child, Geneva. New York: International Universities Press, 1960.

Waddington, C. H. *The nature of life.* London: Allen & Unwin, 1961.

Waddington, C. H. *Principles of development and differentiation.* New York: Macmillan, 1966.

Waddington, C. H. (Ed.), *Towards a theoretical biology.* Chicago: Aldine. 1969.

Weiss, P. The cell as unit. *Journal of Theoretical Biology,* 1963, *5,* 190–195.

Weiss, P. *Dynamics of development: Experiments and inferences.* New York: Academic Press, 1968.

Weiss, P. The living system: Determinism stratified. In A. Koestler (Ed.), *Beyond reductionism: The Alpbach Symposium, 1968. New perspectives in the life sciences.* London: Hutchinson, 1969.

CHAPTER 4

Sequential Order and Plasticity in Early Psychological Development[*]

J. McVicker Hunt

University of Illinois, Urbana, Illinois

The philosophers of nature were exceedingly slow to recognize that organisms go through a series of changes in anatomical substance and structure during their embryonic development. The ancient aphorism that "hair cannot come from not-hair," epitomizing the principle that no substance or structure can come from a substance or structure of a different nature, dominated human thought from the days of ancient Greece to nearly modern times. Over 2,000 years passed from the time of Aristotle's first observations of some of the epigenetic changes that occur in chick embryos until Casper Friedrich Wolff (1759, 1768) detailed the transformations in the circulatory system and the intestine of chick embryos so clearly that he convinced at least those informed of biological matters, brought an end to the doctrine of preformationism, and established recognition of the epigenetic nature of embryonic development.

Preformationism is no more than a historical relic in embryology, yet vestiges of preformationism remain in various of our views of psychological development. All too often we psychologists attribute even to very young infants whatever psychological realities are symbolized by such chapter headings as attention, emotion, perception, and even thought. Moreover, we tend to assume language to be a set of response-produced cues that designate, emphasize, and order things and actions in the world about. It has been the merit of Jean Piaget, perhaps more than of anyone else, to recognize an analogue of epigenesis

[*]This paper was presented at the second annual symposium of the Jean Piaget Society in 1972. The work has had the support of grants (MH-K6-18567; MH-08468; MH-10226; and MH-16074) from the National Institute of Mental Health.

in the development of intelligence (Piaget, 1952a) and knowledge (Piaget, 1952b, 1954), and epigenesis should be recognized in the development of motivation as well.

The potential impact of Piaget's observing and theorizing is great, and the actual impact is growing (Hunt, 1969). Piaget offers a conception of what comes ready made in the human infant at birth that differs sharply from the notion of a multiplicity of minute reflexes envisaged by Watson (1924) and later by Carmichael (1954). In accommodation, assimilation, and equilibration, Piaget offers a conceptual way for environmental encounters to participate inter-actively in psychological development. His interactionistic view of the process of psychological development differs markedly from both the nativism of Gestalt theory and from the predeterminism of Gesell (1954), yet it avoids the extreme plasticity implicit in the idea of a multiplicity of reflexes that can be evoked and combined in an infinite variety of ways—the modern version of John Locke's conception of experience writing on a *tabula rasa* (Hunt, 1969). Piaget's (1952a,b; 1954) observations of development in infants and toddlers during what he termed the "sensorimotor" and "preconceptual" phases lend substantial support to the conception of intelligence, knowledge, and motivation as hier-archically organized through interaction with environmental circumstances in a sequential order of transformations.

Despite the richness of Piaget's observations and theorizing, with their potential impact upon both developmental and general psychological concep-tions, his work has been more in the nature of an exploratory search than of a validation of his own formulations. Although he is the 20th century's "Giant of Developmental Psychology" (Hunt, 1969), the open-endedness of his epistomo-logical views would make it ironic indeed if his writings were to become the basis for yet another orthodoxy in psychology.

In extending the epigenetic view of development from body to behavior and from anatomy to intellect and to epistemology, Piaget has raised, or at least put a greatly increased emphasis upon, four large issues. The first concerns the criteria by which the separate levels, or structures, or stages of psychological development are to be identified. A second concerns the principle by means of which these configurations are to be ordered. A third concerns the nature of the transitions taking place between developmental landmarks, states, or stages. A fourth concerns the nature of the processes within the individual and between the individual and his circumstances that account for the transformations from one stage or state to another. These are large issues. They will keep investigators of psychological development busy for a long time. The following discussion touches in limited fashion upon the first three of these issues, but where the fourth is concerned, new evidence shall be introduced concerning the plastic nature of the processes within the individual and between the individual and his circumstances that account for the transformations in object construction.

Inasmuch as Uzgiris and the author have spent a good deal of time producing a set of six ordinal scales of sensorimotor development (Uzgiris & Hunt, 1975), it may be appropriate to consider briefly the criteria used to characterize the various steps in psychological development to which the terms *landmarks* and *levels* usually refer.

In the course of these investigations, we found ourselves limited by Piaget's six stages of sensorimotor development. First of all, we found a sequence of more than six behavioral "landmarks" on which observers could agree. It occurred to us, moreover, that one could hardly investigate the validity of Piaget's six configurational stages with a measuring tool that assumes their existence. Thus, we ceased to make this assumption in the choice of behavioral landmarks. Instead, as many as could be elicited with fair regularity and with high observer agreement were accepted. Because certain behavioral landmarks that could not be elicited with high regularity seemed to have a high level of theoretical meaningfulness, however, they were retained. Thus, the criteria for "landmarks" became ease of elicitation, observer agreement, and theoretical meaningfulness. The landmarks found served to characterize what has been termed *level* of development. These levels are presumed to persist between transitions, whatever the nature of the transitional processes that serve to alter the observable structure of the behavior. Rarely does an investigator have an opportunity to observe the transitional processes; however, one is able to observe the behavioral landmarks that characterize a level.

Having all the behavioral landmarks grouped together proved to be both practically and theoretically clumsy. Therefore, the landmarks of sensorimotor development were separated into six branches or series. Actually, Uzgiris assumed the major responsibility for separating these developmental landmarks. Such a separation raises the additional issue of the criteria for each branch. The branches owe something to Piaget's schemes ready made at birth and also to his distinction between the organizations of sensorimotor schemes and the constructions and reality. Furthermore, they provided an intuitively meaningful organization for our landmarks.

The six branches have led to seven scales. One is concerned with visual following and the permanence of objects. It has fourteen steps, rather than Piaget's six stages. The second, having thirteen steps, concerns the development of means for obtaining desired environmental events. The third branch concerns imitation and yields two scales: one for gestural imitation with nine steps and one for vocal imitation with nine steps. The fourth branch concerns the epistemological construction of operational causality with seven steps. The fifth branch concerns the construction of object relations in space with eleven steps. And the sixth concerns the development of schemes for relating to objects, with ten steps. Even though these scales appear to be very useful for investigation of a variety of issues, including Piaget's theory of stages, no claim is made for having uncovered the ultimate nature of sensorimotor development.

The principle by which the successive landmarks in each branch of sensorimotor development are ordered brings us to the first substantial term in the title. It is *sequential.* It was the sequentiality of Piaget's stages that first suggested the idea of ordinal scales of psychological development. On the other hand, the hypothesis of sequential ordinality calls urgently for empirical validation of hypothetical sequences of behavioral landmarks. The first empirical test came with data derived from a cross-sectional study of infants differing in age. These infants were examined but once. Here the criterion of sequential ordinality was a matter of whether those who had passed a given landmark in a given branch could also have passed all those landmarks below it. In a cross-sectional study, some presuming was called for. The epigenetic nature of psychological development makes it highly inappropriate for an older infant—say, of 15 months—to be expected to give critical reactions typical of infants of 4 or 5 months to some of the eliciting situations. If an infant gave the critical reactions characterizing two or three of the steps below the final one passed before failure on a couple of more advanced steps, it was presumed that had the infant been examined at an earlier age, he would have shown the critical reactions skipped. For the seven scales, Green's (1956) index of consistency (I) ranges between a high of .991 for the scale concerning the construction of operational causality to a low of .802 for the scale on the development for relating to objects. Except for this latter scale and that concerning the development of means for achieving desired environmental events $(I = .812)$, the remainder of these coefficients are .89 (for vocal imitation) or above. The ultimate test of *sequential organization* must come, however, from longitudinal studies of infants examined repeatedly during their development. Uzgiris has completed the first of such studies, and others are under way. Evidence of *inevitable* sequentiality, moreover, calls for longitudinal studies of infants developing under as wide a variety of cultures and conditions as feasible. Such studies are now under way in parent and child centers in this country and in an orphanage in Tehran.

This principle of sequential behavioral landmarks is far from new. Something resembling sequential organization was recognized by Binet and Simon (1905) in their use of complex psychological functions in order "to assess the intelligence." In starting their investigations with schoolchildren, they were distracted by various aspects of complexity and difficulty. In adopting the conception of mental age, they unfortunately confounded sequential organization with age. Apparently influenced by Galton's (1869) notions on mental inheritance, Wilhelm Stern (1912) suggested the intelligence quotient (IQ) and considered it to be a basic biological dimension of individual differences. In focusing upon rate of development, Stern, moreover, made time (or age) the major independent variable in development. Ever since, the confused arguments over the constancy of this developmental rate have obscured the investigation of the principles by means of which levels or stages of development are ordered.

In the ensuing debates over heredity and environment, maturation was conceived to be genetically preprogrammed, while learning was considered to be under the control of the environment. Thus, when Shirley (1931) uncovered a sequential organization in motor development, she saw it as evidence favoring "the maturation theory." Certainly genetic preprogramming is one factor in the sequential ordering of behavior, but it cannot be the only factor.

In certain instances, sequential order is logically built into behavioral development. Thus, for instance, following an object through 180° of visual arc clearly implies ability to follow an object under lesser degrees of arc. Measures of strength, speed, time of reaction, etc., all follow this principle. Such is the case generally when the assessment of the landmarks is based on the finding of points on continuous variables. In such cases, the matter of sequential organization is trivial.

In certain other instances, the sequential order appears to depend upon the persistence of representative central processes. This appears to be the case for the branch of object construction, which would appear to be basic in the infant's development of knowledge of the world about him.

Sequential organization is far from trivial and far from preprogrammed, not only for object construction but in whatever branch of development the behavioral landmarks imply any of several forms of transformation. It is these forms of transition or transformation that provide the basis within the developmental domain for the hierarchical conception of the organization of behavior and thought. One can hardly discuss the matter, however, without taking into account what appears to be the nature of some of these transformations between successive levels of behavioral organization.

Certain essential features of some of these forms of transformation are implicit in the difference between the characteristics of the observable behavioral landmarks of successive levels of development. This is true for successive levels of object construction. In an early examination, for instance, an infant's eyes may immediately leave the point where an object he has followed with apparent interest disappears. Then, in a later examination, his eyes linger where such an object has disappeared. It would appear that the object, which was without permanence in the first examination, had acquired at least a minimal degree of permanence by the second examination. Let us take another instance. In one examination, an infant will retrieve a desired object that has been completely covered by a single cloth, but when the object is covered by three superimposed cloths, it appears to be lost and the child gives up. At a later examination, however, the child persists in pulling one cloth after another off the object of his desire until he retrieves it. Again, the change in behavior implies that the permanence of the object has increased. Such increases can go on until the child can follow a desired object that has been hidden in a container through a series of disappearances by going first to the place where the container disappeared last and pursuing the places where the container disappeared in reverse order. This reversal between the order of search and the order in which the container disappeared implies that the infant can review his representative central processes backward as well as forward. Such a performance is the top of the scale of object permanence.

Such changes as occur in the behavior of infants seeking objects that have disappeared from sight strongly suggest that the central processes that represent the desired object must have increasing permanence and, at the end, a new level of mobility. Whether this increasing permanence is a matter of preprogrammed neuroanatomical maturation or whether it is a matter of the number and variety of perceptual encounters with objects and events is simply an issue for investigation.

In other instances, the behavioral transition implies a form of transformation consisting of coordination of sensorimotor systems or schemes that were previously relatively separate. Thus, at one point in his development, an infant can follow objects with his eyes, and he can move his hands about, yet, when he is presented with a colorful object, his eyes fixate on it, and his hands are extended generally toward it. He may show evidences of excitement in his breathing and expression, but only accidentally do his fisted hands actually touch the object in the course of crude swipes. White (1967) has termed this "fisted-swiping." Later, when the same infant is presented with the same object, he looks at it, he extends his arms directly toward it, and on the way he shapes his hand or hands for grasping it. Eyes and hands have been coordinated in what White has called "top-level reaching." Similarly, as Piaget (1952a) has pointed out, "sounds heard become something to look at," "things grasped become something to suck," in a series of coordinations of the sensorimotor systems present at birth in what Piaget has called the "primary circular reactions." There is evidence of considerable variation in the age at which such coordinations are achieved (Piaget, 1952a, p. 115). It may be worth noting that the hospital-reared infants in White's (1967) studies of eye–hand coordination achieved top-level reaching considerably earlier than did the home-reared babies who served as subjects in the investigations that led to our ordinal scales. However, our home-reared infants achieved vocal pseudo-imitations much earlier than did White's institutional babies.

Transitions based upon coordination of previously separate systems are not limited to the sensorimotor phase, for symbolic communication through language appears to derive in the course of psychological development from a coordination of object construction with vocal imitation. Object construction provides the perceptual knowledge of what is symbolized, and the acquisition of vocal symbols is apparently motivated by the child's interest in imitating what are to him novel vocal patterns. Such coordinations supply what is perhaps the clearest evidence for the hierarchical organization of behavior, intelligence, knowledge, and thought. From the limited evidence available, we suspect that even these early pseudowords are impossible until an infant has developed object construction to the point where he can follow an object through at least one hidden displacement and has become interested in imitating vocal patterns after hearing them only a few times. It may be worth noting here that, at least hypothetically, both branches of development must have achieved, at minimum, a fairly high sensorimotor level before the transformation comprised of their coordination can occur.

Another form of the implicit nature of the transition between successive behavioral landmarks appears to be motivational in character. The landmarks consist of behavioral evidences that indicate interest in various kinds of environmental circumstances such as prolonged looking, efforts to retain or to regain perceptual contact, and preoccupation with an activity, an object, or a subject. Because the transition appears to be based upon a limited number of perceptual encounters, we have been inclined to think of it as the attractiveness of emerging recognitive familiarity (Hunt, 1963, 1965, 1970). This attractiveness appears to account for the infant's looking longer at familiar patterns before looking longer at novel patterns (Uzgiris & Hunt, 1970, Greenberg, Uzgiris, & Hunt, 1970, Weizmann, Cohen, & Pratt, 1971, Wetherford & Cohen, 1973). It is suspected that this attractiveness may also be the motivation for such repetitive autogenic behaviors as hand-watching and nondistressful vocalization (Hunt, 1965, 1971). Repeated encounters ultimately lead, however, to interest in what is novel, and this interest may well be the intrinsic motivation for exploratory behavior and the imitation of novel gestures and vocal patterns. Such attraction appears to be based, however, on an optimum of novelty, complexity, and challenge. Although the precise nature of what it is in the organism—environment relationship that must be optimal to be attractive is still a matter of debate (Berlyne, 1971; Hunt, 1971), it must be close to the kind of relationship that Hebb (1949, pp. 227–234) considered in his theory of pleasure. Such phenomena will require further investigation before they are completely understood.

Yet another form of the implicit nature of the transition between the landmarks for successive levels of behavioral organization brings to mind what is commonly called *acquired generalization,* what Harlow (1949) called the "learning set." The transition from interest in the familiar to interest in the novel may not be entirely a matter of the hedonic value of recognitive familiarity. Whereas infants appear to be relaxed and pleased when looking at objects that have become recognitively familiar through repeated encounters, they typically wear an intent and concerned expression when they are focusing on unfamiliar patterns. This seems to be true even late in the first half year of life. Perhaps the expression of critical scrutiny reflects the achievement of the first learning set: "things should be recognizable." This is what Woodworth (1947) called the "goal of perceptual activity."

Similarly, a few encounters with an action that leads to an interesting effect produce behavior that implies that the child anticipates the effect. It is this implied anticipation that led Piaget (1952a) to speak of "intentions." In the language of Skinner (1953), these intentional actions would be called "operant responses." Evidence from a variety of sources suggests that the acquisition of a series of such intentional actions, when the infant can obtain—probably with effort—the expected outcome, leads to a "generalized confidence" that Erikson (1950) has termed "trust." The child acts as if he had come to believe, "If I do something, I can make interesting things happen."

The motivational learning sets represent highly tentative formulations, but there is one that is fairly well established in the domain of language development. This formulation's historical origins can be derived from the change in Helen Keller's behavior in the well-known incident at the pump, when "Teacher's" differing manipulations of Helen's hands for *water* and for *cup* led to a sudden change in Helen's behavior. Helen turned to manipulate "Teacher's" hand in such a fashion as to spell the word *water* several times, and then the word *cup*. Then, excitedly, after touching various objects nearby, Helen extended her hand to Teacher to have her spell the names of these objects. Within a few hours, Helen added 30 new words to her vocabulary. A similar change has been observed very commonly in children. After gradually acquiring a number of words, or pseudowords, the referents of which can be recognized by at least those who know the child well, the child begins to ask, in one way or another, the names of objects. It is as if the child had generalized the proposition that "things have names." Such a change in behavior has been repeatedly associated with sharp upward shifts in the rate of vocabulary building (McCarthy, 1954). Such learning sets, or generalizations, may constitute the nature of a good many of the transitions between the behavior characteristics of successive levels of psychological development.

The main point, however, is that the persistence of the central process representative of objects, and the coordinations of previously separate systems, and the generalizations that have been described, are not necessarily preprogrammed. It seems more likely that they derive from the infant's ongoing interactions with his environmental circumstances.

The existence of dependable sequences in several branches of sensorimotor development provides us with a basis for several fortunate modifications in the strategy for assessing development and for studying its structure. First, dependable sequences permit the construction of ordinal scales. Such scales make no assumption of automatic progress in a unitary power without consideration of the interrelationships among the various kinds of behavioral achievements. Second, inasmuch as ordinal scales are based on a series of hierarchically arranged behavioral landmarks for each branch, they provide a method for investigating organizational structures and of testing the validity of those stages described by Piaget (1952a, 1954). Third, ordinal scales disentangle psychological development from age, thereby making it readily feasible to use age as the dependent variable with which to assess the impact of various independent environmental variables on development. Fourth, ordinal scales permit one to get psychological meaning directly from a child's performance. In traditional scales of development, the meaning derives from the interpersonal comparisons of performance implicit in such statistics as percentile ranks, standard scores, IQs, and even mental ages. Although one can readily compare children on ordinal scales, it is unnecessary to make such comparisons in order to obtain the psychological significance of a child's performance. Several of these modifications of strategy in assessment become evident in the data reported on the plasticity of object construction.

Readers of Piaget's works disagree about the underlying implications of what has been listed as the fourth issue, namely, the issue concerning the nature of the causes and the processes underlying the transitions between levels or stages. Although this issue can be refined indefinitely, the broadest division is that between the time-honored poles of maturation and learning. Here, however, learning must be extended to include all of the adaptive effects of informational interaction with the environment. On this issue, the impact of Piaget's work is ambiguous. On the one hand, his theory—with his constructs of accommodations, assimilation, and equilibration and with such aphorisms as "use is the aliment of a schema"—clearly gives a major role in the fostering of development to the ongoing interaction, both social and inanimate, between the infant and his environment. On the other hand, Piaget's empirical method associates each successive stage with an approximate age, and his evidence consists of behavioral landmarks that come at about the same age for all the children within each of his various small samples. So far as sensorimotor development is concerned, the number of subjects in his sample is only three: his own three children. The children in his other samples are presumably from middle-class families of Geneva.

If one takes Piaget's theory more seriously than his evidence, one would expect to find considerable variation in the ages at which infants achieve the successive stages of sensorimotor development. In fact, where visually directed reaching is the behavioral landmark, Piaget (1952a, p. 115) made an explicit point of the role of experience in the fact that his own three children achieved this landmark at ages 3 months, 4 months, and 6 months. He attributed the relatively retarded development of this landmark in Jacqueline to the restraints of clothing dictated by birth in winter.

On the other hand, if one takes the bulk of the evidence that Piaget has presented in his many books more seriously than his theory, one would expect little variation in his successive stages and the ages at which infants achieve the various behavioral landmarks. The matter did not interest Piaget much, but it is clearly one for empirical investigation and calls for the use of ordinal scales of sensorimotor development on children developing under conditions of rearing that vary as much as possible.

It was partly such a consideration that prompted the plan of cross-sectional investigations of sensorimotor development in orphanages with differing regimes. This plan led ultimately to the study done in Athens (Paraskevopoulos & Hunt, 1971) and to the studies under way in Iran and in the kibbutzim of Israel.

Because of an interest in the development of the symbolic processes and symbolic communication, only the Uzgiris–Hunt scales of object permanence and imitation, with emphasis on vocal rather than gestural imitation, have been used in these investigations.

The cross-sectional data reported here derive from the Greek study (see Figure 1). The data were obtained from children developing under three differing sets of rearing conditions. One set consisted of those rearing conditions in the Municipal Orphanage of Athens, where the infant–caretaker ratio was about 10 to 1. The second set consisted of the rearing conditions in Metera, the Queen's orphanage, which aimed to be a model baby center, where the infant–caretaker ratio was 3 to 1 during the time of waking–play. The third set consisted of that variety of rearing conditions to be found in a sample of working-class homes in which most of the babies were examined while they were in a day-care center for working mothers.

The other data presented in Figure 1 derive from two unpublished longitudinal studies, one of which was conducted by Uzgiris. Her sample consisted of a dozen home-reared babies from middle-class families in Worcester, Massachusetts. The babies were examined every other week during their first year, and every fourth week during their second year. The central purpose of this investigation was to get evidence concerning the sequential order of the landmarks in our presumably ordinal scales. The other set of longitudinal data derive from a similar series of repeated examinations, using the Uzgiris–Hunt scales, on eight children from families of poverty where the mother–caretakers participated in a training program for mothers at the parent and child center at Mt. Carmel, Illinois.[1]

Here I present only the evidence concerning object construction from the scale on object permanence (1) because I find that psychologists and educators typically find plasticity in the development of object construction more surprising than they find plasticity in vocal imitation; and (2) because the data on vocal imitation from the longitudinal studies were incomplete when this was written.

In Figure 1, the abscissa represents a selection of 5 of the 14 behavioral landmarks representing the 14 successive levels of development in the scale of visual following and object permanence. For levels below that on the extreme left, the examiner had already determined that the infant subject desired the object being used. The infant demonstrated that desire by reaching for the object: first, when it was completely uncovered and then when it was partially covered. Therefore, we start here with the level at which the infant recovered a desired object that had been completely covered. There are five columns ascending from the abscissa for this level. Under each column is the number of subjects participating in the mean and standard deviation of age for the condition of

[1] These data were gathered in collaboration with David Schickedanz and with the assistance of Earladeen Badger and Melvin Noe, Director.

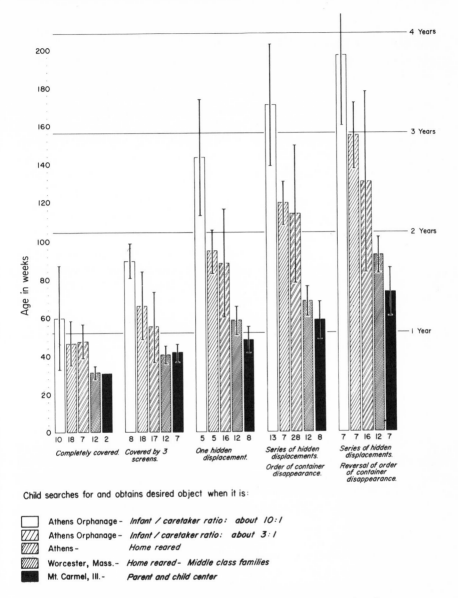

Child searches for and obtains desired object when it is:

	Athens Orphanage –	*Infant / caretaker ratio: about 10:1*
	Athens Orphanage –	*Infant / caretaker ratio: about 3:1*
	Athens –	*Home reared*
	Worcester, Mass. –	*Home reared – Middle class families*
	Mt. Carmel, Ill. –	*Parent and child center*

FIGURE 1. Object construction under differing conditions of rearing.

rearing represented by that column. At the next level represented along the abscissa to the right, the infants recovered an object covered by three screens. At the third level to the right, they retrieved an object that was hidden in a box after that box had disappeared under a cover and had been returned empty. At the fourth level, the infants retrieved the desired object after it had been hidden in a box and the box, in turn, had disappeared under a series of three different covers and had been returned empty. Here, the infant proceeded to look under the covers under which the box that hid the object had first disappeared and proceeded to the other screens in the same order in which the box had disappeared. At the level represented at the extreme right of this figure, the infants retrieved a desired object after such a series of hidden displacements, but each looked first where the box disappeared last, then explored the covers that hid the box in the reverse order in which the box disappeared. Such a performance implies that the infant at this level can replay the central processes representing the events of the eliciting situation in an order opposite to that in which the disappearances occur.

The dependent variable here, represented on the ordinate, is age. The top of each column represents the mean, and the line extending above and below represents the standard deviation of the ages of the children in the sample at that level. The independent variable consists of the rearing conditions for each of the five samples represented by the columns over each level of development.

The first three columns over each level of object construction derive from the Athens study, and the data are cross-sectional in character. The column at the left of each group of five represents a sample of children who had developed from a week or 10 days after birth in the Municipal Orphanage, where the baby—caretaker ratio was 10 to 1. The second column represents babies who developed from birth, or within 10 days after birth, at Metera Baby Centre, where the infant—caretaker ratio was of the order of 3 to 1. The third column, central in each successive group of five, represents home-reared babies from families of working-class status in Athens.

These variations in rearing conditions constitute the independent variable for the means of the ages of the children at each level of development assessed. It should be noted that the Athens study was cross-sectional. Every baby between 5 months and 5 years was examined with the scales of object construction and imitation. A similar sample of home-reared youngsters was examined in day-care centers for children of mothers who worked. Thus, each of these first three columns over the successive levels of object construction represents a different group of children.

The fourth column in each group of five in Figure 1 derives from the longitudinal study of infants from middle-class families in Worcester by Uzgiris. Since this is a longitudinal study, the 12 babies represented in each of the successive four columns are the same children.

The fifth column also represents a longitudinal study. The subjects were the babies from the families participating in the program of the parent and child center at Mt. Carmel, Illinois. Not all of the babies entered the program at the same time. The two represented in the fifth column at the extreme right of the first group of five columns at the left of Figure 1 were children of mothers from the poverty sector who had the status of paraprofessional workers in the Mt. Carmel center. These two infants participated in the day-care program of the Mt.

Carmel center from about a week following their birth and for a time were its only participants. There were ultimately eight children recruited into this program, but the examiner failed to examine one of them at the proper time; therefore, this child has been omitted from the sample represented at the extreme right.

What do the results show? First of all, there was an obvious tendency for mean ages to increase with each successive level of object construction. It is equally clear that the babies of the Municipal Orphanage, where the infant–caretaker ratio was of the order of 10 to 1, were the oldest of those at each successive level. Although the slope for their mean ages appears from inspection to rise more steeply than do the slopes for the mean ages of either the babies from Metera or those home-reared, this apparent interaction between conditions of rearing and rate of development is not statistically significant. On the other hand, these infants of the Municipal Orphanage of Athens were significantly older than the children growing up either at Metera or in their own homes. Although the children of Metera averaged older than those of home-reared children, these differences are not statistically significant.

Note the lines representing the standard deviations for the ages of the Greek children at the three levels at the right of the graph: one hidden displacement, a series of hidden displacements, and a series of hidden displacements with reversal of order. Note how much smaller the standard deviations are for the children of Metera at these levels than for the children of either the Municipal Orphanage or home rearing. This is an interesting finding that was not anticipated. At Metera, where the infant–caretaker ratio was approximately 3 to 1, the caretakers were student nurse–teachers who were carefully supervised. The conditions of rearing among children at Metera differed little. The standard deviations of age reflect this. At the Municipal Orphanage, where the infant–caretaker ratio was 10 to 1, it was extremely hard for a caretaker to be responsive to all 10 or her charges. Inevitably, each caretaker developed favorites, and consequently others were neglected. This is reflected in the standard deviations of age at which the children achieved these upper levels of object construction.

Note that the standard deviations for the ages at which the home-reared children reached the upper levels of object construction are even larger than the standard deviations for those in the Municipal Orphanage and much larger than those for the children at Metera. This finding was unexpected. What this finding suggests is that whatever genotypic variance there may be summates with the development-fostering, or development-hampering, impact of the variations in child rearing within these families. Clearly, the evidence from the differences between the means and these standard deviations indicates that the environmental circumstances encountered have a very substantial influence on the mean ages at which children achieve these higher levels of object construction.

The data from the cross-sectional study are not comparable with those from the two longitudinal studies for two reasons. Cross-sectional studies test children more or less randomly across the ages during which they remain at the given level of development indicated by the behavioral landmark used. Because longitudinal studies measure repeatedly every 2 weeks during the first year and every fourth week during the second year, they detect infants very soon after they have achieved the behavioral landmark indicating any given level of development. Second, the repeated examining inherent in the longitudinal method undoubtedly helps to foster development and make the ages at which samples of children achieve the successive stages younger than those for children in cross-sectional studies. It cannot be determined how much the advantages depicted here for the two samples of children in the longitudinal studies is a matter of such spurious methodological factors and how much is a matter of the development-fostering characteristics of their rearing.

On the other hand, the finding of the means at which the Mt. Carmel sample achieved the following of a desired object through one hidden displacement and then through a series of hidden displacements with reversal of the order in which the container disappeared is of interesting significance. Even though these children of the Mt. Carmel sample came from families of the lowest socioeconomic status in a small Illinois town, the average age at which they followed an object through one hidden displacement was 10 weeks younger than the average age for the Worcester sample of babies from middle-class background. Even more impressively, the age at which these Mt. Carmel babies achieved following an object through a series of hidden displacements with reversal of order averaged 19 weeks younger than the mean of the babies in the Worcester sample. This is a difference of nearly 5 months. This difference is of theoretical importance, for it calls into question the proposition that environmental interaction operates in threshold fashion. It also calls into question the fairly commonly held view that the child-rearing practices of the middle class approximate the optimum.

These bits of evidence clearly imply that the infant's interaction with his circumstances makes a substantial difference in his rate of sensorimotor development. While such investigations yield evidence of the importance of informational interaction with environmental circumstances in development, they have limited value. They do not indicate, for instance, what in the infant–environment interaction is important in fostering object construction. In order to get some inkling of what the infant–caretaker ratio means with respect to the characteristics of the infant–environment interaction, studies are being conducted with Paraskevopoulos regarding that interaction in the Greek orphanages.

One can get some inkling of what in an infant's experience is important from the nature of the program instituted at the Parent and Child Center at Mt. Carmel. This was the training program for mothers developed by Badger (1971a,b,c, 1972). It is an extension and improvement of the one originally employed and tested in the investigative program of Karnes (Karnes, Teska, Hodgins, & Badger, 1970). Conceptually, it is quite simple. First, the mothers and caretakers are encouraged strongly to believe that how they interact with and arrange the situations for their babies will make an important difference in the infants' development and in their future. Second, while their babies are very young, mothers and caretakers are encouraged to be responsive to any behavioral indicators of distress, and to remove the sources of that distress. Third, mothers and caretakers are taught that infants need time for interaction with play materials and with models, and they are taught to observe their infants for behavioral indications of interest, surprise, and boredom and of that distressful frustration which results from an infant's inability to cope with a situation. Fourth, and in close connection with the third aspect, mothers and caretakers are encouraged to provide their infants with materials and models that bring forth the behavioral signs of interest and to remove those that elicit behavioral signs of either boredom or distressful frustration. Fifth, mothers and caretakers are shown something of the sequence to be found in the developing of abilities and interest. From such information, observations of the nature of the materials and models in which an infant is currently interested provide mothers and caretakers with a basis for choosing materials that will shortly become interesting. In this fashion, Badger has attempted to solve what we like to call the "problem of the match." Finally, this approach emphasizes the importance of talking to the infants about the materials with which they are occupied, talking about what they are doing, and utilizing pseudo-imitation—and later, genuine imitation—to encourage vocal interaction. Such evidence as we have presented suggests that this training program for mothers is promising.

In the foregoing:

1. The criteria of levels of development have been outlined; criteria which might also serve for stages or states. We have also noted that our ordinal scales do not assume Piaget's six stages of sensorimotor development.
2. It has been indicated that sequential organization is far from pre-programmed, that it is far from theoretically trivial when there are transformations between successive levels or states.
3. The characteristics of the transformations between successive levels or states have been suggested as implicit in the nature of the differences between the characteristics of the observable behavioral landmarks of successive levels.
4. Evidence has been introduced indicating great variations in the ages at which infants and young children achieve the various levels of object construction. These are correlated with their environmental circumstances.

We hope that the hierarchical hypothesis about the nature of psychological development will be taken seriously. This hypothesis offers at least a fair tool for investigating sensorimotor development in the ordinal scales that Uzgiris and I have developed. We are very much in need of such scales for the preconceptual phase also. If we take the hierarchical conception of development seriously, what Piaget has termed the "preconceptual phase" is a portion of human psychological development about which we are abysmally ignorant. If we are to become more effective in early childhood education, we need instruments for assessment based upon this principle of sequential, hierarchical organization. We need them as tools to learn what kinds of experiences are required to foster psychological development. Moreover, only by taking this hypothesis of an epigenetic hierarchy in psychological development seriously and by determining where investigations based on it will lead can we make relics of history of the vestiges of preformation that still lurk in our theories of psychological development.

References

Badger, E. D. A mother's training program—The road to a purposeful existence. *Children,* September 1971, *18,* 168–173. (*a*)

Badger, E. D. *Teaching guide: Infant learning program.* Paoli, P.: The Instructo Corporation, A subsidiary of McGraw-Hill, 1971. (*b*)

Badger, E. D. *Teaching guide: Toddler learning program.* Paoli, Pa.: The Instructo Corporation, A subsidiary of McGraw-Hill, 1971. (*c*)

Badger, E. D. A mothers' training program—A sequel article. *Children Today,* May 1972, *1,* 7–11; 36.

Berlyne, D. E. What next? Concluding summary. In H. I. Day, D. E. Berlyne, & D. E. Hunt (Eds.), *Intrinsic motivation: A new direction in education.* Toronto: Holt, Rinehart, & Winston of Canada, 1971.

Binet, A., & Simon, T. Méthodes nouvelles pour le diagnostic du niveau intellectuel des anormaux. *L'année Psychologique,* 1905, *11,* 191–244.

Carmichael, L. The onset and early development of behavior. In L. Carmichael (Ed.), *Manual of child psychology* (2nd ed.). New York: Wiley, 1954.

Erikson, E. H. *Childhood and Society.* New York: Norton, 1950.

Galton, F. *Hereditary genius: An inquiry into its laws and consequences.* London: Macmillan, 1869.

Gesell, A. The ontogenesis of infant behavior. In L. Carmichael (Ed.), *Manual of child psychology* (2nd ed.). New York: Wiley, 1954.

Green, B. F. A method of scalogram analysis using summary statistics. *Psychometrika,* 1956, *21,* 79–88.

Greenberg, D., Uzgiris, I.C., & Hunt, J. McV. Attentional preference and experience: III. Visual familiarity and looking time. *Journal of Genetic Psychology,* 1970, *117,* 123–135.

Harlow, H. F. The formation of learning sets. *Psychological Review,* 1949, *56,* 51–65.

Hebb, D. O. *The organization of behavior.* New York: Wiley, 1949.

Hunt, J. McV. Piaget's observations as a source of hypotheses concerning motivation. *Merrill-Palmer Quarterly,* 1963, *9,* 263–275.

Hunt, J. McV. Intrinsic motivation and its role in psychological development. In D. Levine (Ed.), *Nebraska Symposium on Motivation,* Vol. 13. Lincoln: University of Nebraska Press, 1965.

Hunt, J. McV. The impact and limitations of the giant of developmental psychology. In D. Elkind & J. H. Flavell (Eds.), *Studies in cognitive development: Essays in honor of Jean Piaget.* New York: Oxford University Press, 1969.

Hunt, J. McV. Attentional preference and experience: I. Introduction. *Journal of Genetic Psychology,* 1970, *117,* 99–107.

Hunt, J. McV. Intrinsic motivation and psychological development. In H. M. Schroder & P.

Suedfeld (Eds.), *Personality theory and information processing.* New York: Ronald Press, 1971.

Karnes, M. B., Teska, J. A., Hodgins, A. A., & Badger, E. D. Educational intervention at home by mothers of disadvantaged infants. *Child Development,* 1970, *41,* 925–935.

McCarthy, D. Language development in children. In L. Carmichael (Ed.), *Manual of child psychology* (2nd ed.). New York: Wiley, 1954.

Paraskevopoulos, J., & Hunt, J. McV. Object construction and imitation under differing conditions of rearing. *Journal of Genetic Psychology,* 1971, *119,* 301–321.

Piaget, J. [*The origins of intelligence in children*] (M. Cook, trans.). New York: International Universities Press, 1952. (Originally published, 1936.) (*a*)

Piaget, J. [*Play, dreams, and imitation in childhood*] (C. Cattegno & F. M. Hodgson, trans.). New York: Norton, 1952. (Originally published, 1945.) (*b*)

Piaget, J. [*The construction of reality in the child*] (M. Cook, trans.). New York: Basic Books, 1954. (Originally published, 1937.)

Shirley, M. M. A motor sequence favors the maturation theory. *Psychological Bulletin,* 1931, *28,* 204–205.

Skinner, B. F. *Science and human behavior.* New York: Macmillan, 1953.

Stern, W. [*Psychological methods of testing intelligence*] (G. M. Whipple, trans.). Baltimore: Warwick & York, 1914. (Originally published in 1912.)

Uzgiris, I. C., & Hunt, J. McV. Attentional preference and experience: II. An exploratory longitudinal study of the effect of visual familiarity and responsiveness. *Journal of Genetic Psychology,* 1970, *117,* 109–121.

Uzgiris, I. C., & Hunt, J. McV. *Assessment in infancy: Ordinal scales of psychological development.* Urbana: University of Illinois Press, 1975.

Watson, J. B. *Behaviorism.* New York: Norton, 1924.

Weizmann, F., Cohen, L. B., & Pratt, R. J. Novelty, familiarity, and the development of infant attention. *Developmental Psychology,* 1971, *4,* 149–154.

Wetherford, M. J., & Cohen, L. B. Developmental changes in infant visual preferences for novelty and familiarity. *Child Development,* 1973, *44,* 416–424.

White, B. L. An experimental approach to the effects of experience on early human development. In J. P. Hill (Ed.), *Minnesota Symposia on Child Development.* Minneapolis: University of Minnesota Press, 1967, pp. 201–226.

Wolff, C. F. *Theoria Generationis.* Halle, 1759.

Wolff, C. F. De formatione intestinorum praecipue, tum et de amnio, aliisque partibus embryonis gallinacei nondum visis. *Novi Commentarii Academiae Scientiarum Imperialis Petropolitanae,* 1768, *12;* 1769, *13.*

Woodworth, R. S. Reinforcement of perception. *American Journal of Psychology,* 1947, *60,* 119–124.

PART II:
RESEARCH

CHAPTER 5

Information-Processing Tendencies in Recent Experiments in Cognitive Learning

Bärbel Inhelder

University of Geneva, Geneva, Switzerland

Piaget's theory concerns cognitive development and developmental epistemology. It is therefore not surprising that such a theory is itself constantly developing. New problems are being raised, new methods are applied to deal with these problems, and explanatory models are refined and readjusted to account for new findings. Piaget has shown that cognitive development has a direction and proceeds toward better and better adaptation of the knowing subject to the reality that is the object of his knowledge. Through intensive and detailed study of the acquisition of various concepts (number, weight, volume, space, time, causality, probability, and others), it was possible to determine the underlying structures of thought that allow the attainment of these concepts. Subsequently, it was possible to establish a hierarchy within these structures and to hypothesize their possible derivation. These structures have been formalized in algebraic form as grouplike structures and semilattices for the preformal stages of thought and as lattices and groups for the formal stage. The structures are atemporal and reflect the possibilities of a total system but to apprehend the formative mechanisms that can explain the transition from one stage to another, we have to go beyond such structural models. Piaget and his collaborators have become increasingly interested in dynamic models, more specifically in self-regulatory mechanisms.

From a biological point of view, all regulations during development go beyond a mere maintenance of equilibrium. They originate through compensation of perturbations arising either in the organism or in its environment and result in new constructions. Similarly, in psychological development, incomplete systems or partial systems that conflict with one another are enlarged or integrated through regulatory mechanisms. An important aspect of such mechanisms resides in *post hoc* corrections that modify action schemes.

Piaget calls his developmental epistemology "naturalist but not positivist." Cognitive behavior is an outward sign of the assimilatory and accommodatory capacities of a living organism. The biological aspect of Piaget's theory is often difficult to grasp for those psychologists who believe that mental development is infinitely malleable under favorable conditions and with adequate teaching methods, and who are convinced that what they think of as errors of growth can easily be corrected.

A biologically inspired theory that uses concepts such as assimilation, accommodation, and action schemes is very different from a learning theory that tries to account for cognitive development in terms of associations, connections, and conditioning. These latter types of mechanisms always suppose that two events are linked in the subject's mind because he has passively submitted to an outside pressure connecting the two. The concept of assimilation, by contrast, supposes that the subject actively assimilates a new event to already-existing structures. It is not a question of outside events molding the subject's mind but of his own activity on the outside world, plus the feedback from this action, which allows him to construct new concepts and action schemes.

There is thus an interaction between the knowing subject and the objects that are to be known. It is true that Piaget has until recently emphasized the constructive role of the subject and that comparatively little attention has been given to features of the objects favoring the attainment of knowledge. Objects can only be known, in closer and closer approximation, through the activity of the subject himself. The subject never attains complete knowledge of these objects; objectivity is the limit of these convergent processes. As knowledge of objects proceeds, the subject's activity becomes better and better organized. In a sense, this justifies Piaget's theoretical distinction between two types of knowledge: logicomathematical knowledge and the knowledge of the physical world. From the Piagetian point of view, these types of knowledge are the result, on the one hand, of the organization of the subject's activities (logicomathematical knowledge resulting from reflective abstraction) and, on the other hand, of the knowledge the subject gains about the object's properties (knowledge of the physical world resulting from physical abstraction).

From the point of view of developmental psychology, the relations between the two abstraction processes and their reciprocal influence have not yet been sufficiently studied. One of our ambitions is to explore these relations through learning experiments. We suppose that what the child learns about objects influences the way he organizes his own activity and vice versa and that in this link resides one of the dynamic factors of development. Learning experiments seem particularly apt to help us observe transition mechanisms at work. By accelerating the attainment of a concept and by working with the child in several sessions—sometimes as many as six during 2 or 3 weeks—we may observe, or even induce, some of the crucial moments in which "something happens." Evidently, we can never observe the mechanisms but only the behavior that is their result.

We hope that with new facts obtained from the learning experiments, we will be able to get some ideas as to the possible form of a dynamic model of transition mechanisms. In order to study as closely as possible the mechanisms at work in the transition of one substage to another, we chose to conduct learning experiments on the well-explored problems in conservation and class inclusion. As I have already stated, developmental psychology aimed first of all at establishing a hierarchy of underlying structures. Conservation principles and class inclusion operations are important indicators of the existence of a grouplike structure. Logically speaking, an operation transforms a state A into a state B, while its inverse transforms B back into A. Through these transformations, some quantitative property is kept constant, and this invariance can exist only in a coherent system of operations. It is for this reason that when a child understands that, for instance, the weight of a ball of plasticine does not change when the ball is transformed into a sausage or a pancake, we can interpret his understanding as an indicator of the existence of a coherent system of operations. Though the underlying structure of operations may be the same in many concepts of conservation, it is well known that in development they do not all appear at the same time but become established successively over a number of years. One of the very first concepts of conservation, attained by most children around the age of 6, is that of numerical quantity. At that age, children know that a change in the disposition of a set of discontinuous elements does not change its number. When presented with two linear arrangements of discontinuous elements in optical one-to-one correspondence, of which one is then spread out, younger children think that the spread-out elements, because they go "further" than the other elements, are "more" in number.

One of the questions we hoped to elucidate by learning experiments was how children construct more difficult conservation concepts once the conservation of numerical quantity is attained. Since the different conservation concepts had been extensively studied, both cross-sectionally and longitudinally, they appeared to constitute a privileged case in which we might be able to observe supposedly general transition-mechanisms in action.

In one of our experiments designed by Bovet (Inhelder, Bovet, & Sinclair, 1967), we tried to lead children, who in pretests showed an incipient notion of numerical conservation, to a grasp of the conservation of continuous quantities, normally acquired some 3 years later. In the given pretest, the children had to succeed in a test of numerical conservation, consisting of the following items. Two identical glasses, A and B, are filled with large beads. The experimenter and the child simultaneously drop beads, one or two at a time, into the glasses. Glass B then is emptied into a narrower glass (N) or into a larger glass (L). The conservation question is asked. The beads in glass N (or L) are then poured back into B. The beads in glass A are poured into L, and those in B are poured into N at the same time. The conservation question is asked again.

Children who passed the pretest then participated in the experiment. The following types of situations were used (the details of the procedure are not included here). In a preliminary situation, toy houses glued onto matchsticks are first set out in two rows in one-to-one correspondence (Figure 1). Then houses in the second row are displaced.

Questions are asked, first on conservation of the number of houses: "Are there as many black houses as white houses? Or more? Or less? How do you know?" Then on the length of the roads: "Is one of the roads just as long as the other road? Would you be just as tired walking on one road as on the other road? Or more? Or less?"

In other situations, the child himself has to construct paths with matchsticks. Both experimenter and subject have a number of matches at their disposal, but the subject's matches are shorter than those of the experimenter and of a different color. In this situation, seven of the subject's red matches add up to the same length as five of the experimenter's black matches. The experimenter constructs either a straight or a broken line, a "road," and asks the subject to construct a line of the same length, "just as long a road, just as far to walk." Three such problems are presented.

The first problem situation is the most complex: the experimenter constructs a sort of zigzag line and the subject has to construct a straight line of the same length directly underneath (Figure 2).

In the second situation, the subject again has to construct a straight line of

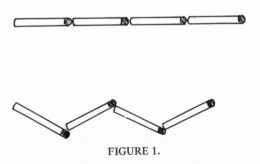

FIGURE 1.

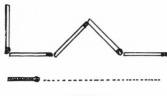

FIGURE 2.

the same length as the experimenter's zigzag line, but no longer directly underneath (Figure 3).

The third situation is the easiest, since the experimenter's line is straight and the subject is asked to construct a straight line directly underneath it (Figure 4). The experimenter uses the same number of matches (five) as in the first and second problem situations, so that in this third situation, when seven of the subject's matches are needed to make a straight line of the same length, a correct solution to the first and second situations is suggested by transitivity.

The three problem situations remain in front of the subject. After he has given his first three solutions, he is asked to give explanations and eventually to reconsider his constructions, while the experimenter draws his attention to one situation after another.

In this experiment, we interviewed a group of children with a mean age of 6 years who had to succeed in a test of numerical conservation without having the concept of conservation of lengths (Piaget & Szeminska, 1952). Not only do the subjects have to give consistent numerical conservation answers, but they also have to be able to justify their answers. Some typical examples of solutions to the three problems follow.

In the first problem situation, the most elementary solution is to construct a straight line whose extremities coincide with those of the experimenter's zigzag line. The child is convinced that the two lines are the same length, although his

FIGURE 3.

FIGURE 4.

line is made up of four short matches and the experimenter's line, of five long matches.

In the second situation, the child finds no ordinal point of reference because he has to construct his line at some distance from the experimenter's line, and so he uses the numerical reference: he constructs his line with the same number of matches the experimenter has used, regardless of the fact that his matches are shorter. When the experimenter now goes back to the first problem situation, the child notices, with some embarrassment, that he has constructed a line that he judged to be of equal length but that does not have the same number of elements as the model line. At this point, we often see amusing and original compromise solutions. For instance, in the first situation, the child may break one of his matches in two, thus creating a line with the same number of elements without destroying the ordinal correspondence (Figure 5). Another solution, again clearly indicating the conflict between ordinal and numerical references, consists of adding one match but placing it vertically instead of horizontally (Figure 6).

When the child is then asked to construct his line in the third situation, he starts by using the same number of matches (five) as the experimenter has used for his line. Since this time both lines are straight and the child's line is directly under the model line, he sees immediately that this does not give the right solution. Because his matches are shorter, his line is not as long as the model (Figure 7).

It is not the purpose of this paper to discuss in detail the purely psychological results of these learning sessions. We intend to use this experiment as one of the many examples of the intricate coordinations and differentiations that take place when a new concept is formed and of the nature of the processes that make this progress possible. In fact, in many other experiments, we observed the

FIGURE 5.

FIGURE 6.

same type of progress, and we feel justified in generalizing from this particularly clear instance.

We were able to observe that our subjects not only made considerable progress but that there were qualitative differences in this progress dependent on the developmental level of the subjects at the beginning of the learning sessions. A good proportion had clearly mastered conservation of length at the end of the sessions. Another group went only part of the way. Some subjects progressed little or not at all, thereby making explicit a number of obstacles that the more advanced or brighter children overcame so quickly that we might have missed their significance.

At the outset of the experiment, as was mentioned above, all of our subjects were capable of conserving simple numerical quantity, which implies that they had already coordinated the initial way of judging quantity by an ordinal relation—"going beyond" or "starting and finishing at the same point"—with a way of judging based on a one-to-one correspondence. It could therefore be supposed that the attainment of conservation of continuous length is a simple result of what in associationist theories is called *generalization.* Nonconservation of length shows that the obstacle is, again, an ordinal or topological way of judging by "going just as far" or "going further than." If lengths constructed from separate but contiguous elements had been presented, a "transfer" would have taken place, and the problem of transition mechanisms would have been solved in a simple but, for our purpose, uninteresting way. A first result of our analysis of the subjects' behavior showed clearly that this was not the way in which the transition took place.

Essentially, it was possible to distinguish four successive steps in the construction process. Those subjects that made hardly any progress at all showed us the importance of the first step. In the preliminary situation with the toy houses

FIGURE 7.

glued to matchsticks of equal length, one asks questions about the number of houses and the length of the road. These children answered correctly the number-of-houses question. They counted the houses and did not talk about one set of houses "going further" than the other. As soon as they were asked a question about the respective lengths of the roads, they did not think of counting the elements or of going back to the one-to-one correspondence. They answered incorrectly, judging according to the "going-beyond" criterion. In this way, it became clear that one or another of two or more different systems of evaluation could be elicited, both in a sense pertinent to the question, but neither sufficiently developed to allow their integration. There was successive activation of two separate systems, and no contradiction was felt by the subject.

A second step in the construction process follows very soon afterward. Instead of the two evaluation schemes arising separately, according to the question asked, both seem to be present practically simultaneously. For example, when the subjects had to construct a road "just as long" as and parallel to the experimenter's road but with shorter matches, they would start off by counting the elements, a scheme activated by the second problem situation, and build their path with the same number of elements. However, no sooner had they finished their construction, than they noticed that one path "went further" and they found their solution no longer acceptable. They could then turn to the other solution, but on noticing that despite the coincidence there were more small matches in the road than long matches in the other, they went back to their first solution. Neither could satisfy them and they could not conceive of a new solution taking both the preceding ones into account, although they were conscious of the contradiction.

The third step did not appear in all the different experiments, but it is perhaps the most significant one. It consists in an inadequate effort at integration and is visible in what we have called *compromise solutions.* The child, as we have already mentioned, breaks one of his matches in several pieces and thus obtains the same number of matches and still does not have a path that "goes beyond"; or he ignores the instruction that he has to make a straight road and puts one of his matches vertically instead of horizontally. In this way, he fulfills both his exigencies in a solution that at least temporarily satisfies him

From here, the fourth step in the construction process follows for many subjects. Instead of one scheme's operating as a *post hoc* correction on the other, we now see a reciprocal adjustment whereby the criterion of coincidence (sufficient provided the two paths are parallel) and that of numerical equility (sufficient provided all matches are of equal length) are successfully integrated into a coherent system that allows the child to solve problems of length in general and no longer only in special cases. Now the different schemes can be integrated, which gives a new impetus to the search for necessary and sufficient conditions for equality of length. This results in a complete understanding of the compensation involved. The children explain, "You need more matches when they are smaller" and "The road goes less far but it has zigzags."

Development takes place in a very similar way in all the processes that have come to light during our training experiments. There is, however, one essential difference. In the logical operations, in the strict sense of the term the regulatory mechanisms that lead sooner or later to an awareness of contradiction are not followed by compromise solutions in the form of partial compensations; instead, they are immediately followed by complete logical compensations that later result in correct solutions. A particularly striking example is the acquisition of logical quantification (Piaget & Szeminska, 1952; Inhelder & Piaget, 1964).

The problem of class inclusion concerns addition compositions. For instance, if B is in the general class and A and A' the subclasses, the following operations obtain: $A + A' = B$, $B - A' = A$, and $B - A = A'$. From this it can be deduced that if both A and A' are nonempty classes, B is larger than A and larger than A'. The inclusion of class A in class B provides the relationship that proves the statements "All A's are some B's" and "A is smaller than B." Certain subjects can agree with the first statement even though they do not understand the second. Complete understanding of the concept of inclusion implies the understanding of the link between the operation $A + A = B$ and the operation $B - A = A'$. This link takes the form of logical compensation. It is only at the level of concrete operations that the child becomes capable of working simultaneously on a general class defined by a general property (e.g., flowers) and on subclasses of this general class that are defined by a more restrictive property (e.g., roses). At the preoperatory level, the child does not conserve the whole when he has to compare it to one of the parts. His mistake is that when he begins by mentally evaluating A, he isolates it from the whole B and can only compare it with A' and not with B. When faced with a bunch of flowers containing a great many roses and a few tulips and asked if there are more roses or more flowers, the child replies that there are more roses. If he is then asked more than what, he often answers, "Than tulips." The main difficulty lies in the fact that the child is asked to compare within only one collection of the logical extension of a subclass A with the logical extension of the total class B.

Sinclair (Inhelder & Sinclair, 1969) has constructed a learning procedure in which the children had to construct by themselves two collections within which the subclasses varied in comparative size while the total collection was kept constant. The experimenter gives one girl doll six pieces of fruit, for example, four peaches and two apples (*PPPPAA*). The child is asked to give the other doll, the boy doll, "just as many pieces of fruit, so that they have just as much to eat, but more apples because he likes them better than peaches." The instruction is repeated as often as necessary, in different forms. The situation can be varied, made easier or more difficult.

Let me cite one typical example. At the beginning of the learning sessions, a 5½-year-old child asserts that the experimenter's instructions cannot be complied with: "It can't be done." Later, when he accepts that it can indeed be done, he gives the other doll an identical collection.

Q. What have you given him?
A. Two apples and four peaches.
Q. Can you remember what I just said?
A. He is to have *the same thing as the girl.*
Q. The same thing as what?
A. The same thing of *the other fruit.*

The experimenter's instructions, "Give the other doll more apples but just as many pieces of fruit," contain two conditions: *more apples* (referring to the subclass) and *just as many* (referring to the total class). In his interpretation of these instructions, the child seems to be incapable of simultaneously taking into account the four components, namely, the *same, more, total class,* and *subclass.* At first he mentions only the condition referring to the total class, "*the same thing as the girl,*" but when the experimenter asks him about the first part of the instructions, the child disconnects this condition from the total class and applies it to the subclass, "*the same thing of the other fruit.*" When the other condition, more apples, is stressed, the child applies it correctly but then neglects the first one. He says, "*We've got to add some then,*" and proceeds to add two apples to the whole collection, so that he now has four peaches and four apples. When he is asked if he is satisfied with his solution, he says that he is not. When we repeat the instructions, he takes away all the fruit he had given the boy doll, ponders, and then seems to make a real discovery: "*We've got to give just apples then?*" And he gives six apples. This solution actually does solve the conflict among the conditions. It does satisfy all the conditions, but vacuously. That is, he solves the problem of including one class in another by identifying the total class with one subclass. He identifies the part and the whole without going through the trouble of having to make compensations for the members of the complementary subclasses. As discussed previously, compensation means taking away one A' whenever one A is added.

The above solution is functionally similar to the third step in the construction process in the preceding experiment: the compromise solution between ordinal and numerical schemes. But here the compensation is immediately complete because it happens to be a special case of the solution. It is specific to logical problems in the strict sense where the ordinal and the extensional aspects of quantification are nondifferentiated.

That this is a special case and not a general logical solution is clearly demonstrated by the fact that when the experimenter's questions reintroduce the two aspects, the child again decomposes his solution into his former disconnected categories:

Q. There we are. Now what's he got?
A. Now he's got more apples than the girl.
Q. Right. Do they have the same *number of pieces* of fruit?

A. No, one's got more.
Q. Who?
A. The boy doll. I gave him two extra apples.
Q. You're sure? How many pieces of fruit has he got then?
A. (*without counting*) He's got eight.
Q. Have a good look and count them carefully.
A. (*very surprised*) He has got six too!

This particular child, who started at the lowest operative level, was not able to go further. However, children who were more advanced at the beginning of the learning sessions resolved the contradiction by a very adequate complete compensation of logical operations and acquired full understanding of class inclusion. This understanding was shown not only in situations involving two collections but also in the more difficult one-collection situation. Finally, for all these children, training in class inclusion had an unexpected positive effect on progress in conservation problems.

These two examples, among many of our learning studies, seem to lead to the following conclusions. Instead of a more-or-less straightforward type of development, with differentiations becoming more and more refined in the form of a treelike diagram the interactions between different subsystems appear to be of the greatest importance. As the first example shows, interactions between numerical and ordinal ways of dealing with problems of judging or constructing lengths lead to a conflict. It is this conflict that leads to the final resolution, through reciprocal assimilation of two different subsystems that do not necessarily belong to the same developmental level. The emergence of conflicts can explain the frequently occurring regressions in the subject's overt reasoning; they are only apparent regressions. In fact, they are observable symptoms of an internal event, announcing the beginning of a structuration of a higher order.

It now seems necessary to relate such a dynamic model to the classical Piagetian structural model. In the first place, the different systems of judging or constructing are internalized schemes. As to their appearance and their possibilities of being integrated into others, these schemes are determined by the general structure of the corresponding level of development.

In the second place, the hierarchical structures are in part common to both types of knowledge: logicomathematical on the one hand and knowledge of the physical world on the other. During the four successive steps in the construction process exemplified in the preceding experiments, either the apprehension of the properties of the subject's own actions or the apprehension of the actual properties or features of the objects may be preponderant at one time. The epistemological nature of their interplay becomes clear only in the structural model.

From our point of view, it is illusory to try to establish process models that are not closely linked to structural ones. Since we are concerned with the specific Piagetian perspective, it would appear that the structural model, since it is based on a developmental hierarchy of structures, can absorb the process model. In fact, if we want to find the components that are common to both, we should think of the all-important concept of compensation.

For each different level of development, the structural model uses specific types of compensation, for instance, the cancellation of a direct operation or, in the case of the logic of relations, reciprocity. Psychologically and even biologically speaking, disturbances always give rise to a reaction on the part of the organism but this reaction is not a passive submission to the environment. On the contrary, it leads to recombination of already existing capacities, in order to reestablish the destroyed equilibrium. In this sense, the reestablishment of an equilibrium involving a novel construction is also a compensation. The process model therefore comprises compensations in the psychological sense. We have seen the example of first a juxtaposition, then an opposition, then a compromise, and finally an integration of different schemes. The final integration, as we have also shown, gives rise to a new set of compensations.

In biology, new combinations take place only inside what are called *reaction norms.* Similarly, we propose that in cognitive development, these new combinations can occur only inside what may be called *zones of assimilation capacity.* The structural levels are at the root of the generation of new combinations, but simultaneously, they impose limits on the novelties than can be produced. The compensations in the structural model thus find their dynamic explanation in the process model; and the way these new combinations act finds explanation in the structural model.

References

Inhelder, B., Bovet, M., & Sinclair, H. Développement et apprentissage. *Revue Suisse de Psychologie,* 1967, *26,* 1–23.

Inhelder, B., & Piaget, J. [*Early growth of logic in the child*] (E. A. Lunzer & D. Papert, trans.). New York: Harper & Row, 1964.

Inhelder, B., & Sinclair, H. Learning cognitive structures. In P. H. Mussen, J. Langer, & M. Covington (Eds.), *Trends and issues in developmental psychology.* New York: Holt, Rinehart, & Winston, 1969.

Piaget, J. [*The child's conception of number*] (C. Cattegno & F. M. Hodgson, trans.). London: Routledge and Kegan Paul, 1952. (Originally published, 1941.)

Piaget, J., & Szeminska, A. 1952.

CHAPTER 6

Some Observations on Early Cognitive Development

Ina C. Uzgiris

Clark University, Worcester, Massachusetts

The issue that I should like to take as my central concern pertains most broadly to organization of achievements in development. If the notion of organization is taken to imply a differentiation of parts in a system and an interdependence of the parts through specifiable relations within the system, the issue of organization may be addressed at the level of actions or at the level of structurations of cognitive processes manifested in actions. One of the attractions of studying development during infancy stems from the relative lack of differentiation between the level of actions and of thought during this period. In the course of this presentation, I should like to share with you some observations on the interrelationships between various achievements stemming from a longitudinal study of a small group of infants as well as some speculations on the implications these observations have for the question of organization in early cognitive development.

Assuming as self-evident the limits imposed by the status of the biological organism, the various achievements observed during infancy may be conceived to be inherently unrelated, at one extreme, or related by virtue of being components in an organized system, at the other. If achievements are thought to be inherently unrelated, the co-occurrence of particular ones tends to be seen as the product of circumstances, the typical environmental conditions provided for individuals, and so forth. This approach invites an attempt to alter the pattern of co-occurrences of achievements by modifying some aspect of the circumstances, thus demonstrating the fortuitous nature of their association. The one aspect of circumstances common to all relates to the passage of chronological time, and thus, chronological time from the moment of birth is used as an anchor for examining the co-occurrence of other achievements. This is basically the approach of traditional infant or intelligence tests. Those achievements that are typically found to co-occur with a chronological anchor point are taken to characterize a level of psychological development, as evidenced in the notion of mental age. The nature of these achievements and their relationship to each other are not considered in themselves as long as they obtain with requisite regularity at that specific point in chronology. Individual departure from the norm creates no serious problem, since variation in individual circumstances can always be invoked to account for such departure.

On the other hand, achievements may be conceived to be related as manifestations of a given form of organization, with necessary and specifiable ties between them. Their co-occurrence becomes central, while their link to chronological time becomes quite unimportant. Piaget has dealt with the problems pertaining to the organization of achievements in development in terms of the concept of stage. Most generally, he has applied the term *stage* to each of the four major periods in development: the sensorimotor period, the preoperational period, the period of concrete operations, and the period of formal operations. At times, discernable levels within each period—namely, the level of entrance into a period, the level of transition, and the level of consolidation—have beem referred to as stages also. In all instances, Piaget has attempted to characterize a stage in terms of an overall structure and to emphasize his lack of concern with the specific chronological age at which it is manifest, except for the claim of an invariant order, arising out of a direct relationship between the structures of successive stages.

Given a notion of structural relationships between achievements of each level in development, lack of synchrony in their occurrence and individual variability in manifesting such achievements become much more critical. These problems have been recognized by investigators of development in the period of concrete operations. Several studies (Dodwell, 1963; Tuddenham, 1971) have observed a considerable lack of correspondence in the same individual in the appearance of achievements taken to be manifestations of the same concrete operational structures. One approach to this problem is to think of structures as specific to particular domains such as quantity, space, causality, etc., or as specific to particular sets of operations. However, Piaget (1971) has recently spoken against such delimitation of cognitive structures, claiming that he is "looking for total structures or systems with their own laws, systems which incorporate all their elements and whose laws cover the entire set of elements in the system" (p. 3). Another approach is to posit variability upon formation of a structure—that is, during initial access to a stage in development—but progressive integration and consolidation of various achievements with its ascendance. There is some empirical support for this suggestion in studies of concrete operational children (Nassefat, 1963; Tuddenham, 1971; Uzgiris, 1964), but the question still remains open. Furthermore, a noncircular specification of the initial phase and the consolidation phase would be required for a strong demonstration of this proposition.

In the sensorimotor period of development, Piaget (1952) has identified six levels, which he also calls *stages*. While he has repeatedly stated that a logic of actions is constructed and culminates in an organization of displacements and positions according to a "group" structure, with practical reversibility and associativity (detours), in a notion of the permanence of objects, and in an objectification and spatialization of causality (Piaget & Inhelder, 1969), he has not been very explicit about the organization of achievements at each of the sensorimotor stages. In view of some of the recent formulations regarding criteria for the identification of stages in development (Pinard & Laurendeau, 1969), it seems almost better to reserve the term *stage* to the sensorimotor period as a whole and to attempt, first, to explicate the structures characterizing identifiable levels in sensorimotor intelligence. The question of synchrony of structuration in different domains at these levels must be also resolved.

It is somewhat surprising that Piaget's theory has not inspired more studies of infant congitive development. There have been attempts to relate the rate of development in various domains—mostly construction of the object—to the environmental circumstances of infants (Golden & Birns, 1968; Paraskevopoulos & Hunt, 1971; Wachs, Uzgiris, & Hunt, 1971) or to relate cognitive achievements to interpersonal behavior (Bell, 1970; Décarie, 1965; Serafica & Uzgiris, 1971). The question of sequential order of achievements in sensorimotor development has received the most systematic study. Corman and Escalona (1969) have investigated the invariance of the sequence of stages pertaining to the development of prehension, object permanence, and spatial relationships. Using both longitudinal and cross-sectional approaches, they confirmed the invariance of the order of ascent to achievements marking the stages in each domain. It is interesting to note that in examining the appearance of achievements deemed characteristic of any one stage, they found neither synchrony, nor a regular sequence, nor even a consolidation of the various achievements prior to progress to the next stage within the same domain. The co-occurrence of achievements in different domains was not studied. Similarly, the work that Professor Hunt and I have carried out to construct scales for assessing development in several domains during infancy was focused on establishing invariant sequences of achievements (Uzgiris & Hunt, 1975), and the problem of correlation between achievements in different domains was treated only secondarily.

The one attempt to look at congruence of sensorimotor achievements across domains was carried out by Woodward (1959), not on infants, but on severely mentally retarded children. On the basis of their performance in a number of situations, the children were assigned to a stage of sensorimotor intelligence and also to a stage with respect to object-concept development, to problem-solving behavior (e.g., the use of means), and to level of circular reactions. Considerable consistency was obtained between the child's stage of sensorimotor intelligence and his level in object-concept development (with 87% of the children classified at the same stage in both), as well as between level of circular reactions and problem-solving behavior (with 52% classified at the same stage in both). In view of the considerable variability in level of development in different domains that has been observed in children attaining concrete operations, Woodward's finding of consistency may be interpreted as due to the nature of her subjects, who may be considered to be almost arrested in their development. On the other hand, it may be that greater consistency in development across domains should be expected at the level of sensorimotor intelligence, with an increase in variability as the complexity of cognitive structures increases with development.

Another impetus for considering the issue of organization of achievements comes from several recent reports of great plasticity in the age at which some of the landmarks of sensorimotor intelligence are achieved by infants in differing circumstances. Some of the earlier studies of object—concept development in infants replicated the ages for various achievements in this domain fairly closely (within a month or two) suggesting only sampling variability. However, the study by Paraskevopoulos and Hunt (1971) on three groups of Greek infants found marked retardation in the orphanage samples, with the highest level of object-concept development being reached from 10 to 20 months later, on the average, by orphanage infants than by typical home-reared infants. On the other hand, in a thesis recently submitted to Brown University, Gaiter (1972) reported that a group of infants given training in activities related to the construction of the permanent object by their own mothers were significantly advanced in object-concept development in comparison to a control group at the end of a 6-month training period. In fact, at the age of 13½ months, 5 of the 12 experimental infants showed behavior indicating the highest levels of object-concept development, about a 6-month advance in comparison to typical home-reared infants. Unfortunately, neither of these studies provides information on whether the retardation or advance, respectively, characterized the infants' functioning in other domains. If circumstances can affect the rate of development during the sensorimotor period to such a marked degree, the generality of their effect becomes a particularly poignant question for the issue of structural organization of sensimotor achievements. Particularly if the notion of stages *within* the sensorimotor period is to be maintained, a consistency of achievements across domains in varied circumstances must be demonstrated.

In order to obtain information on infant development in several domains over time, a group of 12 infants was observed at regular intervals, from the age of 1 month up to 2 years, using the situations from scales we had devised (Uzgiris & Hunt, 1975). The infants came from varied socioeconomic backgrounds, but all had parents sincerely concerned with their well-being. They were observed in their own homes by the same experimenter throughout the 2-year period. The study has been completed recently and will, hopefully, provide information not only on the intercorrelation of achievements across domains at different levels in development but also on the changing interpatterning of achievements during transitions from one level to another. All the analyses on the data have not been completed, and furthermore, they tend to produce complex patterns, resisting succinct presentation (see also Uzgiris, 1973). Therefore, I shall present some general ideas arising from my examination of these results.

First of all, these longitudinal results confirm, with few exceptions, the ordering of achievements that had been obtained from scaling of the observations on infants studied in the construction of the scales. The exceptions are of two kinds: either one or two infants did not follow the expected sequence (in which case the result might be due to error in assessment) or two achievements were as likely to appear in one order as in reverse (in which case the result would suggest that the two achievements are not hierarchically related). I noted with interest Inhelder's (1971) recent comment that in an ongoing study of concrete operational development across various domains at Geneva, they are finding that only some 25% of the children in a replication sample show exactly the same sequence of achievements as was established as modal for a previous sample, and another 50% of the children show a small number of inversions or errors. The results of both of these studies suggest that structurations within the larger developmental stages may be less rigid than originally assumed, allowing some substitutability between achievements and permitting considerable plasticity in the rate of development within specific domains.

Moreover, my first attempt to evaluate interrelationships between achievements in different domains was quite disappointing. Intercorrelations between the infants' ranks in each domain—notion of object permanence, development in means, imitation, causality, schemes for relating to objects, and construction of object relations in space—in terms of the level attained at each month of age were generally low, revealing no particular patterns. There were no periods of higher intercorrelation that might suggest a period of consolidation prior to transition to a new level. However, the use of chronological age intervals was a crude approach to the problem, particularly since the data revealed considerable variability in the rate of development for these infants. Another attempt to look at interrelationships involved setting up contingency tables between achievements in different domains and a search for regularities in the attainment of those achievements. Such contingency tables revealed a number of strong relationships between various achievements and suggested that it may be possible to delineate and characterize at least three levels in the development of sensorimotor intelligence. I have tried to characterize these three levels both in terms of an assumed structuration and in terms of the actual achievements manifested. These three levels may be roughly equated with Piaget's Stages IV, V, and VI of the sensorimotor period, but I hope to give them slightly more detailed articulation. I do not mean to imply that these levels do not have earlier roots; however, at present, it seemed possible to characterize only these particular levels and to relate them to my observations in the longitudinal study.

The first level may be characterized by the appearance of subcomponents in actions. This appearance of subcomponents seems to be initiated by a differentiation between self-initiated actions and environmental outcomes that become progressively more articulated. The appearance of at least two-component actions implies some organization of the components; the relations established between the components may constitute the beginnings of the "logic of actions" mentioned by Piaget (1970). He has suggested that the incorporation of one scheme as a subpart of another may constitute the precursor for the operation of inclusion, while the ordered execution of first one scheme and then another may constitute the precursor for the ordering operation. It seems that the appearance of two-component actions makes both of these relations possible. In the domain of object-concept development, this level seems to be manifest in the achievement of search for an object completely covered by a screen. The mean age for this achievement was 7 months and 8 days in the sample of infants under discussion. This achievement requires the construction of a two-component action, involving the removal of the screen and the grasp of the object, which is initiated by an attempt to obtain the object while the object is perceptually not available. Prior to the attainment of this step in object-concept development, all infants in the sample were observed to engage in examining behavior and in specific attempts to reproduce interesting spectacles, which Piaget has called "procedures." Both of these types of activities imply some focusing on the outcomes of actions and probably facilitate the ensuing differentiation of actions and goals.

There seem to be several grounds for considering this a distinct level in development. Looking again at object-concept development, while the correlations in the age of achievement between one step in the sequence and other steps were not high overall, indicating little individual consistency in the rate of progress, the correlations between the age of beginning search for an object completely covered by a screen and the extension of search to a number of screens were fairly high. For the sample in question, beginning of search for a partially covered object correlated only around .3 with the beginning of search for a completely covered object; however, the beginning of search for a completely covered object correlated around .7 with search for an object under one of two or one of three screens and around .5 with search for an object following a series of visible displacements. A number of associated achievements appeared in other domains during the interval spanned by the extension of search for an object from one to a number of locations; for the sample under discussion, an interval of 4 months was the average. In terms of schemes shown in relation to objects, 10 of the 12 infants were *not* actively dropping objects and observing their fall at the beginning of this interval, but 11 of the 12 were engaging in this activity at the time they searched for objects following a series of visible displacements. It seems that the dropping activity involves a two-component action, since the object is released by the infant to move through space and is then visually relocated. Similarly, while none of the 12 infants showed what I have called differentiated schemes at the beginning of this interval, 11 of the 12 engaged in such activities at the end. I would argue that most differentiated schemes involve two-component actions, often tied by an inverse relation, such as crumpling and straightening, tearing and putting together, putting in and taking out, and so forth. In the domain of imitation, 10 of the 12 infants did not imitate sound patterns familiar to them at the beginning of this interval, but only 2 did not do so by the end. Also, none of the 12 infants imitated complex actions composed of familiar schemes at the beginning, but only 5 did not do so in the end. The development in imitation at this level seems to involve the taking of the modeled action as a goal with an attempt to reconstruct the appropriate action to reproduce it. Some instances of an infant's reproducing only a part of a modeled act are quite instructive. Furthermore, while 11 of the infants did not make use of relationships between objects such as that of support at the beginning of this interval, all did so at the end. It seems that a number of achievements in different domains requiring a differentiation of action from goal in order to commence at least a two-component action are achieved in parallel within a relatively short interval. These achievements manifest the beginning of the structuration of actions and may be considered to form a distinct level in development. It may be of interest to note that in studying the taking into possession of multiple objects, Bruner (1970) noted the appearance of the strategy of setting one object in reserve while picking up another in infants of roughly the same age as the age of infants at this level in development in the present sample. What *does not* occur at this first level is an immediate modification of actions as a result of their outcome. Such modification seems to be characteristic of the next level.

The second level in sensorimotor development may be characterized by the beginning of regulation of actions by their outcomes and thus a gradual modification of actions to attain various goals. The most prominent feature of various achievements at this level is the alteration of actions through gradual approximation, the taking into account of correspondence between outcome and goal. Since new forms of action are thus constructed, it may be that it is in this sense that Piaget has talked of the appearance of an interest in novelty at the fifth sensorimotor stage. The appearance of regulation by outcome is most clearly evident in the infant's activities in relation to objects, in imitation, and in means behavior. For example, at the time when infants begin to search for an object in several locations or under a number of screens, practically none shows activities with objects that indicate a social influence on his actions. However, very soon afterwards, the social influence on his actions becomes evident, so that instead of examining, banging, dropping, and stretching, he begins to push toy cars around, to hug dolls or cuddly animal toys, to build with blocks, and to put a necklace around his neck, the actions specific to each object. The adoption of socially approved ways of acting on toys probably reflects both imitation of models and modification of actions by their outcome. Furthermore, at about the same time, varied relationships between objects—for example, one serving as an extension of another—begin to be exploited in the obtaining of desired goals. The use of these relationships is often achieved through a gradual modification of initially ineffective actions. In regard to imitation, the infant's behavior indicates not only an attempt to reconstruct the model by means of known schemes but also the ability to recognize failure to reproduce the model accurately. It was noticed that infants imitated unfamiliar gestures visible to them more readily when they were performed in relation to an object than when presented as a gesture. For instance, sliding a piece of paper back and forth was imitated more readily than the sliding action alone. This suggests that an act with a definite result may facilitate reproduction by providing an outcome for the infant to reconstruct. The successive modifications in an action that the infants show in gradually approximating the model presented by the experimenter are also illuminating. This level corresponds roughly to the appearance in the domain of object construction of search for objects hidden by means of an invisible displacement in one or a number of locations; that is, the infant has to infer the location of the object when it is not found where it was seen to disappear. For the present sample, between 14 and 15½ months was the average age for such search. Thus, at the appearance of search for an object hidden by an invisible displacement under one of the three screens, 10 of the 12 infants showed socially influenced activities with objects regularly. Similarly, at the same point, the majority of infants (7 of the 12), began to imitate novel sounds presented by the experimenter directly, after a period of responding to them by varied vocal responses. All infants attempted to imitate novel visible gestures by means of gradual approximation at the time they began to search for an object hidden by one invisible displacement, although only 5 of the 12 imitated novel gestures directly. In addition, most infants at this point seemed to recognize centers of causality in objects and therefore learned from demonstrations how to activate objects or produce some spectacle, frequently through gradual approximation. Thus, while a diversity of new achievements may be observed to occur in parallel at this level, including a great deal of specialization in actions, the construction of regulating relationships between outcomes and actions, with compensation and correction of succeeding actions, seems to be the advance in structural organization.

The last level in sensorimotor development may be characterized by implicit representation of objects and events. Piaget has described sensorimotor development as culminating in the construction of a group of displacements that has practical reversibility and thus leads to the first invariant, the notion of the permanent object. It seems that the organization of actions in terms of a network of relations, including combination, inversion, correspondence, and practical reversibility, makes internalized actions possible and thus gives rise to practical inference, evocation of nonongoing events, and modification of actions without overt trial and error. If the achievement of the highest level in object construction—that is, the beginning of search for objects following a series of invisible displacements with the ability to reconstruct the path of an object in reverse—is taken as an index for this level of development (21–23 months of age on the average, in the present sample), a number of parallel achievements in other domains may be found. By the time these infants began to search for objects following a series of invisible displacements, all were engaging in activities with objects showing a social influence, all were imitating novel sounds directly, and all were imitating novel visible gestures directly. They were beginning to imitate novel invisible gestures, for example, facial gestures that one cannot see oneself perform and thus from which one cannot obtain direct visual feedback about the outcome of the attempt. However, by the time these infants began to reconstruct the path of the object in reverse, 9 of the 12 were imitating invisible gestures directly. Similarly, at the same point, 9 of the 12 infants were imitating new words regularly, which they were just starting to do at the beginning of this level. In regard to activities with objects, the naming of objects in recognition appeared often in the context of interacting with another person. The above should be distinguished from the use of a verbal label, as it involves the examining of an object and the use of the name to express the possibilities suggested by the object. Of the 12 infants, 10 were naming objects in recognition by the time they constructed a reverse path in their search for objects. In addition, their activities with objects frequently evidenced evocation of objects or events that were not within their perceptual field at the moment, that is, the beginning of symbolic play. Furthermore, if they found direct access to a desired object blocked, the majority of the infants by this time constructed detours through space and thus were able to reach their goal. Evidence for the construction of solutions to problem situations without overt groping was also obtained at this level. All infants began to show foresightful behavior in one problem situation (involving the necklace and the container), and 8 of the 12 did so in another (the solid ring). It seems that the coordination achieved between the construction of multicomponent actions and the regulation of action sequences by their outcomes at this level allows for a nonovert adaptation of actions or, in other words, thought.

The three levels of organization in sensorimotor intelligence that have been outlined seem to be supported by the occurrence of a number of achievements in rough parallel, all of which may be interpreted as exemplifying that particular level of organization. The parallels are, however, rough, and the question of synchrony in achievements across domains in sensorimotor functioning is still open. The study of this question is important to a theoretical understanding of development, but it demands extensive observation of a sample of subjects at frequent intervals over a period of time. Moreover, it is often difficult to come to an agreement that a particular set of actions in a given situation do, in fact, index the structural relations in question. No one behavior can serve as an index in all instances, and the problems of agreeing on whether a performance does or does not reflect a supposed structuration seen in the field of "conservation" research may be expected to recur in such investigations. Nevertheless, the sensorimotor period seems particularly suited to these investigations, since the length of time involved in a study of the transition from one level to another is not overburdening.

A more detailed articulation of three successive levels in sensorimotor intelligence—the beginning of organization between components of actions in terms of relations of inclusion, order, etc., initiated by differentiation of actions and goals; the beginning of regulation of actions by their outcomes; and the coordination into a structure of multicomponent actions and outcome regulations—hopefully may facilitate further study of the organization of achievements by suggesting additional situations in which evidence of these structurations should be sought. A better grasp of the organization of the various achievements in the sensorimotor period may facilitate not only the study of the plasticity of the organism in varied circumstances but also the understanding of the full impact of a particular modification in circumstances on psychological development.

This chapter is based on a paper presented at the Second Annual Symposium of the Jean Piaget Society on May 24, 1972.

References

Bell, S. M. The development of the concept of object as related to infant–mother attachment. *Child Development,* 1970, *41,* 291–311.

Bruner, J. S. The growth and structure of skill. In K. Connolly (Ed.), *Mechanisms of motor skill development.* London: Academic Press, 1970.

Corman, H. H., & Escalona, S. K. Stages of sensorimotor development: A replication study. *Merrill-Palmer Quarterly,* 1969, *15,* 351–361.

Décarie, T. G. *Intelligence and affectivity in early childhood.* New York: International Universities Press, 1965.

Dodwell, P. C. Children's understanding of spatial concepts. *Canadian Journal of Psychology,* 1963, *17,* 141–161.

Gaiter, J. L. *The development and acquisition of object permanence in infants.* Unpublished master's thesis, Brown University, 1972.

Golden, M., & Birns, B. Social class and cognitive development in infancy. *Merrill-Palmer Quarterly,* 1968, *14,* 139–149.

Inhelder, B. Developmental theory and diagnostic procedures. In D. R. Green, M. P. Ford, & G. B. Flamer (Eds.), *Measurement and Piaget.* New York: McGraw-Hill, 1971.

Nassefat, M. *Étude quantitative sur l'évolution des opérations intellectuelles.* Neuchâtel: Delachaux et Niestlé, 1963.

Paraskevopoulos, J., & Hunt, J. McV. Object construction and imitation under differing conditions of rearing. *Journal of Genetic Psychology*, 1971, *119*, 301–321.

Piaget, J. [*The origins of intelligence in children*] (M. Cook, trans.). New York: International Universities Press, 1952. (Originally published, 1936.)

Piaget, J. [*Genetic epistemology*] (E. Duckworth, trans.). New York: Columbia University Press, 1970.

Piaget, J. The theory of stages in cognitive development. In D. R. Green, M. P. Ford, & G. B. Flamer (Eds.), *Measurement and Piaget*. New York: McGraw-Hill, 1971.

Piaget, J., & Inhelder, B. [*The psychology of the child*] (H. Weaver, trans.). New York: Basic Books, 1969.

Pinard, A., & Laurendeau, M. "Stage" in Piaget's cognitive-developmental theory: Exegesis of a concept. In D. Elkind & J. H. Flavell (Eds.), *Studies in cognitive development: Essays in honor of Jean Piaget*. New York: Oxford University Press, 1969.

Serafica, F., & Uzgiris, I. C. Infant–mother relationship and object concept. *Proceedings of the 79th Annual Convention of the American Psychological Association*, 1971, *6*, 141–142.

Tuddenham, R. D. Theoretical regularities and individual idiosyncrasies. In D. R. Green, M. P. Ford, & G. B. Flamer (Eds.), *Measurement and Piaget*. New York: McGraw-Hill, 1971.

Uzgiris, I. C. Situational generality of conservation. *Child Development*, 1964, *35*, 831–841.

Uzgiris, I. C. Patterns of cognitive development in infancy. *Merrill-Palmer Quarterly*, 1973, *19*, 181–204.

Uzgiris, I. C., & Hunt, J. McV. *Assessment in Infancy*. Urbana: University of Illinois Press, 1975.

Wachs, T. D., Uzgiris, I. C., & Hunt, J. McV. Cognitive development in infants of different age levels and from different environmental backgrounds: An explanatory investigation. *Merrill-Palmer Quarterly*, 1971, *17*, 283–317.

Woodward, M. The behavior of idiots interpreted by Piaget's theory of sensorimotor development. *British Journal of Educational Psychology*, 1959, *29*, 60–71.

CHAPTER 7

Cognitive Development During and After the Preconceptual Period

Jonas Langer

University of California, Berkeley, California

At the heart of structural developmental theory is the thesis that long-term, ontogenetic progress is a self-generated process of equilibration. Equilibration requires both coordination within the subject's functional structures and interaction between the functional structures of the subject and his objects of cognition—the physical, social, and personal environment.

Two facets of coordination within the subject's functional structures are especially important to the understanding of preconceptual development. The first facet is self-generated mental operations that the subject can use to construct physical, social, and personal preconcepts (Langer, 1969b, pp. 168–177). The second facet is the developmental filiations (e.g., genetic prerequisites and parallelisms) between two forms of mental activity, operations, and figurations (Langer, 1974). Previously, we have suggested that logical implication is a more appropriate explanatory model of development than efficient determination or causality. Consequently, we suggested that one of the two major tasks for developmental theory is to specify "the logical structure of each functional stage of action in such a way that the first stage logically implies but does not actually contain the structure of the second, the second logically implies the third, and so on until the end stage" (Langer, 1969b, pp. 168–169). A main derivative of this explanatory model of development is the following structural developmental hypothesis about the form and content of cognition:

> The form of cognition constructed at one stage serves, in part, as intrinsic (subject) content out of which the form of the subsequent stage is self-generated.

When applied to the cognitive development of the preconceptual period, this form—content hypothesis reads as follows:

> The content—that is, material source (determinant or cause)—out of which the form of the young child's preoperations develops is his sensorimotor cognition.

At its most advanced, the form of sensorimotor activity is fundamentally pragmatic and presentational (Langer, 1969b, pp. 112–131). Consequently, the sensorimotor child's physical, social, and personal conceptions remain fundamentally nondifferentiated and uncoordinated.

Once formed, presentational pragmatics constitute the developmental source of the young child's intrinsic cognitive content. This is the intrinsic informational aliment that the young child differentiates and coordinates in order to construct his subsequent stage of cognition. The form that it takes is that of representational preoperations. This is a quasi-deductive, transitional form between the particularities of presentational pragmatics and the generalities of representational (concrete) operations. The general structural character of this transitional cognitive form is transductive. Here is an apt observation of transductive reasoning:

> At 2;1 (13) J. wanted to go and see a little hunchbacked neighbour whom she used to meet on her walks. A few days earlier she had asked why he had a hump, and after I had explained she said: *"Poor boy, he's ill, he has a hump."* The day before J. had also wanted to go and see him but he had influenza, which J. called being "ill in bed." We started out for our walk and on the way J. said: *"Is he still ill in bed?*—No. I saw him this morning, he isn't in bed now.—*He hasn't a big hump now!"* (Piaget, 1962, p. 231).

J. associates Y (ill) with X (hump) and Y (ill in bed) with Z (influenza). She concludes that $\bar{Y}$ (not ill in bed) implies $\bar{X}$ (He hasn't a big hump now!). The structure of J.'s reasoning may be characterized in a negative way as pseudo-transitivity and in a positive way as transductive transitivity.

Transductive preoperations are the developmental precursors of intuitive preoperations, which in turn are the precursors of concrete operations. It would be both a logical and a structural developmental confusion to identify precursory forms, such as transductive transitivity, with more developed forms, such as concrete operational transitivity. In passing, it might be useful to point out that such confusions may well account for much of what we may call the "anything you can find, I can find it earlier" research literature. In general, this literature claims that logical operations may be found in children younger than the ages predicted by structural developmental theory. A recent example is the report of transitive judgments by 4-year-olds (Bryant & Trabasso, 1971). Indeed, there is little doubt that problems could have been presented to J. when she was only 2 years old that would have resulted in "even earlier" correct but transductive judgments.

In sum, the initial intrinsic content of the young child's postsensorimotor cognitions is presentational and pragmatic, while its form is progressively representational and transductive. The preconceptual products may therefore be expected to be diffuse in content and syncretic in form (Werner, 1948; Langer, 1970). A derivative empirical hypothesis then reads:

> The conceptual constructions of transductive representations are relatively nondifferentiated and uncoordinated physical, social, and personal preconcepts.

This general empirical hypothesis about the transductive representational stage, from about 2 to 5 years, is being investigated in a number of related ways in our laboratory (Damon, 1971, 1974; Langer, 1972; Lemke, 1971, 1974). The basic research objective is twofold. The first is to analyze the structural development of transductive preoperations during the representational stage. The second is to trace the manifestations of transductive reasoning in the physical, social, and personal preconcepts constructed by representational cognition.

To ensure that representational rather than presentational concepts were required, part of one investigation (Lemke, 1971, 1974) presented the task material in pictorial form. The pictures represented portraits of the same family at different times from 1949 to 1963. Specifically, the photographs show the family in 1949 (parents and 3 children), 1954 (parents and 5 children), 1956 (parents and 6 children), 1960 (parents and 6 children), and 1963 (parents and 6 children). The child is questioned about the relations between the pictures and between the individuals they portray. Thus, this task requires representational reasoning in order to be dealt with at all, but the operational structure of the representational cognition may range from transductive to concrete operational.

In the fragments of subjects' protocols quoted below, the subject's performance is italicized and the following notation is used. The letter A designates the father. The letters B, C, and D designate the male offspring in order of their birth. The letter W designates the mother. The letters X, Y, and Z designate the female offspring in order of their birth. The numbers 1 to 5 refer to the photographs in the order they were taken from 1949 to 1963. The designations 1a and 1b refer to two copies of the 1949 photographs. Thus, for example, the first notation in the first protocol fragment (presented below) from MAT that $Y3 = X1$ reads: MAT identified the second-born female offspring in the third photograph with the first-born female in the first photograph.

At the beginning of transductive representations, the young child's order or durational prerelations consist of syncretic couplings of members within and/or between pictures by appearance, that is, configurational elements. These configurative elements provide the basis for the preconception of duration, successivity, or simultaneity that is beginning to develop.

MAT (2;7). He constructs the following identifications: $Y3 = X1$. $Z3 = D5$. $X5 = W5 = X3$. $D3 = Z5$. Then he places three pictures in the order 3, 1, 5. Finally, MAT claims that $X1$ is himself. The tester notes some similarity in appearance.

S55 (2;11). "Do you see any people in those pictures (two identical copies, 1a and 1b, of picture 1) that are the same?" *"Yeah," and points to all people, successively, in each photo* . . . "Where is he (C1a)?" *"Right here:" $C1a = B1b$.* "This one is this one?" *"Yeah."*

Marcie (2;8). "Do you see any of the same people in these two pictures (1a and 1b)?" *No response.* "Is he (A1a) in that picture (1b)?" *Marcie constructs: $A1a = A1b$.* "Where's this little boy (C1a), do you see another picture of this little boy?" *Marcie constructs: $C1a = B1b$. $X1a = X1b$. $W1a = W1b$.*

These protocol fragments reveal two related and basic, original characteristics of transductive representation. The first relates to the young child's physical preconceptions. Preorderings are constructed with little regard for—and not consistent with—physical time, whether of succession or of simultaneity. The second relates to the young child's social—personal preconceptions. The syncretic identities constructed are not consistent with and not bounded by elementary properties of age, sex, group membership, and physical lawfulness. For example, the same individual may appear in two guises in one picture.

The first clear structural developmental elaboration upon these initial transductive constructions occurs when the child equates each member within each representation with itself and with an exact copy of itself. However, he still cannot fully relate the members to each other within a single representation, that is, the familial relations. He also cannot relate one representation to another representation within the series. In fact, he cannot even relate one member in two (preselected) successive representations of the family.

S42 (3;0). *"You're going to show me some pictures."* "Did you ever see those pictures before?" *"Yeah."* "Do you see anyone in those pictures that's the same?" *"I see someone in the pictures."* "Tell me, who?" *No response.* "Let's look at these two pictures (1a and 1b). Look at these two pictures. Are they the same?" *"Yeah."* "Or are they different?" *"They're different like mine."* "They're like what?" *"They're different like my pictures."* "Do you see the same people in the pictures? Do you see this man in the other pictures (A1a)?" *"Yeah."* "Where is that man?" *A1a.* *"He's right here."* "And is he in this other picture?" *"Yeah."* "Where?" *"There."* $A1b$. "What about C1a, do you see him in another picture?" *No response.* "Where is he over there?" *C1a.* "Yeah, where is another picture of him?" *C1b.* "That's right. Anybody else the same?" *S is distracted.* "I want to show you one more picture, 1,2. What about that picture, do you see anyone the same in those two pictures?" *"Yeah."* "Do you see the daddy, A1?" *"Yeah."* "Show me." *"The daddy right here."* $B2$. "What about D2, the baby? Do you see that little boy?" *"Right here."* $D2$. "Where's another picture of him?" *"This one."* $Y2$.

Concurrently, the child's personal—social preconception becomes exact as long as his considerations of identity are limited to one representation replicated in two exact copies. These identities are consistent with and are bounded by elementary properties of age, sex, group membership, and physical lawfulness.

The next step in the developmental elaboration of transductive reasoning occurs in the same two basic and related characteristics. First, the child's orderings begin to relate pairs of successive representations. Second, the personal–social preconceptions begin fully to relate the members in one representation to each other as a family and sometimes to relate individual members in two (preselected) successive representations of the family.

> S87 (3;1). "Do you see anybody the same in those pictures?" "Yeah." "Where is he?" No response. "O.K., let's look at this one and this one (2 & 3). Who do you see?" Points to W2. "Who's that?" "I don't know." "That's mommy." "And that's the daddy. A2. And those are the kids." "That's the family. What about the other one?" "And that's the family too." "Is it the same family or a different family?" "Different family." "Do you see A2 in 3?" "Yeah." A2 = A3. "What about the mother?" "Here." W2 = W3. "What about the kids?" Makes general motion to all the children. "What about Y2?" Y2 = Y3. "What about D2?" D2 = D3. "What if I show you 1 & 2?" "This one goes with him and this one goes with him." C1 = D2, B1 = D2. "This little girl's name is X, that's me." "Yeah." "Which picture do you think they took first, which is the first picture?" 1 before 2. "How can you tell?" "T." (S's sister's name.) "Which one is the first here, 2 or 3?" 2 before 3. Counts the people in 3 up to seven. "Let's see if you know who this is, do you see someone you know in that picture?" "Yeah. This:" C5. "Who is it?" "I don't know." "Who's this (X5)?" "You." "And that's my family. Do you see me in this picture, 4?" X4. "And there's your sister, she's outside." "Do you see C4 in 5?" C4 = A5.

Such findings make clear that there is no impression of time in advance of the child's ordering preoperations. The inability to order events has structural implications for the child's preconception of social identity; not only does it set limits to the construction of social knowledge, but it also gives it conceptual definition. Indeed, most of the 3-year-olds could not relate two pictures of the same individual. Some 3-year-olds barely began to identify two individuals in separate photographs as the same person. However, the identification ignored the configurational qualities of the individuals being related, such as their sex. Those children incorrectly claimed, for example, that a boy in one picture was the same person as a girl in another picture. Further, a given individual in one picture might have dual representation in another picture. For example, S87 claimed that D2 was identical with both B1 and C1.

To sum up, we are working on the structural developmental hypothesis that the cognitive form of the 3-year-old's physical, social, and personal preconcepts during this initial preoperational stage is that of transductive representational arrangements in which:

1. Nonobservable events can be linked.
2. Linkages can collate a small number of units.
3. Linkages are becoming physically asymmetrical. (An early manifestation is that 3-year-olds can somewhat imitate a temporal sequence in order.)

4. Temporal linkages are not seriatable. Therefore successive linkages are still not differentiated from simultaneous linkages.
5. Time is not yet continuous. Time remains local time.
6. Linkages are not quantifiable. (Duration, such as age, is not conceivable.)
7. Linkages are neither irreversible nor reversible.

The analysis presented so far should suffice as an indication of our currently ongoing structural developmental inquiries into operational coordinations during and after the preconceptual period. Let us proceed by reviewing in broad outline the rest of the work we are doing.

At age 4, children think that the time is different in two neighboring towns (Oakden & Sturt, 1922). Even though these temporal judgments are inconsistent with physical time, they still indicate some beginning construction of functional temporal relating. Children of 4 cannot yet temporally order the five family photographs. But they can sometimes couple pairs of photographs. This implies that they should also be able to relate a person in one picture with a person in another picture. Analyzing the cognitive structure of functional ordering at this stage into its extensive and intensive components, we hypothesized that the extension of relating is limited to individual members, not to the group, and not even to pairs within the group; and that the extension of relating is limited to couplings, not even to triplings. The consequent expectation, which the data bear out, is that the subject's identity preconcept is limited to transformations of a single member in two and no more than two photographs. We also hypothesized that the intension of relating at this stage composes atemporal (adurational) global configurational properties. Consequently, we expected and found that the subject denies the identity of members in the family across two photographs unless all or most of the properties of the two members are the same in appearance. Therefore, his identification should often be incorrect.

Children of 5 still cannot spontaneously order the series of family photographs. They can collate adjacent pairs into couplings. With much empirical sorting and resorting, plus feedback from the experimenter, they can also arrive at a correct ordering of the couplings, eventually arranging all five photographs. Occasionally, 5-year-olds also understand that a group member need not have the identical global properties in two different photographs to be related; that is, they know that the same person may reappear in two photographs even though his appearance is altered somewhat, such as in height or in dress.

Typically, the 5-year-olds' orderings are based upon proximity. They may still incorrectly identify two members because both look about the same size in the two photographs. Rejections of orderings by 5-year-olds are based upon globalities. Often they claim, incorrectly, that a baby in one photograph does not reappear in a second photograph since there is no baby in the second picture. The incidence of global reasoning increases as the comparison made is between more extreme photographs in the series. For example, more errors are made when the comparison is between photographs 1 and 5 than when the comparison is between 1 and 2 in the series of family portraits. Thus, the structure of the order constructed is a functional relationship based upon global configurational proximities. As the global proximities and the specific objects "between" increase, so the subjects' cognition of temporal linkage and personal identification diminishes.

Six-year-old children spontaneously and immediately arrange the family photographs in proper temporal order. The vestigial preoperational character of the ordering, however, is revealed by the subjects' continuing difficulty with probes about identification of members who have not yet been born and therefore do not appear in any picture. When a member A is younger than a member B at a given time (T_n in the series of photographs), then it can be deduced that in some earlier, intermediate photograph (T_k), B will still appear but in a younger guise, while A will not yet appear because he has not been born. Nevertheless, 6-year-olds still claim that A was already born and does appear in the photograph (on the basis of global similarity) or was simply left out when the picture was taken (by omission of the photographer). A central structural feature, then, of preoperational, intuitive ordering is that it is still not a seriation operation.

In this way, we are structurally tracking one preoperation—constructing ordering transformations—that may be used by the young child to produce coordinated and partially isomorphic physical, social, and personal preconcepts. We are also developmentally tracking the transformations in constructive mental activity from its initial preoperational form of intuitive functional orderings.

There are two coordinative features of our structural developmental findings that should be underscored. The first is the remarkable ontogenetic parallelism between the temporal preorderings of growing people and the temporal pre-orderings of physical motion as constructed by the preoperational child (Piaget, 1971). The second is the partial isomorphism between the preconcepts of physical time and the preconcepts of personal and social identity produced by the young child's ordering preoperations. In this regard, it should be noted that the study referred to here focused upon the child's preconception of the identity of others. In another inquiry, similar results were obtained when the child was probed about his own identity preconcepts (Wolfsohn, 1972).

The above are not isolated instances of structural developmental coordinations. Another investigation, which dealt with very different cognitive problems (Damon, 1974), reported additional confirmatory evidence for the principle of structural filiations outlined above. Children of 4—8 were tested on problems involving ratios, classification, seriation, projective spatial perspectives, and moral judgments. The intercorrelations of subjects' scores on these problems were all statistically significant at the $p > .001$ level. They ranged from a low of .63 to a high of .88. The results outlined so far require that note be taken of studies that have failed to find significant intercorrelations in children's cognitive performances (Green, Ford, & Flamer, 1971). Two general ingredients of our studies may account for the discrepancy. The first is that the aim of our testing is intensive and extensive clinical probing of individual subjects on each task. The second is that the aim of our data analysis is to formalize the structure of operations composing each subject's reasoning.

The second facet of coordination within the subject's functional structures that we are studying is the developmental filiations between two classes of mental activity, operations, and figurations (Strauss & Langer, 1970; Langer, 1974). Figurations are the subject's action systems directed toward constructively extracting and representing empirical information; that is, probabilistic. Extracting schematic knowledge—such as information about the appearance, reality, and predictability of the physical and social environment—is accomplished by symbolic embodiments in a variety of media that have communicative value. Operations are the subject's action systems for constructing transformative concepts that ideally become logically necessary. They range from representational preoperations, such as the one we have just discussed, to formal operations, which develop during adolescence.

In our continuing research on the developmental filiations between operational and figurative structures, we have recently focused upon the subject's understanding and coordination between the appearance and the reality of things, on the one hand, and the transient and the permanent characteristics of things on the other (Langer & Strauss, 1972). In his metaphysical investigation, Bradley (1969) claimed that relating appearance to reality is central to experience: "Appearance without reality would be impossible, for what then could appear? And reality without appearance would be nothing, for there is nothing outside appearances" (p. 432). The first clear ontogenetic manifestations of both distinguishing reality and relating appearance to it were located in the preverbal sensorimotor child's playful pretending, such as the 1-year-old baby who makes believe that he is sleeping. Ontogenetically later manifestations of the cognition of appearance and reality have been found, for example, in the child's developing conception of dreams. Not until about 6–7 years do children begin to distinguish between and relate the appearance and the reality of dreams (Piaget, 1929; Kohlberg, 1969).

These ontogenetic investigations, it seems, can be summarized into two general and related hypotheses, one developmental and the other cognitive. The developmental hypothesis is that the cognition of the appearance and the reality of things follows a long and varied course. This course begins early, in the form of sensorimotor presentational activity. It requires a long intellectual history to achieve the abstract conceptual form it takes in adult theoretical thought, particularly in its epistemological and scientific embodiments. Given the long-standing interest in the problem of appearance and reality, it is surprising that most of the details in this ontogenesis have yet to be determined. The cognitive hypothesis is that much of the person's knowledge about the appearance and the reality of things comes from his figurative activity (Langer, 1974; Piaget, 1970). Here *figurative activity* refers to those cognitions that are primarily directed toward extracting empirical information from the physical and social configuration of the environment. To illustrate, one way for a child to determine whether two perpendicular lines merely look different or really are different lengths is to place them on top of each other. This way of extracting information from the configuration of the two lines is a plausible source of empirical knowledge about the appearance and the reality of illusory versus nonillusory physical objects.

As is well known, an early focus of considerable epistemological and psychological inquiry was the cognitive development of the identity of objects (Cassirer, 1957; Meyerson, 1962; Werner, 1948). The ontogenetic course of the cognition of identity begins with the infant's preverbal, sensorimotor activity. By 12 months, this infantile activity has well established the presentational permanence of objects, notwithstanding transient spatiotemporal displacements that are observable (Piaget, 1954). The cognition of identity culminates ontogenetically, during adolescence, in the formal operational concept of the conservation of objects notwithstanding spatiotemporal and qualititative deformations in their configurations (Piaget, 1952).

Again, it seems that the ontogenetic investigations of the identity of objects can be summarized into two general hypotheses, one developmental and the other cognitive. The developmental hypothesis (outlined in more detail in Langer, 1969a, p. 97) is that working out the identity of objects requires a long and varied history of subject–object interactions that passes through numerous stages. The cognitive hypothesis is that much of the subject's knowledge about the identity of objects comes from his operational reasoning (Langer, 1974; Piaget, 1970). Here *operational reasoning* means those cognitions that are primarily directed toward mentally transforming observed things and their deformations in a logical fashion. Operational reasoning constructs mental structures about the logic of things. These logical conceptions supersede the character of immediate observations. To illustrate the obvious, if a child understands that a deformation in the shape of a ball of clay may be transformed in thought to reestablish its initial state, then this mentally constructed reversibility enables him to know that the quantity of objects is conserved under all conditions of observed shape deformation.

In his metaphysical investigation, Bradley (1969, pp. 62–63) argued that the flux of deformative changes in objects constitutes reality, while the identity of objects is an idealization created by thought. Interestingly, some recent psychological investigations are based on the opposite metaphysic; namely, that deformations are illusory appearances of things that have not changed (are identical) in reality (Braine & Shanks, 1965a, b; King, 1971; Murray, 1965). The claim is that the young child confuses the way illusory objects appear (that is, unequal and unchanged) with the way they really are (that is, constant and conserved). Consequently, it is argued, distinguishing between the appearance and the reality of objects should be the sufficient condition for cognizing identity. Older children who distinguish between the appearance and the reality (AR) of objects should therefore judge them to be conserved even when they are deformed.

Our findings on the 5-year-olds' conception of objects are not consistent with either metaphysical view. We found that AR judgments and conservation concepts are not coextensive cognitive phenomena. At least half the 5-year-old subjects produced nonparallel performances between these cognitive activities. Furthermore, conservation concepts are not the cognitive products of AR judgments. Most of the spontaneous, nonparallel performances were featured by more advanced operational reasoning about identity than figurative AR judgments. Morever, neither training to distinguish the appearance from the reality of illusory objects nor training to distinguish the appearance from the reality of deformed objects produced progress in operational reasoning about the conservation of discontinuous quantity, length, or continuous quantity.

The structural developmental relations between AR judgments and conservation conceptions are complex. The conservation concepts of our subjects were not influenced by AR training, whether the spontaneous operational structure of the subjects was mixed operational—that is, partially intuitive and partially concrete—or was purely intuitive operational. Rather, our best, but still initial and therefore tentative. indication is that the coordination is probably more delimited and precise. Subjects were most likely to progress if their initial operational structure was intuitive preoperational about the more difficult deformations and mixed or concrete operational about the easier deformations (discontinuous quantity deformations). But the cognitive progress of these subjects was limited to their conservation concepts of length deformations. The progress did not generalize to another form of deformations of equal difficulty (continuous quantity deformations).

Whatever the validity of Bradley's metaphysical speculation that identity is an appearance, "an idea which at no actual time is ever real," our empirical research indicates that this is not the case for the developing cognition of the young child. Little coordination was found within the young child's cognitions of appearance, reality, and identity, with the possible but still-to-be-replicated exception of the child who is in a transitional phase between intuitive preoperations and concrete operations.

In concluding this consideration of coordination within the subject's functional structures, I find two additional hypotheses worth noting. The first hypothesis requires a structural epistemological metric that we do not have. If we did, then we would expect the coordination to be greater, at any given developmental stage, between the physical, social, and personal concepts produced by the same operation than between the facts produced by figurations and the concepts produced by operations. This is so even when the facts and concepts are in the same knowledge domain, such as the cognition of physical objects. Greater disparity should obtain between concepts and facts than between physical and social concepts.

The second additional hypothesis is that the disparity between related concepts and facts constitutes the kind of perturbation that may be a source of cognitive progress. Interestingly, it was found that factual knowledge about the appearance and reality of objects did not seem to be relevant to the young child's conceptual knowledge about the same object's conservation, with the possible exception of when his conceptual knowledge was in transition from preoperational to concrete operational.

In general, from our perspective, the structural developmental filiations between figurations and operations is an orthogenetic process of equilibration. The basic organization of the sensorimotor stage is a global fusion of assimilatory operations (such as playful transformations) and accommodatory figurations (such as imitative reproductions). The observable result is syncresis of perception, action, and affect. The sequence of stage development, starting with the sensorimotor stage, is marked by progressive differentiation and integration of these functional structures. The orthogenesis of accommodatory figurations and assimilatory operations constitutes a central feature of the coordinative equilibration that is the source of stage development, that is, progressive alteration of functional structures. The functioning of one structural system of action may lead to the feedback of information that modifies its organization. In turn, this may result in intrinsic disequilibrium between it and the organization of other functional structures. Disequilibrium is a necessary condition for progressive reorganization and feedforward to the child's schemes of action. The manifest symptom may then be some observable modifications and advances in acts and their products, constructed facts and theories.

Finally, we may turn briefly to the second part of the equilibration thesis, which refers to the interaction between the subject and his environment. In a recent analysis (Langer, 1969a), I hypothesized that establishing disparity between a child's and a model's level of reasoning may be one way of studying interactive disequilibrium leading to developmental change. The general idea is that cognitive development is a progressive approximation to a potential, ideal equilibrial state that is never fully achieved. In particular, this means that if the child is perturbed by an event that he lacks the structural competence to deal with, then he will be in a heightened state of disequilibrium. This leads the child to act so as to compensate for the perturbation so that his existing functional structures are transformed. Thus is developed the competence for new forms of action that more intelligently anticipate and efficiently deal with future events of the same class.

Several types of experiments have been performed in the study of the interactive aspect of cognitive development. Beginning with Smedslund's (1961) initial investigations, a series of experiments have sought the developmental consequences of presenting children with a confrontation and/or conflict between logical mental operations such as addition—subtraction and reversibility (Wallach, Wall, & Anderson, 1967; Langer, 1969a; Mermelstein & Meyer, 1969). Another set of experiments has been begun to assess the consequences of conflict in children's predictions and outcome judgments (Bruner, Olver, & Greenfield, 1966; Inhelder & Sinclair, 1969; Strauss & Langer, 1970).

A third experimental approach is the one with which we are specifically concerned. The basic research design is to examine the effect of structural disparity between the child's own judgments and explanations—and those of a model—upon the subsequent conceptions of the child. Thus, the interactive disparity refers to the differing level of the child's and the model's reasoning.

A fair amount of research has been done along these lines on moral (social) concepts (Turiel, 1969), and we are beginning to work along these lines on logical and physical concepts. In the first study of this kind on logical conceptions (Kuhn, 1970, 1972), 4-, 6-, and 8-year-old children were exposed to models dealing with classification problems (taken from Inhelder & Piaget, 1964) at different levels in relation to the childrens' predominant pretest stage. Very little change was induced. Insofar as change was obtained, the children observing a model performing at a slightly higher structural level than their own were most affected. Children observing a model performing at a considerably higher level than their own were affected less. The least affected were children observing a model performing at a slightly lower structural level than their own.

It may come as no surprise that it is impossible to induce progress to stages that have not yet developed, because the requisite functional structures are not yet present in the subject. But the difficulty in interactively inducing regression in reasoning to a stage that the person has just passed through is on its face highly surprising. After all, the child is simply in the position of merely having to exercise reasoning capacities that he has already developed. The finding is, however, completely consistent with the conservative rules of self-regulatory coherence proposed elsewhere as the source of resistance to extrinsic inducement to change, whether progressive or regressive (Langer, 1969b).

Now we can bank on the conservative nature of developmental processes to result in phenotypical actualization at the stage of concrete operations and conventional morality. Most children reach that level of development, some a bit faster or a bit slower. However, they will actualize their potential for concrete operations and conventional morality. At the same time, we have begun to find that the genotypical potential for the development of formal operations and principled morality is not always actualized by adolescents and adults (Kuhn, Langer, Kohlberg, & Haan, in press). These findings suggest the pedagogical hypothesis that if you have to pick only one period for educational intervention to support mental development, adolescence is a prime target. An obvious question that follows is the optimal relation between speed of overall development and the most mature stage of development that will be actualized. It may well be that the child has to progress through the sequence of early developmental stages within an optimal rate-range, or he will not actualize his full potential. But we do not know, and this must therefore remain an open research hypothesis.

This is not, however, the research route we have been taking. Rather, as we have sketchily described, we have been trying to track the coordinative, filiative, and interactive facets of the equilibration thesis of structural stage development of operations and figurations. The thesis is that the orthogenesis of operations and figurations produces physical, social, and personal concepts that are transformed at each stage of development.

References

Bradley, F. H. *Appearance and reality: A metaphysical essay.* London: Oxford University Press, 1969. (Originally published, 1893.)

Braine, M. D. S., & Shanks, B. L. The conservation of a shape property and a proposal about the origin of the conservations. *Canadian Journal of Psychology, 1965, 19,* 197–207. (*a*)

Braine, M. D. S., & Shanks, B. L. The development of conservation of size. *Journal of Verbal Learning and Verbal Behavior, 1965, 4,* 227–242. (*b*)

Bruner, J. S., Olver, R. R., & Greenfield, P. *Studies in cognitive growth.* New York: Wiley, 1966.

Bryant, P. E., & Trabasso, T. Transitive inferences and memory in young children. *Nature, 1971, 232,* 456–458.

Cassirer, E. [*The philosophy of symbolic forms*] (Vol. 3). *Phenomenology of knowledge.* (Ralph Manheim, trans.). New Haven: Yale University Press, 1957. (Originally published, 1929.)

Damon, W. *A developmental analysis of the positive justice concept from childhood through adolescence.* Unpublished Master's thesis, University of California, Berkeley, 1971.

Damon, W. V. B. Early conceptions of justice as related to the development of operational reasoning. (Doctoral dissertation, University of California, Berkeley, 1973). *Dissertation Abstracts International, 1974, 35,* 2400B–24001B. (University Microfilms No. 74-24, 631.)

Green, D. R., Ford, M. P., & Flamer, G. B. (Eds.). *Measurement and Piaget.* New York: McGraw-Hill, 1971.

Inhelder, B., & Piaget, J. [*Early growth of logic in the child*] (E. A. Lunzer & D. Papert, trans.). New York: Harper & Row, 1964.

Inhelder, B., & Sinclair, H. Learning cognitive structures. In P. H. Mussen, J. Langer, & M. Covington (Eds.), *Trends and issues in developmental psychology.* New York: Holt, Rinehart, & Winston, 1969.

King, W. L. A nonarbitrary behavioral criterion for conservation of illusion-distorted length in five-year-olds. *Journal of Experimental Child Psychology, 1971, 11,* 171–181.

Kohlberg, L. Stage and sequence: The cognitive-developmental approach to socialization. In D. A. Goslin (Ed.), *Handbook of socialization.* New York: Rand McNally, 1969.

Kuhn, D. Mechanisms of change in the development of cognitive structures. *Child Development, 1972, 43,* 833–844.

Kuhn, D., Langer, J., Kohlberg, L., & Haan, N. The development of formal operations in logical and moral judgment. *Genetic Psychology Monographs,* in press.

Kuhn, D. Z. Patterns of imitative behavior in children from 3 to 8: A study of imitation from a cognitive-developmental perspective. (Doctoral dissertation, University of California, Berkeley, 1969). *Dissertation Abstracts International, 1970, 31,* 900B–901B. (University Microfilms No. 70-13, 092.)

Langer, J. Disequilibrium as a source of development. In P. H. Mussen, J. Langer, & M.

Covington (Eds.), *Trends and issues in developmental psychology*. New York: Holt, Rinehart, & Winston, 1969. (*a*)

Langer, J. *Theories of development*. New York: Holt, Rinehart, & Winston, 1969. (*b*)

Langer, J. Werner's comparative organismic theory. In P. H. Mussen (Ed.), *Carmichael's manual of child psychology*. New York: Wiley, 1970.

Langer, J. *Stages of temporal schematizing*. Paper presented to the Colloquium of the Department of Mathematics, University of California, Berkeley, 1972.

Langer, J. Interactional aspects of cognitive organization. *Cognition*, 1974, *3*, 9–28.

Langer, J., & Strauss, S. Appearance, reality, and identity. *Cognition*, 1972, *1*, 105–128.

Lemke, S. P. *Children's identity concepts*. Unpublished manuscript, University of California, Berkeley, 1971.

Lemke, S. P. *Identity and conservation*. Unpublished doctoral dissertation, University of California, Berkeley, 1974.

Mermelstein, E., & Meyer, E. Conservation training techniques and their effects on different populations. *Child Development*, 1969, *40*, 471–490.

Meyerson, E. [*Identity and reality*] (K. Loewenberg, trans.). New York: Dover, 1962. (Originally published, 1908.)

Murray, F. B. Conservation of illusion-distorted lengths and areas by primary school children. *Journal of Educational Psychology*, 1965, *56*, 62–66.

Oakden, E. C., & Sturt, M. The development of the knowledge of time in children. *British Journal of Psychology*, 1922, *12*, 309–336.

Piaget, J. [*The child's conception of the world*] (J. Tomlinson & A. Tomlinson, trans.). London: Routledge and Kegan Paul, 1929.

Piaget, J. [*The child's conception of number*] (C. Cattegno & F. M. Hodgson, trans.). London: Routledge and Kegan Paul, 1952. (Originally published, 1941.)

Piaget. J. [*The construction of reality in the child*] (M. Cook, trans.). New York: Basic Books, 1954. (Originally published, 1937.)

Piaget, J. [*Play, dreams and imitation in childhood*] (C. Gattegno & F. M. Hodgson, trans.). New York: W. W. Norton, 1962. (Originally published, 1951.)

Piaget, J. Piaget's theory. In P. H. Mussen (Ed.), *Carmichael's manual of child psychology*. New York: Wiley, 1970.

Piaget, J. [*The child's conception of time*] (A. Pomerans, trans.). New York: Ballantine, 1971. (Originally published, 1927.)

Smedslund, J. The acquisition of conservation of substance and weight in children: I–VII. *Scandinavian Journal of Psychology*, 1961, *3*, 85–87.

Strauss, S., & Langer, J. Operational thought inducement. *Child Development*, 1970, *41*, 163–175.

Turiel, E. Developmental processes in the child's moral thinking. In P. H. Mussen, J. Langer, & M. Covington (Eds.), *Trends and issues in developmental psychology*. New York: Holt, Rinehart, & Winston, 1969.

Wallach, L., Wall, A. J., & Anderson, L. Number conservation: The roles of reversibility, addition–subtraction, and misleading perceptual cues. *Child Development*, 1967, *38*, 425–442.

Werner, H. [*Comparative psychology of mental development*] (E. B. Garside, trans.). New York: International University Press, 1948. (Originally published, 1924.)

Wolfsohn, A. *Aspect of the development of identity concepts*. Unpublished doctoral dissertation, University of California, Berkeley, 1972.

CHAPTER 8

The Emergence
of the Child as Grammarian[*]

Lila R. Gleitman, Henry Gleitman, and Elizabeth F. Shipley

University of Pennsylvania, Philadelphia, Pennsylvania

Abstract

Demonstrations of some young children's awareness of syntactic and semantic properties of language are presented. Rudiments of such "metalinguistic" functioning are shown in 2-year-olds, who give judgments of grammaticalness in a role-modeling situation. The growth of these abilities is documented for a group of 5- to 8-year-old children, who are asked explicitly to give judgments of deviant sentences. Adultlike behavior, in these talented subjects, is found to emerge in the period from 5 to 8 years. Possible relations of metalinguistic functioning to other "metacognitive" processes are suggested.

Introduction

What do we mean when we say a speaker "knows the rules" of language? Transformational linguists have been guarded in explicating this claim, for surely there is a difference between what the speaker knows and what a professional grammarian knows. There is broad agreement that speakers "follow the rules" and, in fact, have trouble *not* following them (as in memorizing deviant sentences and the like; e.g., Miller & Isard, 1963). But performances of this kind are hardly equivalent to our everyday understanding of what it means to *know* rules.

*This paper is reprinted with permission from *Cognition, International Journal of Cognitive Psychology,* 1972, *1*(2–3), 137–164.

Used in this ordinary sense, the term *knowledge* implies awareness of generality; in its strongest form it involves the capacity to articulate the rule system itself, as in a chess player who can readily recite the rules of the game that constrain his behavior. The elite linguistic informant is rather like the chess player: he follows the language rules, but on demand he can do much more. He can demonstrate some awareness of the existence of a rule system by performing the one task that provides the main data base for modern grammatical theories: he can indicate whether a sentence is or is not well-formed. A rule system may be followed and yet not be known in this sense. The spider weaves his web according to a well-defined set of arachnid principles, but we hardly expect him to note any deviance if he weaves under the influence of LSD. Rule following *per se* implies knowledge of a weaker sort than that which linguists have generally been interested in. The very tasks they impose upon their informants require more than mere obedience to the rule system: the rules themselves must be engaged in the service of a further cognitive act. In a way, the linguist assumes not only that the speaker knows the rules but that he knows something about his knowledge.

This paper is concerned with the development of this aspect of linguistic behavior, the ability of a speaker to reflect upon the rules that he follows. There is little doubt that this metalinguistic skill has been a critical methodological prerequisite for the construction of linguistic theories during the last two decades. We are here concerned with the emergence of this skill in young children.

Developmental psycholinguists have shown us that the young child already honors the rules for English sentence formation, at least within very wide limits. Children of 4 and 5 speak the language fairly well, have trouble—like adults—in repeating and memorizing deviant sentences, and so forth (e.g., Labov, 1970). But this work tells us only that children follow the rules, "know how" to speak English.[1] The question is whether they can also contemplate the structure of the language, whether they know that they know. We will claim that at least some 5-, 6- and 7-year-olds possess this metalinguistic ability to a remarkable degree and that a germ of this capacity can already be seen in the 2-year-old. Thus, in part we are pursuing a claim some of us have made elsewhere (Gleitman & Gleitman, 1970), a claim that is, we believe, implied—though usually cautiously—in the writings of most generative grammarians: it is the speaker's potential abstract awareness of language structure, and not merely his orderly behavior in

---

[1] We do not wish to overstate the case for the sophistication of children's speech. Although many developmental psycholinguists state the language-learning process is essentially complete at age 4 or 5 (e.g., McNeill, 1966; Lenneberg, 1967), this is by no means clear. We do know that gross errors in speech have largely disappeared at this time, except where morphophonemic irregularities (*bringed,* etc.) are involved; but we have no firm data on the complexity and variety of structures in early child speech.

accord with these rules, that lies at the heart of the generative–transformational hypothesis.

The Child's Garden of Syntax

At first glance, there seems to be something of a paradox for students of cognitive development in the preschooler's linguistic precocity: if language is simply a tool of thought, then it is surprising that language abilities seem to emerge so much earlier than other cognitive skills. The child's progress to logic, to a belief in the conservation of quantities, to concepts of number, seems painfully slow, but almost any mother can attest to leaps of apparently abstract thought in the particular areas of phonology and syntax. For example, no 3-year-old lisps out his syllables so poorly that he does not feel entitled to employ a self-conscious baby talk to dolls and other social inferiors (Gelman & Shatz, 1976; Shipley & Shipley, 1969). Such aspects of juvenile competence are rarely studied, in part because of the widespread belief that they cannot be dealt with experimentally (e.g., Brown, Fraser, & Bellugi, 1964). Yet anecdotally, it is easy to point to cases where young children manifest great sensitivity to identifiable subtle features of language. For example, here is a question about segmentation from a 4-year-old:

Mommy, is it AN A-dult or A NUH-dult?,

a query made doubly intriguing by the fact that this child did not make the *a/an* distinction in spontaneous speech until 2 years later. And a 4-year-old with a question about adverbial complements:

Mother (*taking car around a sharp bend*): Hold on tight!
Child: Isn't it *tightly*?

A precocious first-grader, unacquainted with formal punctuation marks, delicately observes the distinction between use and mention:

Child (*writing*): They call Pennsylvania Pennsylvania because William Penn
          had a (Penn) in his name.
Mother: Why did you put those marks around the word Penn?
Child: Well, I wasn't saying Penn, I was just talking about the word.

This child quite apparently does more than speak in accordance with the rules of grammar. She recognizes paraphrases, laughs at puns, and rejects deviant though meaningful sentences. We believe that these features of behavior, far from being the icing on the linguistic cake, represent our best clues to central aspects of language competence. We will show in this paper that the capacity to reflect on linguistic structure is available to some very young children. First, we demonstrate the rudiments of this abstract attitude in 2-year-olds. Second, we document evolution of this capacity in the young school-aged child. No normative data are presented. We intend the work as an existential comment on linguistic creativity in some young children. We cannot speculate on how widespread such talents may be in the population at large.

Judgments of Grammaticalness from the 2-Year-Old

The Problem of Doing Developmental Psycholinguistics

Fruitful linguistic inquiry can hardly begin unless the speaker–listener can provide firm judgments on at least some sentences of his language. The primary data are not the subject's utterances, but rather a set of sentences he judges, upon reflection, to be well formed. The theory of grammar that emerges is an account of these judgments. Precisely how such an account is related to a description of language performances (other than judgment-giving performances) is currently something of a mystery. What is important for our purposes here is the fact that these judgmental data have not been available to the developmental psycholinguist. Even if we had a complete description of the child's speech and a complete description of the adult's linguistic judgments, this would be a dissatisfying state of affairs, for there is no obvious way to compare these accounts in the interest of describing language acquisition. Brown, Fraser, and Bellugi commented in 1964 on this methodological gap separating the linguist's study of the adult from the psychologist's study of the child:

> The linguist working with an adult informant gets reactions to utterances as well as the utterances themselves. . . . Can such data be obtained from very young children?
> With Abel [a 2-year-old] we were not successful in eliciting judgments of grammaticality. Of course there was no point in asking him whether an utterance was "grammatical" or "well-formed." We experimented with some possible childhood equivalents. The first step was to formulate tentative grammatical rules, and the next to construct some utterances that ought to have been acceptable. For Abel "The cake" should have been grammatical and "Cake the" ungrammatical. How to ask? The experimenter said: "Some of the things I say will be silly and some are not. You tell me when I say something silly." Abel would not. If Abel had a sense of grammaticality, we were unable to find the words that would engage it. (Brown, 1970, pp. 72–73)

Given this outcome, psychologists have used various indirect methods in the study of the very young language learner. Almost all of the techniques represent attempts to get at the classificatory system. Large contributions to our knowledge of the emerging speaker have come from careful observation of spontaneous speech (e.g., Braine, 1963; Miller & Ervin, 1964; Brown, Cazden, & Bellugi, 1969; Bloom, 1970), which must, in some admittedly cloudy way, reflect something of the speaker's underlying organization of the language.

Similarly, studies of repetition, memory, and the comprehension of various syntactic and semantic structures (e.g., Brown & Bellugi, 1964; Menyuk, 1969; Chomsky, 1969) are in many ways analogous to solicitation of judgments of well-formedness. These latter methods are to some extent validated by their success with adult informants for whom concordant judgmental data can be provided (e.g., Savin & Perchonock, 1965; Johnson, 1965; Bever, Lackner, & Kirk, 1969; and many others).

At present, then, we are able to get a fairly coherent picture of the course of speech acquisition and some hints about the mechanisms of language learning from the work of these investigators. But the fact remains that the insights incorporated into modern generative grammar could probably not have been achieved by the use of such indirect methods (see, for discussion, Chomsky, 1965). Judgments of grammaticalness have always been used to provide the primary data. Comparable data from child informants would obviously be very useful. They would enable the developmental psycholinguist to proceed just like a linguist who studies some exotic adult language. But so far no one has found a little child who gives stable judgments on his own primitive language.

Why is the young child unable or unwilling to provide these judgments? Does he merely fail to understand the instruction? Is this failure orthogonal to his linguistic capacities—perhaps representing a general cognitive immaturity? The work of Shipley, Smith, and Gleitman (1969) was designed to examine this issue. Perhaps the child does make judgments of well-formedness but simply cannot understand an instruction to report on them. If so, we might get classificatory data from the child by developing some behavioral indices of differential responsiveness to various language forms. An examination of this study will help set the problem toward which the present paper is directed: the growth of metalinguistic reflection in the language learner.

Shipley *et al.* had mothers give commands (mild imperative sentences) to children aged 18–30 months. Some commands were well formed (e.g., *Throw me the ball!*), but some were "telegraphic" or foreshortened, as in the children's own speech (*Ball!* or *Throw ball!*). We found that children discriminate among these formats, as shown by their differential tendency to obey these commands. More specifically, the holophrastic children (who do not yet put two words together in speech) tended to obey foreshortened commands. In contrast, telegraphic speakers ignored, repeated, talked about, laughed about telegraphic commands, but obeyed well-formed commands. Shipley *et al.* assumed that children fail to obey commands that they perceive as linguistically deviant; thus, differential tendency to obey these commands was interpreted as an implicit judgment on the "acceptability" or "naturalness" of their format.[2]

---

[2] A simpler hypothesis—that the child fails to obey only because there isn't enough information in the shortened commands—is falsified by the outcome: a child is more apt to obey *Ball!* than *Gor ronta ball!* though the two contain identical intelligible information. Further, at these ages, information outside the noun itself has no effect on the specific

This study revealed that the spontaneous speech of children provides a limited data source for the study of their linguistic knowledge, in practice as well as in theory. Clearly, the telegraphic speech of these children did not reflect the fact that they could discriminate telegraphic syntax from the adult syntax. Perhaps the children "preferred" the well-formed sentences that they themselves never produced at this stage, as indicated by their tendency to act on just these. But such behavioral indices can be at best crude indicators of the child's "judgments" on the sentences offered to him—if indeed he can make such judgments. These indices do not come to grips with the question of classification.

Soliciting Judgments from 2-Year Old Children

Can the 2-year-old child be induced to give judgments of grammaticalness more directly? Some curious hints began to appear among the subjects of Shipley *et al.* Every once in a while, a child seemed to behave much like an adult when confronted with a linguistically bizarre stimulus:

Mother (*delivering stimulus*): Joseph: Gor ronta ball!
Joseph:[3] Wha', Momma? "Gor ronta ball"?

We have punctuated this sentence advisedly. The child seemed to be querying the format directly—not asking whether or not his mother really wanted him to gor ronta ball. Other children would grab the list of stimulus sentences from their mothers (obviously they could not read) and say "Now I do one!" Such behavior suggests that these children were regarding the sentences apart from their communicative function.

In a longitudinal variant of this work, in which eight children were studied at successive stages of language development, these sophisticated responses became too frequent to ignore.[4] To be sure, in the first run of the experiment, the children behaved as we had anticipated. By and large (but with the usual enormous noise), the telegraphic speakers obeyed well-formed commands more often than telegraphic commands. In successive runs some months later with these *same* children, we expected to see the culmination of this development:

---

behavior of the child given that he looks at the stimulus object in the first place: if he does anything at all with the ball, he is equally likely to throw it if you say *Ball, Throw ball, Throw me the ball,* or *Gor ronta ball.* Only the likelihood of his coming into contact with the ball in the first place differs under these formats.

[3] In all instances, names have been changed to protect the innocents.

[4] The longitudinal study was undertaken, in part, to replace spontaneous speech measures with a better external criterion of each child's development. Thus, each child served as his own control. This experiment differed in various ways from the 1969 study, most relevantly by the inclusion of some word-order reverses (e.g., *Ball bring; Ball me the bring*) which allow us to ask whether the child who rejects telegraphic sentences does so merely because they lack the intonation contour of well-formed sentences.

the subjects would now more uniformly respond to well-formed sentences and balk more often at deviance. But this was not the outcome. On successive runs, the distinction between well-formed and telegraphic commands became *less* potent in predicting the children's tendency to obey.

Obviously these subjects had not been unlearning English. On the contrary, they seemed to have learned to cope with anomaly. Our feeble operational techniques thus are well-foiled:

Mother: Allison: Mailbox fill!
Allison: We don't have any mailbox fills here.

Assuming the subject is playing it straight, she has interpreted the stimulus as a compound noun (albeit one whose referent she cannot discern) and has responded accordingly. But in light of Allison's 10-month-long experience as a subject with such sentences—and with her favorite ready-to-be-filled mailbox toy not 2 feet from her eyes—it is more likely that she is putting us on. Accordingly, we had to reopen the question of whether she had become a functioning linguistic informant at all of 2 years old.

Abandoning the indirect route, we now performed an experiment designed to solicit judgments of grammaticalness directly. The subjects were three girls, all about 2½ years old, who had participated in the longitudinal study. Two of the girls (Allison and Sarah) had responded preferentially to well-formed sentences in the first part of the longitudinal study (the expected result for the "telegraphic speaker") and had become indifferent to this distinction ("posttelegraphic") by the last run, as we have just discussed. The third (Ann) had responded preferentially to telegraphic sentences in her first run through the experiment (the expected result for the "holophrastic speaker") and responded preferentially to well-formed sentences by the time of the final run (the telegraphic stage). Thus, by the behavioral measures, Allison and Sarah were a step ahead of Ann in language development when the present experiment was run.

In designing the test situation, we exploited the children's willingness to imitate adult roles. The child was told "Today we have a new game." Mother, experimenter, and child would take turns being "teacher." As a preliminary step, the experimenter (as teacher) read a list of sentences to the mother, who judged them "good" or "silly" and did so correctly in all cases. She also repeated the good sentences verbatim and "fixed up" the silly ones. If the child hadn't quickly clamored for her turn, she was now offered it. The mother became teacher and the child was asked to judge the sentences, repeating the good ones and fixing the silly ones. Finally, the child became teacher. She was handed the stimulus list (needless to say, she could not read) and was told to offer sentences to the experimenter, who gamely undertook to judge these (as correctly as he could) for grammaticalness.[5]

---

[5] We have frequently been asked how we succeeded in telling the children to deal with

The stimuli were 60 sentences, all short imperatives. The noun object of each sentence was the name of a toy or other object known to the child. The sentences varied along two dimensions:

1. Intonation contour: the sentences had either the contour of a well-formed imperative (*Bring me the ball; Ball me the bring*) or that of a telegraphic sentence of the kind these children sometimes still produced in speech (*Bring ball; Ball bring*).
2. Order: the serial order of words might be correct (*Bring me the ball; Bring ball*) or the order of noun and verb might be reversed (*Ball me the bring; Ball bring*).

Thirty of the sentences were those used in the prior study and thus were familiar to the child. The other thirty sentences were new. The familiar sentences were presented at one session, the new ones a week later.

All three children undertook to judge the sentences offered to them. The mere fact that they did so, and that the results were nonrandom, suggests that these 2-year-olds could view language "as an object." That their classificatory skills were quite feeble. nevertheless, can be seen from Table 1. Each child tended to judge well-formed sentences (those that were full in contour and correct in serial order) as "good," though this outcome is far from categorical (combined probabilities from chi-square test, $p < .02$). There were no differences between the familiar and the unfamiliar sentences. For all subjects, the reversed-order sentences resulted in more judgments of "silly" (combined probabilities from chi-square test, $p < .001$). But only Allison judged telegraphic sentences with word order preserved as sillier than well-formed sentences. Recall that all three subjects distinguished telegraphic from well-formed sentences by the behavioral index (tendency to obey such commands) in earlier runs through that test.

Two of the three subjects (Allison and Sarah) were willing to repeat those sentences they had judged to be good. Sarah's repetitions were with one exception verbatim; her single "error" was a recognizable correction of a telegraphic sentence. Allison judged 20 of the 30 sentences of session 2 to be good, and she was asked to repeat these. Of these 20 sentences, 10 were actually well formed, and she repeated all these verbatim. Of the 10 that were actually deviant, she repeated 5 verbatim and changed 5 in some way. That is, she gave verbatim repetitions of well-formed sentences 10 times out of 10 and of deviant sentences 5 times out of 10 (Fisher test, $p = .025$). Four of the five nonverbatim "repetitions" were partial corrections. This outcome is similar to that achieved by Labov (1970), whose 12-year-old subjects unintentionally, and in spite of the

---

"sentences" when these children could hardly be expected to understand the word *sentence*. Indeed that is a puzzle, but nevertheless the children acted as if they understood what to do.

TABLE 1
Sentences Judged "Good" by Three 2-Year-Olds (in percentage)

Subjects	Normal order		Reversed order	
	Well-formed	Telegraphic	Well-formed	Telegraphic
Sarah	92	100	75	58
Ann	80	82	50	58
Allison	80	58	58	58

task requirements, "corrected" sentences offered for repetition to conform with their own dialect.

The repetition data, coupled with Labov's findings, give some independent evidence of these children's language organization. More relevant to the issue of metalinguistic functions are Allison's and Sarah's attempts to correct those sentences they had judged to be silly (Ann refused to attempt this). The corrections are shown in Table 2. Inspection of the table shows that Allison

TABLE 2
Sentences Judged "Silly" and Corrected by Two 2-Year-Olds[a]

Subjects	Sentences judged "silly"	Correction
Sarah	Pull wagon	Pull the wagon me
	Chair look	Chair look
	Clothes iron	Iron clothes
	Door shut	Door shut
	Put on a coat	Put me in a coat
	Make up the bed	Make the bed
	Wash the dishes	Wash the dishes
	Song me a sing	Sing me a song
	Box the open	Get in the box
Allison	Find cup	Drink out of the cup
	Push sweeper	The rug sweeped
	Bring book	Close book
	Mailbox fill	Mailman, put the mail in the mailbox
	Cup find	Fill the cup
	Pick up the iron	Iron the clothes
	Fill the mailbox	Put mail in the mailbox
	Ball me the throw	Throw the ball
	Sweeper the push	The sweeper push on the rug
	Iron up the pick	Iron the clothes

[a]The table shows all cases in which correction was attempted. Some other sentences were also judged to be "silly" but no corrections were offered for them. One subject, Ann, refused to provide any corrections at all.

usually (about 7 times in 10) and Sarah sometimes (about 4 times in 9) made a change in the direction of well-formedness. It appears that the children understood the question that was asked and made a conscious attempt to restructure the output.

There is a further curiosity in Allison's repsonses: some of them were nonparaphrastic (e.g., *Bring book / Close book; Cup find / Fill the cup*) We must admit that the instructions were vague; when we told the child to "fix it up if it is silly," we did not stipulate that the correction had to mean the same thing. But it is worth noting that one need not so instruct an adult. If we ask an adult to correct the expression *The dog bit cat the,* we expect the response *The dog bit the cat.* If informants responded *The dog bit the rat* with any measurable frequency, linguistic theory would look a good deal different than it does. Nor would we ever expect as responses *The cat was bitten by the dog, The domestic canine bit the cat, It was the dog who bit the cat,* or any of a host of other paraphrastically related responses. The adult informant has a surprisingly precise notion of what "it" means in the instruction "Fix it up" in the context of a deviant sentence. We show later on that at least some 6- and 7-year-olds interpret the task just as adults do.

In the last experimental condition (the child as "teacher"), we got some further suggestive evidence from Allison, who invented 20 sentences for her mother to judge. Of these 20, 18 were well-formed imperatives of the type she had been tested on in this and the earlier experiment (e.g., *Sit on the horsie; Put pants on yourself; Look at that chair*). One was a reversed-order imperative (*Rug put on the floor*) and the last a peculiar declarative (*Hair is on yourself*). It is of some interest that all save one of these inventions were imperatives, reproducing in minute detail the syntactic structure of the sentences we had offered to her. It seems unlikely that a child asked simply to "say sentences" will produce imperatives so exclusively; thus, it is probable that Allison was capable of developing a set for a unique grammatical structure in response to her perception of the requirements of the task. On the other hand, she showed no tendency to be rigid on semantic grounds, for her inventions varied over a wide range of topics.

In sum, we have found that the method of Shipley *et al.* (1969) rapidly becomes unworkable as the child passes out of the telegraphic stage of speech. The sophisticated 2-year-old, like his seniors, seems to fiddle around with deviant material. He may somehow internally "correct" it and then respond to the corrected material (the general paradigm hypothesized for adults by Katz, 1964; Ziff, 1964; and Chomsky, 1964; see Gleitman & Gleitman, 1970, for some experimental evidence). Thus, no simple behavioral index now gets close to his recognition of the distinction between well-formed and deviant sentences. At this stage, some of his knowledge can be tapped by direct query: *Tell me if the following sentence is good or silly.* Tenuously, but quite clearly, some 2-year-olds can follow this instruction in the role-modeling situation. Further, two of the three subjects studied gave evidence of going beyond simple classification. Isolating the deviance, at least in some measure, they often provided partial corrected paraphrases of deviant material. Indirect data from their spontaneous speech and from corrected repetitions were also consistent with these interpretations.

We believe that with appropriate refinement of these elicitation procedures, it may be feasible to inquire quite directly into aspects of young children's language organization. However, we do not know how far this judgmental capacity extends. In this study, we dealt only with very simple sentence types. We do not know if these subjects could have provided stable judgments if we had edged closer to the limits of their knowledge (a matter which is after all in some doubt even for adults; see, e.g., Maclay & Sleator, 1960; Hill, 1961). What has been demonstrated here is at least a minimal capacity in some children under 3 to contemplate the structure of language.

The Child as Informant

We will now show that some children from 5 to 8 years old come up with intuitions about syntactic and semantic structure so subtle that they are often overlooked even by professional grammarians. We will not argue that most or even many children can perform such feats of reflection. Since extreme differences in linguistic creativity have already been demonstrated for adults (Gleitman & Gleitman, 1970; Geer, Gleitman, & Gleitman, 1972), it would be surprising if we did not find great differences among children. We have not, then, looked for subjects who are in any way representative of the dialect population. On the contrary, we have taken some pains to interview children we suspected were highly articulate, either from personal knowledge or from aspects of their background. After all, the adult informants whose judgments provide the empirical basis for linguistic theory are at least as far from being a random sample of the population.

Having granted the bias of our sample, we begin with a transcription of a dialogue between one of us (LRG) and one of her children.

An Interview with a 7-Year-Old Child

At the time this dialogue was taped, Claire was 7 years old, in her second year of grammar school. She had had a good deal of exposure to language games and had participated when very young in pilot studies of the sort reported by Shipley *et al.* (1969). We are not suggesting, then, that Claire was average in either linguistic capacity or experience, although some of the results we report below for children of less special background suggest that her approach to syntactic questions is by no means unique.[6]

LG: Are you ready to do some work?

CG: Yes.

LG: We're going to talk about sentences this morning. And I want your opinion about these sentences.

CG: Yes, I know.

LG: Are they good sentences, are they bad sentences, do they mean something, are they silly, whatever your opinions are. Do you know that your opinions can't really be wrong?

CG: I know because you told me.

LG: Do you believe me?

CG: Yes, I believe you, because everybody has his own opinion.

LG: You and I may disagree; would you like me to tell you when I disagree with you?

CG: Yes, but you won't tell me!

LG: Okay, okay, I'll tell you. The important thing is you should know it's all right to disagree. Okay: *John and Mary went home.* (1)

CG: That's okay.

LG: That's an okay sentence?

CG: Yes.

LG: Does it mean the same thing as: *John went home and Mary went home?* (2)

CG: Yes, but it's sort of a little different because they might be going to the same home—well, it's okay, because they both might mean that, so it's the same.

LG: Here's another one: *Two and two are four.* (3)

CG: I think it sounds better *is.*

LG: *Two and two is four?*

CG: Am I right?

LG: Well, people say it both ways. How about this one: *Claire and Eleanor is a sister.* (4)

CG: (*laugh*): *Claire and Eleanor are sisters.*

LG: Well then, how come it's all right to say *Two and two is four?*

CG: You can say different sentences different ways! (*annoyed*)

LG: I see, does this mean the same thing: *Two is four and two is four?*

CG: No, because *Two and two are two and two* and *two and two is four.*

LG: Isn't that a little funny?

CG: *Two and two more is four,* also you can say that.

LG: How's this one: *My sister plays golf.* (5)

---

[6] All sentences presented to Claire and all of her initial responses appear in this transcript. A few tedious interchanges resulting from probes have been deleted.

CG: That's okay.

LG: How about this one: *Golf plays my sister.* (6)

CG: I think that sounds terrible, you know why?

LG: Why?

CG: Poor girl!

LG: Well, what does it mean?

CG: It means the golf stands up and picks up the thing and hits the girl at the goal.

LG: How about this one: *Boy is at the door.* (7)

CG: If his name is *Boy.* You should—the kid is named *John,* see? *John is at the door* or *A boy is at the door* or *The boy is at the door* or *He's knocking at the door.*

LG: Okay, how about this one: *I saw the queen and you saw one.* (8)

CG: No, because you're saying that one person saw a queen and one person saw a one—ha ha—what's a one?

LG: How about this: *I saw Mrs. Jones and you saw one.* (9)

CG: It's not okay—I saw—*You saw Mrs. Jones and I saw one* (ha ha). Besides there aren't two Mrs. Jones.

LG: Is that the problem there? Is that why the sentence sounds so funny?

CG: No, the other problem is *I saw—You saw Mrs. Jones and I saw one*—a one.

LG: A one, you mean like a number one?

CG: No—a one, whatever a one—well, okay, a number one.

LG: How about this: *Be good!* (10)

CG: That sounds okay.

LG: How about this: *Know the answer!* (11)

CG: That's the only way to say it, I think.

LG: The only way to say what?

CG: *You better know the answer!* (*threatening tone*)

LG: How about this one: *I am eating dinner.* (12)

CG: Yeah, that's okay.

LG: How about this one: *I am knowing your sister.* (13)

CG: No: *I know your sister.*

LG: Why not *I am knowing your sister*—you can say *I am eating your dinner.*

CG: It's different! (*shouting*) You say different sentences in different ways! Otherwise it wouldn't make sense!

LG: I see, you mean you don't understand what that means, *I am knowing your sister.*

CG: I don't understand what it means.

LG: How would you say it?

CG: *I know your sister.* Do you disagree with me?

LG: It so happens I agree with you. How's this one: *I doubt that any snow will fall today.* (14)

CG: *I doubt that snow will fall today.*

LG: How's this: *I think that any snow will fall today.* (15)

CG: *I think that some snow will fall today.*

LG: That way it's okay?

CG: I don't think snow will fall taday cause it's nice out—ha ha.

LG: How about this: *Claire loves Claire.* (16)

CG: *Claire loves herself* sounds much better.

LG: Would you ever say *Claire loves Claire?*

CG: Well, if there's somebody Claire knows named Claire. I know some-body named Claire and maybe I'm named Claire.

LG: And then you wouldn't say *Claire loves herself?*

CG: No, because if it was another person named Claire—like if it was me and that other Claire I know, and somebody wanted to say that I loved that other Claire, they'd say *Claire loves Claire.*

LG: Okay, I see. How about this: *I do, too.* (17)

CG: It sounds okay but only if you explain what you're trying to say.

LG: How about: *The color green frightens George.* (18)

CG: Doesn't frighten me, but it sounds okay.

LG: How about this one: *George frightens the color green.* (19)

CG: Sounds okay, but it's stupid, it's stupid!

LG: What's wrong with it?

CG: The color green isn't even alive, so how can it be afraid of George?

LG: Tell me, Claire, is this game getting boring to you?

CG: Never-rrrrrrrrrrrrrrrr.

LG: Why do you like to play a game like this? What's the difference how you say things as long as people understand you?

CG: It's a difference because people would stare at you (*titter*). No, but I think it's fun. Because I don't want somebody coming around and saying—correcting me.

LG: Oh, so that's why you want to learn how to speak properly?

CG: That's not the only reason.

LG: Well, what is it?

CG: Well, there's a lotta reasons, but I think this game is plain fun.

LG: You want to go on playing?

CG: Yeah, and after this let's do some spelling; I love spelling.

Other Subjects

As a further check on the incidence of skills apparent in Claire's responses, we tested six more children with these same materials. Listed in ascending age, they were: S1—female, 5 years; S2—male, 5 years; S3—male, 6 years; S4—male, 7 years; S5—male, 7 years; S7—female, 8 years (S6 was Claire Gleitman, 7 years). All of the subjects were children of academic families. The interviewer for S1 and S5 was their mother, an undergraduate psychology student. The interviewer for S2, S3, S4, and S7 was an undergraduate linguistics student who had never met the children before the interview. All sessions were taped.

Results

Rather to our surprise, all of the children we interviewed were prepared to play the game; all classified the sentences in fair conformance with adult judgments; and all, including the youngest, gave interesting and relevant accounts of what is wrong with the deviant sentences, at least some of the time.

Classification of the Sentences. Table 3 presents the conformance of the children's judgments on these sentences with our own. There are many reasons to be embarrassed by so formal a presentation of these data. Most centrally, the accuracy of the child's response was often dependent on the wit of the interviewer in making the correct probe. In particular, the youngest subjects would accept almost any sentence unless some further question was asked:

E: How about this one? *Boy is at the door.*
S1:   Good.
E: Good? Is that the way you would say it?
S1:   No. *A boy is at the door. Boy is at the door* isn't a good sentence.

More generally, it should be clear that this test was performed simply to ascertain whether children of these ages can in principle adopt the attitude of judging and classifying in a manner similar to that of adult informants: with respect to this point, the results are clear cut. But since the choice of test sentences was haphazard in terms of any metric of well-formedness, complexity, and the like, we can make no general statement about the judgmental capacities of children as compared with adults; the percentage of agreement with adults would almost certainly be changed by a varying of the proportion of one or another kind of deviance. In the absence of normative data, these subjects' responses are useful only to expand the picture drawn in the original interview. But the results leave little doubt that a variety of delicate questions of syntax and semantics were handled rather neatly by these children. Below we give a number of examples, organized according to several rough syntactic subcategories.

Stative verbs: Sentences 13 (*I am knowing your brother*) and 11 (*Know the answer!*) contained stative verbs in deviant environments. As can be seen from these examples, this verb class has no forms in the present progressive or in the imperative. As Table 3 indicates, the younger children failed to notice the problem. The older ones rejected the deviant forms. S6 suggested the so-called

TABLE 3
Conformance of Children's Judgments to Those of Adults[a]

		Subject						
		S1	S2	S3	S4	S5	S6	S7
		Age						
	Adult judgment	5	5	6	7	7	7	8
(1) John and Mary went home	wf	+	+	+	+	+	+	+
(2) John went home and Mary went home	wf	+	+	+	+	+	+	+
(3) Two and two are four	wf	+	+	+	+	+	+	+
(4) Claire and Eleanor is a sister	d	−	−	+	+	+	+	+
(5) My sister plays golf	wf	+	+	+	+	+	+	+
(6) Golf plays my sister	d	+	+	+	+	+	+	+
(7) Boy is at the door	d	+	+	+	+	+	+	+
(8) I saw the queen and you saw one	d	−	−	−	−	+	+	+
(9) I saw Mrs. Jones and you saw one	d	+	+	+	+	+	+	+
(10) Be good!	wf	+	+	+	+	+	+	+
(11) Know the answer!	d	−	−	−	+	−	+	+
(12) I am eating dinner	wf	+	−	+	+	+	+	+
(13) I am knowing your sister	d	−	−	−	+	+	+	+
(14) I doubt that any snow will fall today	wf	+	−	+	+	+	−	+
(15) I think that any snow will fall today	d	−	−	+	+	+	+	+
(16) Claire loves Claire	wf/d							
(17) I do too	wf	+	−	+	−	+	+	+
(18) The color green frightens George	wf	−	+	+	−	−	+	−
(19) George frightens the color green	d	+	+	+	+	+	+	+
Total "+" judgments for all sentences		12	10	15	15	16	17	17

[a] Adjust judgments were provided by three independent judges who indicated whether each sentence was well-formed (wf) or deviant (d). The children's judgments are marked "+" if they agreed with those of the adult and "−" if they did not, regardless of their explanation. Sentence 16 cannot be scored in this manner; whether or not it is deviant depends upon whether the same referent is assumed for both nouns. The names in sentences 4 and 9 were chosen to be familiar; in sentence 16 the child's own name was used.

pseudo-imperative interpretation (an ellipsis for an *if*-clause), which is acceptable for such verbs (*Know the answer = You better know the answer = If you don't know the answer,* *≠!*).

Collective versus distributive use of and: All children stated that (1) *John and Mary went home* and (2) *John went home and Mary went home* mean the same thing. Claire spontaneously brought up the collective/distributive issue in response to this comparison. She first tried to distinguish the two sentences on this basis ("they might be going to the same home") but then recognized that both forms share both construals ("they might both mean that, so it's the same").

Pronominal referents: Sentences 8 and 9 display the anomaly that arises when a definite noun-phrase is the apparent antecedent of an indefinite pronoun:

(8) *I saw the queen and you saw one.*
(9) *I saw Mrs. Jones and you saw one.*

The oddity is clearer in (9), for while there may be only one Mrs. Jones in the world, *one* cannot have that same Mrs. Jones as its grammatical antecedent. The four younger children accepted (8) without question, which is consistent with their tendency not to notice syntactic deviance when no semantic anomaly arises. On the other hand, all of the subjects rejected (9). The responses to these questions are displayed in full below. It is quite clear that the quality of the explanations improves with the age of the children; put another way, there is an increasing conformance of their judgments with our own. Note that the younger children gave explanations that accorded with their judgments: they rejected only the case with the proper noun, and they explained by claiming that this structure is incorrect with a name. (The stimulus sentence is tagged by its number; the experimenter's comments, somewhat abbreviated, are bracketed):

S1: (8) Good. (9) No, 'cause there's only one Mrs. Jones. [Then how would you say it?] *I saw Mrs. Jones* [and?] *I did, too.*

S2: (8) Yeah. (9) I would hate that 'cause they're not—I got two reasons. They're not the same age and they don't look the same. [So how would you say it?] I don't know. It's silly. Because it don't say the name and—it don't say the name—it's—*I saw Richard Jamison, and you saw one.* Don't give no reason.

S3: (8) Good. (9) It sounds funny 'cause *You saw Mrs. Jones* is okay, but *I saw a one*—it should mean something like *I saw—You saw a tree and I saw one, too.* You can't say it with a name. [So what's the problem?] Because you have to say something like *You saw a tree and I saw one.* But you can't say something like *You saw Mrs. Jones and I saw one.* You have to say *You saw Mrs. Jones and I saw her, too.*

S4: (8) That's a good sentence. (9) That's silly, 'cause there might not be two Mrs. Jones that I know. [So how would you say it?] *I saw Mrs. Jones and so did you. Both of us saw Mrs. Jones.*

S5: (8) No, *I saw the queen and you saw the same queen that I saw—you and me saw the queen.* (9) No, *I saw a Mrs. Jones and so did you.*

S6: (8) No, because you're saying that one person saw a queen and one person saw a one—ha ha—what's a one? (9) It's not okay—*I saw—You saw Mrs. Jones and I saw one*—ha ha—besides, there aren't two Mrs. Jones. [Is that the problem here?] No, the other problem is *You saw*

> *Mrs. Jones and I saw one—a one.* [Like a number one?] No—a one—
> whatever a one—well, okay, a number one.

S7: (8) That doesn't really make sense. *You saw a queen*—no, I'll say *me—I saw a queen and you saw a queen, too.*(9) That doesn't make sense because there's only one Mrs. Jones that you saw and you have to see the same one, probably. *I saw Mrs. Jones and you saw her, too.* [But if there were two Mrs. Jones?] *You saw her*—I don't know. I guess if there were two you could say *one.* It would sound funny. [Suppose your grandmother and your mother are both Mrs. Smith, so you might be able to see two of them at the same time.] *I saw Mrs. Smith and you saw them, too*—ha ha—that sounds—*and you saw them, too—I saw Mrs. Smiths*... I don't know.

Explanations of Deviance. While our subjects very often rejected syntactically deviant but meaningful expressions, they ordinarily, and improbably, explained their rejection on semantic grounds, e.g.:

E: How about *Kari and Kirsten is a sister.*
S4: Funny.
E: Why is it funny?
S4: Because that doesn't make sense.
E: How would you say it?
S4: *Kari and Kirsten are sisters.*

This happened with trying consistency. Since the subject easily provided a paraphrase, he had obviously grasped the sense of the sentence; but even so he often "explained" the peculiarity of the sentence by denying its meaningfulness. Again, this confusion is not restricted to children; one has only to make the case a bit more difficult. Thus, adults given the sentence *I saw the queen of England and you saw one, too* will often reject it on the grounds that there is only one queen of England. The fact that the sentence would sound just as odd if there were fifty queens of England entirely escapes their notice (Gleitman, 1961).

Of course very often a semantic explanation is appropriate; here is an example from a 5-year-old:

E: *George frightens the color green.*
S1: No, because green is used to boys.
E: If there was a color that never saw children, it could be frightened?
S1: No. It couldn't be frightened because—'cause—I'm thinking, okay, Mom? ... No, 'cause colors don't have faces of paint. You talking about paint?

We have seen that semantic "explanations" were common among our subjects, even where they were inappropriate. Yet, there also were many instances in which the children, including the 5-year-olds, pointed quite precisely to a syntactic violation; e.g.:

E: *I think that any rain will fall today.*
S3: You can't say *any* there.
E: *I am knowing your brother.*
S4: It's not right English. It should be *I know your brother,* not *I am knowing your brother.*
E: *Two and two are four.*
S6: I think it sounds better *is.*

It is worth noting that these children, not yet exposed to grammar exercises in school, nonetheless had definite opinions that took the form "you can't say . . . you have to say."

To this extent, the children seemed to adopt a frame of reference in answering these questions that is similar to our own. The nonparaphrastic responses often observed in the 2-year-old subjects (see Table 2) had disappeared. The quality of explanation changed markedly with age (whether it also changes with intelligence, schooling, and the like is a question we cannot speculate on).

Some further ticklish differences in the frame of reference for dealing with our experimental question are left unanswered here. As a final comment, however, the following kind of response would probably be exceedingly rare in adult subjects, but it occurred more than once in our sample. (We were trying to find out whether *is* and *are* are both acceptable in sums):

E: *Two and two are four.*
S3: Yeah.
E: Can you think of any other way to say that?
S3: Three and one?

Discussion

We now consider the factors that determined the behavior of these subjects in responding to the question: *Is the following sentence "good" or "silly"?* A number of tangled issues of truth, plausibility, meaningfulness, and syntactic patterning enter into the interpretation of these findings. Did our subjects distinguish between implausible or false expressions and linguistically anomalous ones? Even if they did, did they really contemplate the constraints on arrangements of words and phrases (syntax) or did they consider only the meanings of such arrays and the entities that comprise them (semantics)? Below we comment on our subjects' approaches to these fine distinctions. These matters are presumably of some importance, perhaps especially to those psychologists who claim that "semantics is what is important" about language and language learning and that the transformational foray into syntax is in some ways uninteresting or not cogent for psychologists of language. In our view there are really two issues. One is the immediate question about the factors that determined our subjects' judgments. The other concerns the general problem of distinguishing syntax from meaning.

What Makes a Sentence "Silly": Falsehood or Ill-Formedness? There are many ways that a sentence can be "silly." For example, there are quite different oddities involved in *Mud makes me clean* versus *Mud drinks my ankle.* Notice that the negative of the first is entirely unexceptional (*Mud does not make me clean*), while the negative of the second is precisely as odd as the positive (*Mud does not drink my ankle*). Stated more generally, *Mud makes me clean* is implausible to the extent that mud is rarely a cleansing agent, but it is a "good" sentence of English.

Is this true of *Mud drinks my ankle?* Again, some would say that this is a good sentence of English on the grounds that it is a case of a noun phrase followed by a verb phrase in which the right completion of the verb *drink* (a noun phrase) is also correct, given the gross patterns of English. But most linguists would respond that a description of the English language that fails to account for the oddity of this sentence is primitive and incomplete (after all, if linguists disclaim responsibility for this phenomenon, who is to handle it?). In the standard transformational formulation, such oddities are described as violations of *selectional restrictions* that obtain among the words and phrases of the language (for discussion, see Chomsky, 1965): *drink* requires an animate subject while *mud* is not an animate noun. Knowledge of selectional restrictions on words is claimed to be part of the lexical information that speakers have internalized. (Whether this information is "semantic" or "syntactic" is a question to which we will return.) Linguists are less concerned (although not utterly unconcerned) to account for the implausibility of *Mud makes me clean,* which more clearly turns on the language user's "knowledge of the world" as opposed to "knowledge of language."

How do speakers interpret the instruction to tell whether or not a sentence is "silly?" By and large, adults accept *Mud makes me clean* with only mild waffling, and they reject *Mud drinks my ankle.* They accept implausible sentences and reject violations of selectional restrictions.

In contrast, 2-year-olds, as already mentioned, seem to reject implausible sentences. For example, *Find book* was "corrected" as *Close book.* Our guess is that these nonparaphrastic responses were attempts to come up with more plausible expressions. Similarly, the 5-year-olds studied here sometimes rejected sentences on these grounds:

E: *I am eating dinner.*
S2: I would hate that.

E: Why?

S2: I don't eat dinner anymore.

E: How about *I am eating breakfast?*

S2: Yum, yum, good!

On the contrary, the older subjects rarely rejected sentences on the basis of implausibility or falsehood. If the experimenter suggested that they do so, they considered this only a joke:

E: *I think that any rain will fall today.*

S3: Well, *any* is not the right word. You should say *I don't think that any rain is going to come down.* Right?

E: Okay. It's a pretty nice day anyway.

S3: So it's not gonna rain, so that's why I'm probably right (*gails of laughter*).

Similarly, Claire pointed up this distinction in one response:

E: *The color green frightens George.*

S6: Doesn't frighten *me*, but it sounds O.K.

On the other hand, violated selectional restrictions—which indeed lead to a bizarre meaning—were uniformly rejected. For a simple case such as *Golf plays my brother*, all subjects said that it is "backwards" or that "it doesn't make sense." They might also provide a reading for the deviant sentence:

S3: Ha ha. That doesn't sound right. You should say *My brother plays golf* instead of *golf plays brother*—that would mean a golf ball or something bats the boy over the thing.

It is also worth noting that S1, who for mysterious reasons of his own rejected *I am eating dinner*, rejected *Golf plays my brother* on appropriate grounds:

S1: I hate it cause it's backwards

While the tendency to reject implausible but "correct" sentences diminished with the older subjects, it did not disappear. All subjects rejected *George frightens the color green*, which violates a selectional restriction on *frighten*. But some also rejected *The color green frightens George* on the grounds of implausibility:

S7: No, because green is just still. It isn't going to jump up and go BOO!

Nor should we expect categorical acceptance of implausible expressions in the light of the vagueness of these instructions. The point here is not whether categorical behavior was found: given these instructions, some adults also reject such sentences (after all, the idea *is* silly). Much more centrally, the plausibility

dimension seemed highly salient for 2-year-olds (see Table 2), was still sometimes apparent in 5-year-olds, and became much less salient as the determinant
of judgments among the older children and adults. As we will now discuss,
syntactic dimensions become more potent with age.

*What Makes a Sentence "Silly": Syntactic Deviance or Semantic Ano-
maly?* We have so far seen that what differed among our subjects, and what
differentiated them most clearly from adults, was the precise understanding of
the question: *Is the following a good sentence of English?* Did they respond in
terms of meaning or form? (Of course this further question raises serious
problems of definition, most of which we regretfully ignore, for they reach well
beyond the scope of this paper.)

While syntactic structure appears to be the basis of many of the rejections of
sentences we have cited thus far, it may be argued that semantic anomalies arise
from the syntactic deviations and that it was the semantic anomaly to which
these subjects responded. In that event, the best test cases for sensitivity to
syntax would be those sentences whose syntactic deviations have the least
semantic force. These are usually low-order violations of phrase-structure constraints. Examples among our stimuli are sentences in which number concord is
violated (*John and Jim is a brother*) or in which determiners required by count
nouns are missing (*Boy is at the door*). Similar to the last instance are the
foreshortened forms without particles and determiners presented to 2-year-olds
(*Bring book*). These cases can be contrasted with deviations from well-formedness that, at least intuitively, do more radical violence to meaning, such as *Golf
plays my brother, I think that any rain will fall today,* and, for the 2-year-old,
Ball me the throw. If the children noticed only semantic anomaly and ignored
syntactic patterning, they should have accepted sentences of the first sort (*John
and Jim is a brother*) and rejected sentences of the second sort (*I think that any
rain will fall today*).

The youngest subjects were indeed most responsive to deformations which
obscured or complicated semantic interpretation. Thus the 2-year-olds gave
clear-cut data only for sentences with word-order reversals, such as *Ball me the
bring,* whose meaning is obscure. Similarly, the 5-year-olds often accepted a
deviant sentence if it was odd only in its word arrangement but still clear in
meaning (e.g., *John and Jim is a brother*). Nevertheless, there are some indications that even the youngest children were sensitive to syntactic issues as such.
For example, one of the 2-year-olds (Allison) was much more likely to judge a
telegraphic sentence as "silly" than a well-formed one. The sensitivity to syntax
was more obvious in the 5-year-olds, who sometimes noticed syntactic oddities
that yielded no semantic problems. One of them rejected *Boy is at the door* and
spontaneously added, *"Boy is at the door* isn't a good sentence." From 6 years
on, the salience of syntactic deviance was no longer in doubt. All children over 5
years of age rejected *Boy is at the door* and *John and Jim is a brother.* Each

provided the appropriate paraphrase, so they obviously understood these expressions. They were then rejected solely on grounds of syntactic nicety.

Beyond the immediate issue we have just considered is the question of whether a relevant distinction can in general be drawn between syntax and semantics. Certain psycholinguists seem to believe that it can. They seem to assume that constraints on word order and the like, insofar as these are not merely historical accidents, are relevant only to the nature of memory, sequencing of outputs, and other issues of linguistic information-processing. What they fail to notice, or misinterpret, is that very much of what we mean by *meaning* is expressed through syntactic devices. Notions such as subject, predicate, noun, adverbial phrase, and the like are the categories and functions described in the syntax of the language; but of course these are not semantically empty notions. The movement within transformational linguistics known as *generative semantics* (e.g., Lakoff, 1972) is an attempt, as we understand it, to merge the semantic and syntactic descriptions of the language in a way more perspicuous than in Chomsky's (1965) formulation. But whatever success this venture may have, it is bizarre that any version of transformational–generative grammar could be viewed as describing "merely" the semantically empty syntax of the language. Clearly, these theories have always been attempts to describe the complex interweave of form and meaning that natural languages represent.

This being our view, it is hard for us to argue any more strenuously than we have that our subjects were aware of English syntactic structure. If it can be shown that the features of syntactic structure that these children noted and commented on always have some semantic content, that can come as no surprise to us and cannot mitigate our interpretations of these findings.

Conclusions

The Child as Language Knower

All of the children we have studied showed at least a muddy capacity to be reflective about knowledge. Even the 2-year-olds provided nonrandom classifications of simple sentences: the fact that they undertook this task at all is evidence of at least the rudiments of a metalinguistic skill. A child who can do this must already be said to know something about language that the spider does not know about web weaving.

The ability to reflect upon language dramatically increases with age. The older children were better not only in noting deviance but also in explaining where the deviance lay. By and large, the 5-year-olds offered only paraphrastic corrections. They did not add much in the way of explanation, even though they indicated that there are ways "you have to say it" and that some of the sentences are just "not right." In contrast, the older children often referred to linguistic categories (e.g., "You can't say it with a name") and occasionally changed the lexical classification of a familiar word, thus rendering a deviant sentence well formed (e.g., "You can't say that unless you are 'a Green' "; "*One person saw a queen and one person saw a one*—whatever a 'one' is"). This achievement is all the more impressive considering the fact that many adults have serious difficulty when required to change the categorial status of a word (Gleitman & Gleitman, 1970). But even when the subjects offered only example or paraphrase, the older ones sometimes came up with all of the data relevant to the writing of a rule of grammar, Claire's response to *Boy is at the door* is a case in point:

> If his name is *Boy. The kid is named John,* see? *John is at the door,* or *The boy is at the door,* or *A boy is at the door,* or *He's knocking at the door.*

Most of the main distinctions among noun and noun-phrase types (count, proper, pronoun; definite versus indefinite noun-phrase) are neatly laid out in this response. Such manipulation of linguistic data is a not inconsiderable accomplishment. It is after all the *modus operandi* of the practicing linguist.

We should reiterate that the abilities we have demonstrated in some children do not necessarily appear in very many. Our claims are simply existential. The lack of normative data is only one of the reasons for this caution. A number of studies (e.g., Pfafflin, 1961; Gleitman & Gleitman, 1970) have shown that there are substantial individual differences among adults in the ability to deal with classificatory problems. These differences in metalinguistic skills are not attributable solely to differences in nonlinguistic matters such as memorial capacity (Geer, Gleitman & Gleitman, 1972). Under the circumstances, it is only reasonable to suppose that such differences already exist among young children. Chomsky's demonstration (1969) of individual differences in the recognition of transformational features of verbs in 6- to 10-year-olds gives further grounds for this belief.

Metalinguistic Functions Compared to Other Metacognitive Processes

At least in adults, there are some other "metacognitive" processes which seem to be similar in some ways to the metalinguistic functions we have just considered. We think and we sometimes know that we think; we remember and sometimes know that we remember. In such cases, the appropriate cognitive process is itself the object of a higher-order cognitive process, as if the homunculus perceived the operations of a lower-order system. But the lower-order process often proceeds without any metacognition. This is certainly true of language, whose use (even in professional grammarians) is often unaccompanied by metalinguistic reflection. Similarly, for other cognitive processes such as memory: we see a friend and call him by name without any awareness that we have just recognized and recalled. The important point is that we *can* deal with memory in a metacognitive way, just as we can reflect metalinguistically. Examples of metacognition in memory are recollection (when we know that we remember) and intentional learning (when we know that we must store the material for later retrieval). Another example is the phenomenon of knowing that one knows—that is, has stored in memory—some item of information even though one cannot recall it at the moment (e.g., the "tip-of-the-tongue" phenomenon, Brown & McNeill, 1966; memory monitoring, Hart, 1967).

Developmental evidence suggests that these various metacognitive processes may be closely related. In particular, their time of emergence seems suspiciously close to the 5- to 7-year age range in which we found adultlike performance on metalinguistic tasks. Whether Piaget's stage analysis can handle such findings is another matter, but it is interesting to note that the period from 5 to 7 is just about the time when children begin to explain their judgments of space and number (Ginsburg & Opper, 1969). Similarly for monitoring processes in memory. Several Russian investigators have shown that intentional strategies for remembering are rarely adopted before 5 years of age but are increasingly utilized thereafter (Yendovitskaya, 1971).

Whether these relations among the various metacognitive functions will turn out to be more than mere analogies remains to be seen. The primary emphasis of the present paper has been on the metacognitive aspect of language behavior, for it is this that allows us to say that language is not only used but known. The results indicate that this kind of knowledge is found even in children. Consider a reaction to Chomsky's paradigm (1969) in which the child is shown a blindfolded doll and is asked: "Is this doll easy or hard to see?" (Claire, age 8):

CG: Easy to see—wow! That's confusing.
LG: Why is it confusing?
CG: Because it's hard for the doll to see but the doll is easy to see and that's what's confusing.

Or again, on the ambiguity of *ask to:*

LG: What would it mean: *I asked the teacher to leave the room.*
CG: It would mean *I asked the teacher if I could leave the room to go to the bathroom* or it would mean *I asked the teacher to leave the room so I could go to the bathroom in privacy.*

Here knowledge is explicit. The child has moved from mere language use to serious innovation and creativity, to contemplation of language as an object. Such skills are frequently manifest in 6-, 7-, and 8-year-olds. We believe it is this kind of language activity that is most intriguingly engaged and convincingly explained by transformational theory; this is hardly surprising because just such data are the methodological prerequisite for grammar construction.

ACKNOWLEDGMENT

The work reported here was supported by the National Institute of Health under grant number 20041-01. Thanks are due to Rochel Gelman and Francis W. Irwin for helpful comments on the manuscript, and to Harris Savin for many useful suggestions and criticisms in developing this work. We also wish to thank Betsy Alloway and Judy Buchanan, who carried out some of the experiments. The change of judgments from semantic to syntactic over the age range studied here was first pointed out to us by Marilyn Shatz, to whom we are much indebted.

References

Bever, T. G., Lackner, J. R., & Kirk, R. The underlying structures of sentences are the primary units of immediate speech processing. *Perception and Psychophysics,* 5, 1969, 225–234.

Bloom, L. *Language development: Form and function in emerging grammars.* Cambridge, Mass.: M.I.T. Press, 1970.

Braine, M. D. S. The ontogeny of English phrase structure: The first phase. *Language,* 1963, *39,* 1–13.

Brown, R., & Bellugi, U. Three processes in the child's acquisition of syntax. In E. H. Lenneberg (Ed.), *New directions in the study of language.* Cambridge, Mass.: M.I.T. Press, 1964.

Brown, R., Cazden, C., & Bellugi, U. The child's grammar from I to III. In J. P. Hill (Ed.), *Minnesota Symposium on Child Psychology.* Minneapolis: University of Minnesota Press, 1969.

Brown, R., Fraser, C., & Bellugi, U. Explorations in grammar evaluation. *Monographs of the Society for Research in Child Development,* 29 (1) Serial No. 92, 1964. Reprinted in R. Brown, *Psycholinguistics.* New York: The Free Press, 1970.

Brown, R., & McNeill, D. The "tip of the tongue" phenomenon. *Journal of Verbal Learning and Verbal Behavior,* 1966, *5,* 325–337.

Chomsky, N. *The acquisition of syntax in children from 5 to 10.* Cambridge, Mass.: M.I.T. Press, 1969.

Chomsky, N. Degrees of grammaticalness. In J. A. Fodor & J. J. Katz (Eds.), *The structure of language.* Englewood Cliffs, N.J.: Prentice-Hall, 1964.

Chomsky, N. *Aspects of the theory of syntax.* Cambridge, Mass.: M.I.T. Press, 1965.

Geer, S., Gleitman, H., & Gleitman, L. Paraphrasing and remembering compound words. *Journal of Verbal Learning and Verbal Behavior,* 1972, *11,* 348–355.

Gelman, R., & Shatz, M. Appropriate speech adjustments: The operation of conversational constraints on talk to two-year olds. In M. Lewis & L. Rosenblum (Eds.), *Communication and language: The origins of behavior,* Vol. 5, New York: Wiley, 1976.

Ginsburg, H., & Opper, S. *Piaget's theory of intellectual development.* Englewood Cliffs, N.J.: Prentice-Hall, 1969.

Gleitman, L. Pronominals and stress in English conjunction. *Language Learning,* University of Michigan, Ann Arbor, Michigan, 1961.

Gleitman, L., & Gleitman, H. *Phrase and Paraphrase.* New York: Norton, 1970.

Hart, J. T. Memory and the memory-monitoring process. *Journal of Verbal Learning and Verbal Behavior,* 1972, *6,* 385–391.

Hill, A. A. Grammaticality. *Word,* 1961, *17,* 1–10.

Johnson, N. F. The psychological reality of phrase-structure rules. *Journal of Verbal Learning and Verbal Behavior,* 1965, *4,* 469–475.

Katz, J. Semisentences. In J. A. Fodor & J. J. Katz (Eds.), *The structure of language.* Englewood Cliffs, N.J.: Prentice-Hall, 1964.

Labov, W. The logic of non-standard English. In F. Williams (Ed.), *Language and Poverty.* Chicago: Markham Press, 1970.

Lakoff, G. Generative semantics. In D. Steinberg & L. Jakobovits (Eds.), *Semantics: An interdisciplinary reader in philosophy, linguistics, anthropology and psychology.* London: Cambridge University Press, 1972.

Lenneberg, E. *Biological foundations of language.* New York: Wiley, 1967.

Maclay, H., & Sleator, M. Responses to language: Judgments of grammaticalness. *International Journal of American Linguistics,* 1960, *26,* 275–282.

McNeill, D. The creation of language by children. In J. Lyons and R. J. Wales (Eds.), *Psycholinguistics papers.* Edinburgh: Edinburgh University Press, 1966.

Menyuk, P. *Sentences children use.* Cambridge, Mass.: M.I.T. Press, 1969.

Miller, G. A., & Isard, S. Some perceptual consequences of linguistic rules. *Journal of Verbal Learning and Verbal Behavior,* 1963, *2,* 217–228.

Miller, W., & Ervin, S. The development of grammar in child language. *Monographs of social research in children development,* 1964, *29,* 2–34.

Pfafflin, S. M. Grammatical judgments of computer-generated word sequences. Murray Hill, N.J.: Bell Telephone Laboratories (mimeo), 1961.

Savin, H., & Perchonock, E. Grammatical structure and the immediate recall of English sentences. *Journal of Verbal Learning and Verbal Behavior,* 1965, *4,* 348–353.

Shipley, E. F., & Shipley, T. E., Jr. Quaker children's use of *thee:* A relational analysis. *Journal of Verbal Learning and Verbal Behavior,* 1969, *8,* 112–117.

Shipley, E. F., Smith, C. S., & Gleitman, L. R. A study in the acquisition of language: Free responses to commands. *Language,* 1969, *45,* 322–342.

Yendovitskaya, T. V. Development of memory. In A. V. Zaporozhets & D. B. Elkonin (Eds.), *The psychology of preschool children,* Cambridge, Mass.: M.I.T. Press, 1971.

Ziff, P. On understanding understanding utterances. In J. A. Fodor & J. J. Katz (Eds.), *The structure of language.* Englewood Cliffs, N.J.: Prentice-Hall, 1964.

CHAPTER 9

Environment, Experience, and Equilibration

Celia Stendler Lavatelli

University of Illinois, Urbana, Illinois

We are witnessing today in America a phenomenal growth in early childhood education. The number of states making kindergarten mandatory is increasing rapidly, as is the number of states and communities offering public school education for 4-year-old children. Unfortunately, while opportunity can be legislated, quality of program cannot. All too many preschool programs are basing their curricula upon modified primary programs of the kind Silberman (1970) decries in *Crisis in the Classroom* for being dull and joyless. One curriculum suggests the following for the fall months:

1. Arithmetic: Introduction of numerals 0–5, worksheets, games on the chalkboard, exercises on the feltboard. Introduction to commercial arithmetic blocks.
2. Reading: Alphabet recognition and sounds. Games with initial consonant sounds.
3. Social studies: People and animals prepare for cold weather. Columbus Day—dramatic plays and crafts centered around voyage. Halloween—stories of ghosts and witches.
4. Art: Boat pictures.

And so on, for a completely preplanned, academic curriculum, based upon the notion that the best preparation for first grade is to be taught the first-grade curriculum in the preschool and that education goes on when the teacher is directing the class, teaching a specific skill or concept. It assumes that learning follows such teaching. It provides little or no opportunity for children to explore, to become involved in something they want to do, to stretch their minds as they solve problems meaningful to them. However, it is only as we change the emphasis from a view that education is direct teaching to one that education is learning, and as we begin to view the child as the agent of his own learning, that classrooms become joyous places, warm and humane, where intelligence is nurtured and grows during the critical preschool years.

This view of education is not new; John Dewey elaborated on it over 50 years ago. Piaget's developmental theory has provided fresh impetus for the notion that the school is an environment for learning and that school environments can facilitate the development of intelligence. Some teachers interpret this to mean that the teacher's role is to make available to the child the conventional preschool materials—doll-play equipment, blocks, wheel toys, art media, puzzles, books, and games—and let the child choose what he wants to do and how he wants to do it. The teacher steers the work and play into constructive social channels, encouraging the shy and timid and redirecting the child who is acting out. The child's own play activities will contribute to his cognitive development, the argument goes; as the child plays, he will make important discoveries about the properties of objects and relations between objects. Anything more in the way of teacher direction is considered to be imposition.

It *is* true that as they play children make discoveries contributing to their cognitive growth, but what children discover is a function of the mental structures they can impose upon data. What children get out of play is what they bring to it. When I was in high school, I chose to do a project in biology class—keeping a diary of observations of birds. Daily, I recorded the kinds of birds I saw, where I saw them, whether they were eating or flying, and so on. I had little to bring to my observations, for I did not have the structures from ethological research available to today's student to interpret certain behaviors as courting behaviors, signals of distress, and so on. There *is* a structure to a discipline composed of generalizations that have mileage.

Similarly, as Piaget has suggested, there is a structure to mental processes that allows logical processing of data, bringing order to what we see when we look at particular stimuli. Perhaps we subordinate some data to others, establishing superordinate and subordinate classes; perhaps we relate what we are experiencing to past experiences in a one-to-one mapping. These structures are not innate; they are constructed by the child out of his interactions with objects or events. Observe the behavior of the preoperational child—whose structure for dealing with classification is not complete. When we ask him to sort objects varying in size, shape, and color into three different piles, he is very reluctant to put red circles and red squares in the same pile and equally reluctant to put green circles and red circles in the same pile. That an object can belong to the class of circles and also to the class of redness is a notion of multiple classification that does not exist, nor does the notion of subordinate and superordinate classes. It is only as the child constructs a classificatory structure out of many actions of combining subclasses and taking classes apart that an elegant way of classifying emerges.

I propose that the cognitive task of the preschool should be to aid in the construction of classificatory structures as well as to facilitate the construction of number and ordering structures identified by Piaget that develop along with classification during this period. A preschool academic program will not do this; conventional reading-rediness activities do little to promote intellectual growth. Furthermore, in a completely unstructured preschool, some children may make marvelous discoveries; however, not all do, and not all do in every domain. We overestimated the child's ability to discover in the days of progressive education, and one hopes that we do not make the same mistake in the name of open education. There are college students who have difficulty in preparing outlines of papers because they do not subordinate some ideas to others or who have other difficulties with hierarchical classification. And there are others who have difficulty with spatial relationships. Man's greatest evolutionary achievement is logical intelligence, and it is found in man in all cultures; individuals, however, have vulnerable areas.

Logic Is Logic: The Structuralist View

Piaget's (1970) position, that mental structures are the same for all men, is supported by cross-cultural data. As human beings, we all have the same biological structures and functions. These interact with the common features of the natural world, leading to the development of the same mental structures and functions. Logical thought is universal.

The French anthropologist Lévi-Strauss pioneered in analyzing social structures to examine the workings of the mind. From his analysis of thought in primitive cultures, Lévi-Strauss (1963) concluded that "the kind of logic in mythical thought is as rigorous as that of modern science . . . the difference lies not in the quality of the intellectual process, but in the nature of the things to which it is applied . . . in the discovery of new areas to which it may apply its unchanged and unchanging powers" (p. 28). He maintained that logic is logic whether it is professed by Australian aborigines or a theoretical physicist. The mind imposes forms upon content, and one can find examples of forms common to all societies.

Lévi-Strauss (1966) discounted the notion of a "savage mind" in a "creature barely emerged from an animal condition" (p. 42) and incapable of logical thought. He examined classifications in primitive societies and found in them an inherent logic. The Aymara Indians in Bolivia, for example, developed a taxonomy of the genus *Solanum* that included over 250 varieties (the eggplant and the potato are examples), divided and subdivided into an elaborate binominal taxonomy, a high-order achievement of logical thought. Similarly, structural analysis of kinship systems reveals evidence of logical structures. In totemic societies, for example, clans are divided on the basis of relationship to some object or animal (a totem) not only in a methodological way but also according to a classification scheme based upon carefully built theoretical knowledge of the plant or animal. These groupings are instances of algebraic structures. "The savage mind," Lévi-Strauss (1966) concluded, "is logical in the same sense and the same fashion as ours" (p. 268).

Still another structuralist, Chomsky (1968), applied the structuralist point of view to language, claiming that the human mind is programmed at birth with a mental representation of a universal grammar that makes possible the learning of a natural language. Chomsky believes that there is some innate equipment for processing certain kinds of phenomenal entities, which accounts for the common structure underlying language learning.

Piaget, too, has been concerned with mental structures and is sympathetic to the work of both Chomsky and Lévi-Strauss. However, he parts company with Chomsky on the issues of innate syntatic laws, preferring instead, like Lévi-Strauss, to explain stability in structures across cultures in terms of equilibrium mechanisms. For Piaget (1971, p. 114), mind, at any point in life, is the unfinished product of continual self-construction. Structures are not preformed but are self-regulatory transformational systems, with the functional factors in that construction being assimilation and accommodation.

For Piaget, any critical account of structuralism must begin with a consideration of mathematical structures. The first known structure to be identified and studied is the mathematical "group," a system consisting of a set of elements and having certain properties. These properties are not derived from properties of things but from ways of acting upon things, for example, reversing them or combining them. The properties (Piaget, 1970, p. 18) are such that:

1. When performed upon elements of the set, the combinatory operation yields only elements of the set.
2. The set contains a neuter or identity element that, when it is combined with any other element of the set, is unaffected.
3. Each element of the set has an inverse that, when combined with the former, yields the neuter or identity element.
4. The combinatory operation (and its inverse) is associative ($[n + m] + 1 = n + [m + 1]$).

A discovery of Piaget's that has had a profound effect upon his thinking is that there is a resemblance between the structures of thought and mathematical structures, with the mathematical group being a prototype of logical structures; that is, thought, when it is logical, has the same properties as mathematical group structure, both being governed by an internal logic. We can carry on thought displacements upon data; we can reverse an operation (go back to the starting point) with a realization that the starting point will be unchanged. We can be certain that the end result in thought is independent of the route taken; we can figuratively put 2 and 2 together in different ways and still get 4. We can compare sets of data, knowing that if for every element in one set there is a corresponding element in the other, the sets must be equal. These displacements are derived from group properties.

One can identify structure in children's responses to Genevan tasks most readily in those involving physical causality. Here it is the structure of knowledge that the child reveals, as well as the structure for comparing events. Over and over again, for example, the child offers explanations of a phenomenon that show his growth, and confusion, in the area of gravity. Given a task in which he must assess the height of two towers, one constructed on a lower base, the child often places a stick across the top of both and says, "They're the same because the stick doesn't go down." The child never lacks for an explanation; he has notions and schemes, which he uses to explain many different phenomena. The way in which he applies his structure of knowledge to compare events depends upon his developmental state of mental structures for processing data. Most preschool children have not yet developed the mathematical group structure; their thought is preoperational. The teacher can play a role in helping them build the group structure Piaget has identified.

Logical Development in Cross-Cultural Studies

The brief review of the structuralist position presented here may help to dispel the naïve viewpoint of "the savage mind" and the young disadvantaged as children who "do not just think at an immature level; many of them do not think at all" (Bereiter & Engelmann, 1966). All children think and all attain logical thought, but the timing may be different, and the logic may be applied to different problems in different cultural environments.

We turn next to a consideration of the impact of environment upon logical development.

The Genevan tasks, adapted for particular cultures, have been useful in revealing differences between nonindustrialized and industrialized societies. Investigators have compared the development of thinking processes among the Uganda (Almy, 1967), the Zulu (Cowley & Murray, 1962), Australian aborigines (DeLemos, 1967), and the Papual (Prince, 1968). The reasons children gave for their responses had a universal quality; "you didn't add anything and you didn't take anything away" was a way of reasoning expressed in many languages. However, children growing up in an aboriginal environment achieved conservation on the Genevan tasks at a later age than did European children in the same country.

There is the very real possibility that certain terms that express equivalence in administration of conservation tasks may have different meanings in different cultures. However, as Maccoby and Modiano (1966) pointed out, differences in cognitive demands between industrialized and primitive societies, between urban and rural environments, may very well be the source of differences in cognitive strengths. For example, it may be that urban man must make "more abstract formulations as to how things are, how they are alike and how they are different" (p. 268).

Is schooling a factor? Goodnow's (Goodnow & Bethon, 1966) research is relevant here. She tested European and Chinese boys in Hong Kong, between 10 and 13 years of age, on Genevan tasks of combinatorial reasoning and conservation of space (area), weight, and volume. She reported that similarities across milieus were more striking than differences, with both European and Chinese children in Hong Kong performing much as children performed in Geneva, although space and volume tasks were more difficult for the Hong Kong sample. An examination of the data, however, reveals that one of her groups, consisting of Chinese boys with less than a year of schooling, did the poorest on the tasks. Only 60% of the boys who were between 10 and 13 years of age had attained conservation of area, whereas 70% of the Genevan children passed this task successfully at 7–8 years.

Additional light on the effects of environment comes from studies showing that effects of schooling can differ for different tasks. Price-Williams's (1961) study on the Nigerian and Vernon's (1966) on the Canadian-Indian and Eskimo both show that while performance of their sample was roughly comparable to that of the Genevan children, some tasks were more vulnerable to lack of schooling than others.

The work of Siegel and Mermelstein (1965) and Mermelstein and Shulman (1967) is relevant to the question of environmental setting and development. They found that children denied schooling in Prince Edward County, Virginia did as well as disadvantaged children in Flint, Michigan on conservation tasks, with neither group performing as well as the Genevan group. Girls, however, did somewhat better than boys on a conservation-of-quantity task, perhaps, the authors speculated, because of participation in certain household tasks. Wei's (1967) study of classifactory behavior of preschool white children from educationally advantaged and disadvantaged families indicated that vulnerability in some areas may begin before school; she found significant differences favoring the advantaged between the two groups.

My own work on logical development among the Houk-Lo, the boat people living in Aberdeen Harbor in Hong Kong, reveals that it is not low socioeconomic status (SES) *per se* that sets the pace of logical growth, but rather the opportunities provided in natural settings for interactions contributing to logico-mathematical development. The Houk-Lo families are among the poorest of the Hong Kong poor, and since the British Crown Colony provides no free compulsory education, the children grow up with only minimal schooling, if any, in the overcrowded settlement-house classes. These children leave the sampans each day, some to find work on the streets, others up to 7 years of age to play on shore, where I observed them. I was struck with their vitality and industry. Hong Kong is a city that teems with life, and there is a hustle and bustle on the streets, a vitality that is reflected in the vim and vigor with which the children throw themselves into their games. I was also struck with the children's inventiveness at games and with the fact that the games provided a natural setting for the acquisition of certain logical concepts.

There were four separate play areas along the shore, each featuring a particular game or set of games. The children divided themselves among each of the play areas, moving from one area to another as they tired of one kind of activity. The number of children in the total play area averaged 60 per day. A random sample of 12 of the children was selected for scheduled observation. Two games, described below, were selected for special observation because of their inherent logic. Of the 1 hour of observed play each morning, 6 of the 12 children tended to stay with one of these games for at least half of each session and spent the rest of the time as active observers of the other games. There were 4 who divided their time almost equally between the two games and 2 who were "flitters," going from game to game and back again. During the 1 week of observation, the actual time spent on one of the two games being observed varied from 100 minutes (1 child only) to 40 minutes (2 children).

The two games selected were, as stated previously, chosen for their potential contribution to development of logical thinking. They were:

1. *Playing cards.* This game was played with paper cards picturing characters from Chinese history. Two children played at one time. A card was held in the palm of one hand. The children dropped the cards simultaneously. Each pictured character had a certain value attached to it (as in our system, in which a queen is worth 2 points, a king 3 points, and so on). The child whose character had a lower value had to give to his opponent enough cards to make up the difference. Thus the game involved attaching a value to a particular card, recognizing the difference in value between it and other cards, and counting out the proper number of cards to make up the difference. The game was therefore excellent preparation for conservation of number, where conservation is achieved by compensation.

2. *Bottle caps.* For this game, a 2 X 2 matrix was drawn in the dirt:

1	3
4	2

Each child had a supply of bottle caps to begin with, and each stood at the same distance from the diagram to pitch a bottle cap at one of the numbers. The child who landed his cap in the highest number was rewarded by being paid in bottle caps the difference between his score and that of each of the other players. Like playing cards, this game, too. contributed to conservation of number.

The "natural" curriculum, then, the one devised by the children themselves, provided opportunity for acquiring conservation structures. The natural setting in which the children lived provided opportunity for acquiring certain spatial concepts. The sampans where the children lived were lined up, three or four deep, several hundreds of them along the shore. All looked more or less alike in size, shape, and state of deterioration. To find one's own sampan required certain spatial skills, such as attending to cues denoting position (in front of, in back of, on the other side of) and using a frame of reference with points away from the boat (toward the far end of the shore line, toward the middle of the shore line, toward the street end of the shore line). The need for certain spatial skills might conceivably facilitate development of certain aspects of spatial relations in Houk-Lo children.

One would expect these children on the basis of their low SES to score low on Piagetian tasks in comparison with a Genevan sample. But it was hypothesized that when the "natural" curriculum and natural settings provide for the kind of interactions conducive to logical growth, the disadvantages of low SES were compensated for. I am suggesting that one must analyze the kind and quality of interactions in natural settings for their possible contribution to logical development and not assume an inevitable connection between SES and development of intelligence.

To assess the children's progress in logical thinking, I administered three of the Genevan tasks, with some changes to allow for cultural differences: conservation of number, conservation of quantity, and rotation of an object in space.

A complete account of procedures and findings is presented in a paper, "The Acquisition of Conservation in a Natural Setting: A Study of Houk-Lo children in Hong Kong" (Lavatelli, Hotvedt, & Lee, 1976). Here I want to report only a brief summary of results.

Task 1, Conservation of Number

Of the children tested, 81% gave a conservation response, with 71% being able to justify conservation with evidence of reversibility. The mean age of these children was 7.07 years. For this same task, 70% of Genevan children passed at 7 years.

Task 2, Conservation of Quantity

Conservation was achieved by 66% after the first transformation (rice poured from a larger bowl into two smaller ones), while 58% maintained conservation after the second transformation (rice poured from a larger bowl into seven smaller ones). Full conservation with evidence of reversibility was achieved by 38%. Again on this task, the Houk-Lo children compared favorably with Genevan children. While 38% of Houk-Lo subjects achieved full conservation at 7.02 years, 32% of Genevan children reached this stage at 7 years.

Task 3, Rotation of an Object in Space

Of the Houk-Lo children, 62% solved the simplest of reversals on a task involving rotation of an object in space by 180° at 7 years of age, and 10% solved a double reversal. The task involved two identical boats with the same easily identifiable parts on each (mast and difference in levels, for example). A man was placed in the middle of one of the boats while the two boats were lying side by side facing in the same direction. Then one of the boats was rotated 180°, and the child was asked to place a second man in the same place on the second boat as the first man in the first boat. The next step was more complicated, since the man was at the edge of the boat and so a double reversal was necessary. Again the Houk-Los' performance was in line with that of more advantaged subjects, although subtle differences in procedure made precise comparison difficult.

While the study is not definitive, findings certainly lend support to the proposal of several investigators that social settings be examined for interactional opportunities contributing to logicomathematical development. Play experiences of varying cultural groups might be analyzed for the extent to which participant action contributes to construction of number, classification, ordering, and spatial structures.

Experience and Equilibration

A word here about experience and success on Piagetian tasks. Piaget has discussed experience as a possible contributing factor but has discounted its effectiveness as the unique factor. Certainly, merely being exposed to a particular experience is not necessarily conducive to cognition. Some children make brilliant discoveries in the course of play; others do not. Watching a laboratory experiment or even conducting one may or may not help a child to acquire a particular concept. The key factor for Piaget is *equilibration*. The child assimilates data from an interaction into existing mental structures that may produce disequilibrium. The mind goes to work to restore equilibrium, as structures change to accommodate to the new. The process is one of autoregulation: the child regulates input and regulates the transformation of data. Accommodation as well as assimilation may result in disequilibrium when there is disparity between notions. In either case, the child must convince himself of what he will accept and then modify the existing framework of thought in order to incorporate the new data.

Natural settings provide learning situations in which the child is highly motivated. He may want to be competent because of some inner need for competence, as White (1959) has suggested. Or the social setting may provide a stimulus to do well in the eyes of one's peers or perhaps to strive for success because everyone else is striving. Or a competitive spirit may urge the child to better his peers. Child development specialists and educators prefer that a child be motivated by a drive for competence rather than a drive to "better one's peers."

The process of equilibration may be facilitated in the social setting. Watching what one's peer does can contribute to assimilation. The child can, of course, copy without assimilating. A child may sometimes say in the course of clinical interviews, "I'll say they're the same because he said it, and he's smarter than I am, but I don't really believe it." The child is telling us that seeing is not necessarily believing. But seeing what another is doing may click with the child whose cognitive growth is far enough along not only to assimilate but to accommodate to what he sees.

What is done with the data depends upon the mental structures the child has available for processing data. We turn next to how teachers can facilitate their development.

Implications for Early Childhood Education

Piaget has described important developments in cognitive growth that occur during the period of early childhood. At that time, sensorimotor schemata are elaborated into conceptual structures. Setting up correspondences becomes quite systematic; subordination schemes develop.

At the present time, preschool teachers are trying to influence developments in classification, number, and ordering, but all too often, they do not understand that there is a *structure* to classification, to number, and to ordering. Because they are not aware of structure, they provide learning activities of the *Sesame Street* genre; children learn to count by rote, to identify letters of the alphabet by name, and to separate objects according to color, size, or shape when directed to do so. In all such activities, the teacher has imposed a structure upon the data; the teacher has done the thinking, while the children simply carry out directions for tasks that they can solve perceptually. There is no great intellectual challenge to the child in putting all red objects in one pile and all yellow objects in another when told to do so. Under such a system, the script writer or the teacher becomes smarter, but not the child.

How can the teacher provide learning opportunities for children to build logical structures during the preschool years? The first prerequisite is for the teacher to understand the properties of logical classification, number, and ordering and to understand the teaching role in the educational process. I am going to describe what it means, in terms of structure, to classify logically and suggest activities in which children may engage, working in small groups with the teacher for short periods at a time. The activities are adapted from Genevan tasks and from science and mathematics learning experiences in American and British experimental programs. There is a sequential order in which the characteristics of classificatory behavior emerges; this order has been described by Inhelder and Piaget (1964) as a result of investigations with more than 2,000 children in Geneva. With minor variations, the order has been confirmed by Kofsky (1966), who found six different levels of difficulty in her tests of classificatory logic, with success on the tasks at each step differing significantly from tasks at the preceding level. Teachers can observe where children are on the developmental ladder by examining the structure of the class the child forms when asked to group objects together. The structure he imposes upon objects is a reflection of the mental structure he has already constructed.

The Characteristics of Logical Classification

Those characteristics of particular concern to the development of young children are:

1. There are no isolated elements, that is, elements not belonging to a class. If an element is the only one of its kind, then it gives rise to its own specific class.
2. For every specific class, there is a complementary class characterized by the property of not having the property of the specific class. The class of oranges, for example, might be said to consist of oranges and all the fruit-not-oranges.
3. For a class of wire-haired dogs, we have the class of dogs-not-wire-haired.
4. A specific class includes *all* the members having the property common to that class.
5. A specific class includes *only* members having the property common to that class.
6. The class of things that belong both to As and *not* As is the empty set. Or there is no such thing as a dog belonging to neither the class of wire-haired or the class of dogs-not-wire-haired.
7. A complementary class has its own characteristics.
8. A particular class is included in every higher-ranking class that contains all its elements: "all" A or "some" B.

With these characteristics of classification in mind, it is possible to construct a model of a training program to foster development of logical classification. First, the characteristics listed above have to be translated into separate operations, and then the operations must be arranged in order of difficulty to match as nearly as possible a developmental sequence.

For children to be able to carry on classification activities according to the logic of the characteristics mentioned, they must be capable of certain mental operations. They have to be able to take in information from an object or experience in the environment and transform that information, *do* something to it, as follows:

1. Identify properties of objects (size, color, shape, etc.), and match objects with more than one property.
2. Keep in mind two or more properties of objects at the same time while searching for any object to complete a set.
3. Combine objects to make up subclasses, combine subclasses to make supraclasses, and recognize the existence of complementary classes.
4. Change from one criterion for grouping to another.
5. Take a whole class apart to find subclasses and make comparisons of "all" and "some."
6. Discover intension and extension of a class.
7. Visualize an object as having simultaneous membership in two classes.
8. Put together elements from several groups so that none is repeated.
9. Make all possible combinations of elements.

Some classification activities designed to facilitate development of logical classification are described below.

Identifying properties of objects and matching objects by more than one property. The goals for this set of activities include not only identifying properties of objects but also matching objects by more than one property. The equipment used is a specially selected set of kindergarten beads in two sizes, two shapes, and three colors. The teacher makes a model string and the children copy the string. Activities are sequenced, beginning with the very simple one in which the child copies a model necklace made up of all the red beads on a shoelace. He does the other colors in turn and, in subsequent lessons, shapes and sizes. Next, there are additional models that the teacher makes, models that begin with a simple alternation of red bead with yellow bead and end with a complex pattern demanding that the child attend to the number, size, shape, and color of the beads all at the same time.

The overall objective of having children identify properties of objects and match objects by more than one property is to enable children to find the common property of a class and to extend that class to include all objects possessing that property. Thus, the teacher may vary directions on subsequent days to say, "Find all the beads that are alike in some way and string them" and "Tell me how they're alike."

Accompanying the actions are verbal activities, with the teacher presenting models of certain grammatical structures. As with the actions the child carries out, grammatical structures modeled for him are sequenced, beginning with simple declarative sentences and progressing to transformations upon those sentences that include coordinate sentences with directions for more than one action. In each case after the teacher gives the directions and the child begins the action, the teacher says, "Tell me what you're doing. Why did you choose that one?" This exercise forces the child to attend to not one but several properties of an object at the same time and to describe the object using noun phrases: "It's a round bead" or "It's a small yellow bead." If the child cannot put words together to frame a response properly, the teacher models the correct response and again asks the question. The child may not repeat the response letter perfect; research on imitation (Slobin, 1971) shows that children repeat correctly only those grammatical structures that they already have in their repertoire, but word-for-word repetition is not necessary.

There are follow-up activities to be carried out in connection with each set of materials that are designed to reinforce and extend what has been taught. For example, in one activity, two children may be hidden from each other's view by a screen. The child puts a bead on his string and says to the other, "I'm putting a round yellow bead" (note use of noun phrase, with adjectives to describe two properties). The other child then puts a round yellow bead on his string, plus another that he describes to his unseen companion, and the game continues for a specified number of beads, at the end of which time the children can physically compare their strings. A number of investigators have commented on the need to have children use the language of referents—to talk about events and objects not visible or not in the immediate present. The follow-up activity just described provides training in this very important skill.

Keeping in mind two or more properties of objects in searching for an object to complete a set. This activity in the Piagetian program requires that the child put to use the skill developed in the beads activity; he must keep two or more properties of objects in mind as he searches for an object to complete a set. The vehicle of instruction is the matrix puzzle. A matrix is an ordered series of elements designed in such a manner that the elements in one pair are related to the elements in another in the same way. Readers are familiar with matrices in intelligence test items: "Black is to white as night is to ____." The subject must supply the necessary word. The puzzles in this program are picture puzzles. The first puzzle in the series makes use of the training in recognizing properties of size, shape, and color provided in the beads activity. The picture shows one large red flower and one small yellow flower in the top horizontal row; beneath are one large red apple and a blank space for which the child must select the appropriate card from a number of choices of flowers and apples. The puzzles become more difficult, demanding attention to three variables at the same time. At first, an adult is likely to think that the puzzle is too difficult for the preschool child, that he will not be able to follow the verbal directions. This, however, is not the case. The young child can solve the puzzle without much difficulty; however, he solves it at a perceptual level rather than a conceptual one. Inhelder and Piaget (1964) have described how the child uses symmetry to do this. Instead of thinking of how each of the first pictured pair of objects is related and finding a picture that will establish the same relationship in another pair, he simply thinks, "I've got a red one here, and this one's yellow, so the answer card must be yellow. And there's one here and one here and one here, so it's got to be one here." By a simple matching of elements that stand out perceptually, he can solve a puzzle.

How can one find out at what level the child is operating? Ask him. This is what Inhelder and Piaget did and what the Piagetian program described here urges teachers to do. Furthermore, the teacher who says, "Tell me about it. Why did you choose that card?" is developing both language and logic. With many children, such a question is often greeted with a look of surprise, as if this were the first time the child had been asked to explain his action to another person. Regardless of the answer, the teacher then selects another answer card, puts it in place of the child's choice, and asks, "Would this one do just as well?" "In what way?" or "Why?" We have found in our experimental work that time and time again a child who has chosen the correct card without hesitation will abandon his choice, also without hesitation, and justify the incorrect response by finding a different symmetry. If he cannot think in terms of two variables at once, he will agree to any card containing one of the properties in question.

Complementary classes. The next set of activities in the series is designed to provide training in the ability to recognize complementary classes. Given pictures of dogs of which two are collies, can the children separate the set into collies and dogs-not-collies? The object is to make two classes of dogs, no more. The young child may make collections of as many classes as there are kinds of dogs, but this is not the task. In fact, teachers who are new to teaching classification skills often characterize such behavior as "creative"; they remark proudly on the number of classes the child can make. Actually, such behavior is more characteristic of the younger child; it is not at all difficult to match dog for dog on a perceptual basis. A much more creative task is demanded of the child in dealing with complementary classes.

The actual materials used in our Piagetian program were an assortment of miniature vehicles, consisting of trucks, airplanes, and a car, to make up the class of trucks and the complementary class to things not-trucks. Since the vehicles were in three colors, it was possible also to form a class of red objects and a complementary class of objects-not-red or, more simply, other objects. As Inhelder and Piaget (1964) have explained, the relationship here is important in helping children to understand what is included in a class: when we talk about collies or airplanes, there is understood a complementary class of dogs-not-collies or vehicles-not-planes, and both the specified class and its complement make up the total class. Often adults disregard the complementary class in discussing a specified class and, as a result, make illogical remarks.

Taking the whole class apart to find subclasses and to make comparisons of "all" and "some." The reader must bear in mind that one of the characteristics of the preoperational child is that of making judgments on the basis of perception. Shown 20 wooden beads of which 18 are yellow and 2 are red, and asked if there are more wooden beads or more yellow ones, the child may be overwhelmed by the visual display of so many yellow beads. Because he is not yet making transformations upon data, because he cannot reverse a process, he fails to go back in his mind to the whole class of wooden beads and to compare the whole class with subclass, or all with some. His answer, therefore, is that there are more yellow beads because there are only two red beads.

How can we induce development of the classification structures essential to solving such tasks? The way suggested in this program is to have children carry out many activities in which they combine subclasses to make a class and break a class down into its subclasses. They can combine yellow roses and red roses to make bunches of roses and combine roses and daisies to make bunches of flowers. They answer questions about the classes that they make: Are all of the roses yellow? Are all of the yellow flowers roses? Are there more daisies or more white daisies? Are there more roses or more flowers? Suppose all the flowers died, would there be any roses left? Such questions force the child to think about groupings that he is composing, to make comparisons between classes, and to break classes down into subgroups. As the child forms various subclasses and classes, the teacher asks him to explain what he is doing and to justify his actions, with the teacher supplying language models when they are needed.

Abstracting the common property of a class and extending the class to include all objects possessing that property. The set of activities that develop the skills of "intension" (abstracting the common property) and extension involves hindsight and foresight, memory and prediction. Given a collection of miniature objects—tools, eating utensils, animals—and three boxes in which to place objects alike in some way, and required furthermore to use all the objects, the child must both abstract the common property and then, remembering that property, discover it in each object that he puts into a particular class. He must be able to look back at what he started with and look ahead at the same time.

Such behavior is very different from that of the younger child (3–4 years old). As Inhelder and Piaget (1964) pointed out, children at an earlier stage do not arrange elements in collections and subcollections on the basis of similarity alone. They are unable to overlook the spatial configuration of the objects, and what they do is unite them in "graphic" collections.

Making such graphic collections may take the form of laying objects in line, or making a geometrical figure or pattern out of them, or making a pretend picture out of them. Thus, given a set of circles, squares, and triangles, the child may place a triangle on top of a square to make a house with a roof top, because "they go together to make a house," instead of abstracting the common property of squareness or triangularity or roundness out of the figures.

At the next stage in classification, the child is capable of spontaneous anticipation, even if it is imperfect. He may be unable to foresee the details of a classification, but he is no longer operating on the basis of perception. One object may strike his fancy in a particular way, and he will choose the next object to go with it on the basis of a common property, although he will not be able to maintain the system for all objects. Gradually, as children have more and more experience in classifying objects, the operations of hindsight and foresight appear.

In addition to the special activities conducted in the structured periods, there are many opportunities during the preschool day for the teacher to stimulate actions upon classes as well as relations between classes. In the housekeeping corner, the teacher may begin by naming the common property: "Put all the things-to-eat-with, or eating utensils, on this shelf." Later, however, the teacher may say, "Let's put all the play clothes in separate boxes. Here are three boxes. Put the clothes that are like each other, that go together in some way, in each box." Note that there may be several schemes for classifying the clothes—by color, by category, by material—provided the child adheres to the rule of classifying all the clothes. In fact, the teacher may call attention to the various classification schemes developed by different children and encourage flexibility in changing from one criterion to another.

Finding an object to fit the intersection of two classes. Finding an object to fit the intersection of two classes is a skill that depends upon a skill developed earlier in the classification sequence, namely, abstracting the common property in a group of objects. The task used in Geneva involves pictures of a red leaf, a brown leaf, a green leaf, a purple leaf, and a yellow leaf, all lined up in a horizontal row. In the vertical row are pictures of a green hat, a green jacket, a green dress, a green book, and a green umbrella. The child is asked to choose from a group of pictures the one to put in a blank space where horizontal and vertical rows meet, a picture that will "go" with both sets of objects. The groups of pictures from which the child must choose includes pictures of all the objects listed above. To solve the puzzle, the child must abstract the common property from the objects in both the vertical and the horizontal rows, keep each property in mind, and find the picture of an object that contains both properties simultaneously. Since the common property of the vertical row is green-ness, he must search for a green leaf to put in the intersection of the two classes. The activity demands abstracting ability, memory, and the concept of simultaneous membership in two or more classes. Earlier training experiences in this program have attempted to build these. Here there is the opportunity to apply all three mental processes to the problem of finding an object to satisfy several conditions simultaneously.

The next activity is also designed for training in finding an object to fit the intersections of two classes. The equipment needed for each child consists of two nylon rope rings and colored geometric shapes. The first step in the activity requires that each child arrange the rings so that a green square is in neither ring, and then inside one ring, and finally inside both rings. The first two directions are carried out without difficulty; even the third, inside both rings, is carried out with considerable success. Children quickly catch on to the fact that they can put the figure inside both rings by putting one ring on top of the other. Then the teacher asks, "Can you find another way to put the figure inside both rings?" Gradually, children come to see that they can slide one of the rings to one side, more and more, until there is barely room enough in the intersection for the figure. Then more figures are introduced until, finally, there are several miscellaneous red figures in one circle and several squares of various colors in the other, and the problem is to determine which of the remaining shapes will fit in the intersection. The activity can be carried out with a variety of materials, including those used in other activities in the program. An outcome of the activity is the child's awareness that whatever he puts in the intersection must satisfy the conditions of both sets of objects and his awareness that the object in the intersection belongs to both sets, regardless of how small the intersection is.

Making all possible combinations of elements. The two final sets in the classification series involve combinatorial and permutation problems: "Given a certain number of elements, how many combinations can you make?" The high school student meets such problems in algebra when he is asked to find all possible arrangements of three elements, *a b c.* He can make *abc, acb, bac, bca, cab,* and *cba,* for a total of six different combinations. If he has an unlimited supply of each element—that is, a quantity of *a*s, *b*s, and *c*s—and is asked to make combinations of two elements, he can, of course, make nine. It comes as a surprise to many high school students that the number of arrangements is limited and that it is possible to predict in advance what the number of arrangements will be. Arranging and rearranging elements abstractly are mental transformations that are possible because of the concrete operations the child has carried on at an earlier stage. A little girl who has two different skirts and two different sweaters may discover that she can make a total of four outfits, while a little boy who has one engine and three different kinds of freight cars, with several of each kind, may discover that he can make nine different arrangements of trains of two cars each.

Note that the child *may* make such discoveries in the course of daily living, but as we pointed out earlier, children vary considerably in their level of logical development. What the child gets out of a particular experience depends in part upon what he brings to it. However, it also depends upon the teacher's role of problem maker, upon the teacher's ability to raise pertinent questions that will lead to fresh insights on the child's part.

The complete preschool program (Lavatelli, 1970) includes activities in number and ordering, as well as in classification. The activities are based upon the number and ordering structures as described by Piaget and Inhelder (Piaget, 1952; Inhelder & Piaget, 1964). All of the activities in the program, in all three domains, have basically the same ultimate goal: to facilitate development of those properties of logical thought that correspond to the properties of the mathematical group.

The teaching method, a modification of the clinical method, is also the same for each activity. For a short period each day, each child works with his own set of concrete materials in a small group. After exploratory play, the teacher suggests a transformation of the materials and poses a problem about the before-and-after that the child is to solve with the materials. The teacher asks of an individual child. "Tell me what you're doing," or after response to a question of fact, "Why do you think so?" The teacher sometimes proffers a counter-suggestion, "The other day a boy told me . . . ," and describes either a correct or an incorrect solution. At this point, a child in the transition stage may give up his correct, albeit tentative, solution when an incorrect response is suggested, or he may assimilate enough from the mythical child's reasoning to withstand the countersuggestion. The help the teacher offers is to call attention through questions to certain elements the child may not have noticed or to suggest a gradual transformation of the stimulus display. For example, to help the child deal with conservation of number, the teacher may suggest a very gradual bunching together of one set of elements, so that the child can build a mental representation of the process. The teacher does *not* tell the children they are "wrong" or give them the "right" solution. As Piaget (1970) has suggested, "each time one prematurely teaches a child something he could have discovered for himself, that child is kept from inventing it and consequently from understanding it completely" (p. 715). In fact, the teacher should not regard developmentally immature responses such as the graphic collections of the 3-year-old as *wrong* any more than crawling or painting with one color is wrong.

Specific teaching techniques suggested within the program are derived from research on the factors contributing to the transition from preoperational to concrete operational thought. Techniques include addition–subtraction (Wohlwill & Lowe, 1962), perceptual conflict (Smith, 1968), reversibility procedures (Wallach, Wall, & Anderson, 1967), and verbal-rule instruction (Beilin, 1965). In general, the maxim of the Geneva school is observed: training is effective only within the limits imposed by the equilibration model.

Research has made it abundantly clear that short-term restricted types of training are ultimately ineffective in inducing logical thought structures. These structures are pervasive and powerful; they take time to develop and require the background of a broad spectrum of experiences before they can be generalized and applied universally. In addition to short instructional periods that serve the purpose of bringing into focus certain elements of structure, the teacher must be on the alert during periods of self-directed play for opportunities to strengthen training begun during the instructional period. Only in this way will transfer of training be facilitated.

The question arises: If logical operations appear anyway, why not sit back and wait for time to make the child logical? Piaget is very clear on this point; the child does not become logical by virtue of maturation alone. Intelligence grows through successive assimilations and accommodations; a training program can provide opportunities for these to occur. As Piaget (1970, p. 715) suggested, the teacher can devise experimental situations to facilitate the pupil's invention of knowledge. Also individuals and even ethnic groups, as we have seen, may vary in cognitive strengths and weaknesses; there are some who are strong in domains such as classification and weak in spatial concepts, and vice versa. A training program can provide the foundations that help to prevent development of spatial idiots, or any other kind.

The question also arises: Why carry on training in *groups?* Why not have the teacher intervene when the opportunity occurs and on an individual basis? The group training is less haphazard and also provides a social situation that facilitates development. Children look at one another's work and listen to one another's responses. As we have pointed out, no child is convinced by what another says or does; each must convince himself. But as Piaget (1970) has stated, "One of the fundamental processes of cognition is that of decentration relative to subjective illusion, and this process has dimensions that are social or interpersonal as well as rational" (p. 729). In a group setting organized along nonauthoritarian lines, the child comes to realize that there are points of view other than his own. His egocentricism is challenged and he moves toward an equilibrium between assimilation and accommodation.

Environment and experience influence cognitive growth, but equilibration is the key to the process. The teacher plays a critical role. Piaget has pointed out that listening to children's responses to the Genevan tasks helps the teacher become more aware of thinking processes. With increasing sophistication in the area of structure, the teacher will be better prepared to ask the adroit question or suggest a new line of inquiry to individual children during their periods of self-chosen, self-directed activity. No daily 10-minute period of mental gymnastics is going to work miracles in building mental structures, but the teacher must be aware of the structures. Only then can the teacher set up a learning environment conducive to autoregulation that will facilitate equilibration.

References

Almy, M. The usefulness of Piagetian methods for early primary education in Uganda: An exploratory study. In *Child growth and development projects.* Makerere University College National Institute of Education (mimeo), 1967.

Beilin, H. Learning and operational convergence in logical thought development. *Journal of Experimental Child Psychology,* 1965, *2,* 317–339.

Bereiter, C., & Engelmann, S. *Teaching the disadvantaged child in the preschool.* Englewood Cliffs, N.J.: Prentice-Hall, 1966.

Chomsky, N. Language and the mind. *Psychology Today,* February 1968, *1,* 48–51; 66–68.

Cowley, J. J., & Murray, M. Some aspects of the development of spatial concepts in Zulu children. *Journal for Social Research,* 1962, *13,* 1–18.

DeLemos, M. M. *Conceptual development in aboriginal children: Implications for aboriginal education.* Research Seminar on Education for Aborigines, Center for Research into Aborginal Affairs, Monash University, Melbourne (mimeo), 1967.

Goodnow, J., & Bethon, G. Piaget's tasks: The effects of schooling and intelligence. *Child Development*, 1966, *37*, 574–582.

Inhelder, B., & Piaget, J. [*Early growth of logic in the child*] (E. A. Lunzer & D. Papert, trans.). New York: Harper & Row, 1964.

Kofsky, E. A scalogram study of classification development. *Child Development*, 1966, *37*, 191–204.

Lavatelli, C. S. Early childhood curriculum. *American Science and Engineering.* Newton, Mass., 1970.

Lavatelli, C., Hotvedt, & Lee, E. The acquisition of conservation in a natural setting. A study of Houk-Lo children in Hong Kong. (In process).

Lévi-Strauss, C. *Structural anthropology.* New York: Basic Books, 1963.

Lévi-Strauss, C. *The savage mind.* Chicago: The University of Chicago Press, 1966.

Maccoby, M., & Modiano, N. On culture and equivalence: I. In J. S. Bruner, R. R. Olver, P. M. Greenfield, (Eds.), *Studies in cognitive growth.* New York: Wiley, 1970.

McCarthy, D. Language development in children. In L. Carmichael (Ed.), *Manual of child psychology* (2nd ed.). New York: Wiley, 1954.

Mermelstein, E., & Shulman, L. S. Lack of formal schooling and the acquisition of conservation. *Child Development*, 1967, *38*, 39–52.

Piaget, J. [*The child's conception of number*] (C. Cattegno & F. M. Hodgson, trans.). London: Routledge and Kegan Paul, 1952. (Originally published, 1941.)

Piaget, J. Piaget's theory. In P. H. Mussen (Ed.), *Carmichael's manual of child psychology.* New York: Wiley, 1970.

Piaget, J. [*Structuralism*] (C. Mafchlere, trans.). New York: Harper & Row, 1971.

Price-Williams, D. R. A study concerning concepts of conservation of quantities among primitive children. *Acta Psychologica*, 1961, *18*, 297–305.

Prince, J. R. Science concepts in New Guinean and European children. *Australian Journal of Education*, 1968, *12*, 81–87.

Siegel, I. E., & Mermelstein, E. *Effects of nonschooling on Piagetian tasks of conservation.* Paper presented at American Psychological Association meeting, September 1965.

Silberman, C. E. *Crisis in the classroom.* New York: Random, 1970.

Slobin, D. I., & Welsh, C. A. Elicited imitation as a research tool in developmental psycholinguistics. In C. Lavatelli (Ed.), *Language training in early childhood education.* Urbana: University of Illinois, 1971.

Smith, I. C. The effects of training procedures upon the acquisition of conservation of weight. *Child Development*, 1968, *39*, 515–526.

Vernon, P. E. Educational and intellectual development among Canadian Indians and Eskimos. *Educational Review*, 1966, *18*, 79–91.

Wallach, L., Wall, A. J., & Anderson, L. Number conservation: The roles of reversibility, addition–subtraction, and misleading perceptual cues. *Child Development*, 1967, *38*, 425–442.

Wei, T. T. D. Piaget's concept of classification: A comparative study of advantaged and disadvantaged young children. (Doctoral dissertation, University of Illinois, Urbana, 1966). *Dissertation Abstracts*, 1967, *27*, 4143A (University Microfilms No. 67-6769).

White, R. W. Motivation reconsidered: The concept of competence. *Psychological Review*, 1959, *66*, 297–333.

Wohlwill, J. F., & Lowe, R. C. Experimental analysis of the conservation of number. *Child Development*, 1962, *33*, 153–167.

CHAPTER 10

Application of Piagetian Theory to Remediation of Reasoning

Beth Stephens

University of Texas, Richardson, Texas

A decade or more has elapsed since Piaget was "rediscovered," and during the intervening years there have been continued and varied attempts to incorporate his theory into classroom practices. Although Piaget has been a prolific author, he has not supplied a guide book on "How to Practice Piaget" and probably will not! Yet guidelines do evolve as one reviews his theoretical writings. Throughout his work there is a recurring theme: intellectual development proceeds as the child interacts with his environment—with the objects and people around him. He states that "a child knows an object only to the extent to which he has acted upon it." When urged to cite the educational approach that was most compatible with his theory, he stated that perhaps it was Dewey's learning by doing—an active student situation.

Another recurring theme is that understanding and/or successful reasoning occurs only if the child's mental structures are sufficiently advanced to meet the demands of the situation. A child, as Piaget has noted, may be impervious to a particular learning opportunity if it requires thought structures that he has not yet achieved.

Thus, there are three guidelines that can be deduced. First, provide a child with learning opportunities that are commensurate with his level of cognitive development. Commensurate activities may be defined as activities that are far enough in advance of a person's present level of functioning to be motivating but not so much in advance that they will be frustrating. Because tempos of development vary from person to person, individual appraisal of a person's current level of functioning is necessary to determine the individually appropriate level for reasoning activities. Second, after a student is provided cognitively appropriate activities, he then must do the interacting—you can't do it for him. Such an approach serves to challenge the traditional "passive pupil–active teacher" roles and suggests instead an action-oriented student who explores and manipulates, hypothesizes and experiments, as the teacher provides necessary structure. In addition, the teacher provides questions that challenge reason and thought, questions that motivate a person to explore and to thrust a bit further. Emphasis is on the process of learning rather than on the product of learning. Third, for a teacher to assume the role just described he or she must be trained in Piaget's theory of cognitive development; that is, the teacher must know how development proceeds and what characterizes a child's past, present, and succeeding levels of functioning. The teacher also must have knowledge of the reasoning assessments used by the Geneva group and be skilled in providing opportunities for the pupil to apply reasoning to ongoing problem situations. Some teachers have difficulty in the implementation of Piagetian theory because they don't clearly understand what constitutes reasoning as defined by the Geneva school.

Teachers of school-aged children will gain insight concerning these thought processes if they review the assessments for analyzing concrete and formal thought that were devised or adapted by the Geneva group. As a review is made of the numerous concrete-level measures, one realizes that several basic abilities are represented.

One concrete-level measure is conservation of substance, an assessment in which the child agrees that two identical balls of clay contain the same amount of clay and also agrees that there continues to be the same amount even when one ball is successively transformed into a "hot dog," a "pancake," or into a dozen small pieces. This involves understanding of the invariance of quantity, the realization that quantity is constant although the shape of an object may undergo changes. The task actually requires reversibility of thought processes. In order to realize that the ball and the hot dog contain the same amount of clay although the hog dog looks longer, the child must reverse his thought processes and think back in time to remember that before the clay was rolled into a hot dog it was a ball the same size as the other ball. The child must also realize that nothing was added and nothing was taken away, therefore (his thought moves from the past back into the present) they must still be the same. The numerous Piagetian conservation experiments all tap this reversibility of thought processes (Inhelder, 1968).

Assessments involving logical classification represent another area. Some experiments deal with elementary logic-classification. One example is class inclusion—animals (Piaget & Inhelder, 1964). The task requirements are to sort a set of 17 pictures into three related piles (ducks, birds, and animals). After the initial classification, the subject is questioned on class inclusion and possible class extensions (e.g., "Can you group the ducks with the birds and keep the label "birds" for that group?"). Another example is class inclusion–beads (Piaget & Inhelder, 1964). A box containing 10 wooden beads, 8 of which are red and 2 of which are yellow, is displayed, and the subject is required to judge whether there are more *wooden* beads or *red* beads in the box. Additional questions are derived from modifications of the basic experimental arrangement. A third example is that of intersection of classes (Piaget & Inhelder, 1959). Two rows of pictures are presented. One, a horizontal row, contains five pictures of the same object with each picture a different color; the other, a vertical row, contains five pictures of the same color but of different objects. Instructions are to pick a single picture from an assorted array and to place it at the intersection of the two rows, a picture that relates appropriately to both rows. The tasks previously described require flexibility of thought, the ability to group and regroup objects, to categorize and sub-categorize, and to classify and reclassify.

Memory and mental imagery are involved in two assessments that measure the ability to rotate a mental image of an object prior to its actual rotation. Assessments that involve this operativity and symbolic imagery include rotation of squares and rotation of beads. In the rotation of squares (Piaget & Inhelder, 1963), the subject is required to draw the anticipated rotations of two cardboard squares, one red and one blue, that are mounted on a board. In a second procedure, the subject is asked to select the one drawing that represents the way the red square will appear at a specific position as it is rotated clockwise. In the rotation of beads (Piaget, 1952), three differently colored beads mounted on a stiff wire are exhibited. Then the beads are placed in a tube and the tube is rotated. The task is to judge which of the three beads will emerge first from the tube.

An assessment that involves *mental imagery and spatial orientation* requires a person to consider how objects will appear from another person's perspective, a viewpoint or perspective different from the one he currently is experiencing. One example is changing perspectives–mobile and stationary (Piaget & Inhelder, 1964). A cardboard tower, house, and tree are placed in specified positions on a table. After moving to consecutive positions around the table, the subject is required to find a drawing that represents the complex when viewed from these perspectives. In a second task, the subject, while seated, is asked to indicate where a doll will have to stand in order to see the perspective corresponding to the drawing shown him.

Formal or abstract thought involves the ability to reason abstractly and/or to hypothesize ways in which an answer may be obtained. It also involves the ability to carry out actions that will check these hypotheses. Formal thought is required in the following assessment, which involves combinatory logic. In a task involving combination of liquids (Piaget & Inhelder, 1964), five identical bottles, each filled with a colorless liquid, are placed on a table. Three bottles contain chemicals that, when mixed together, produce a brown-red color. The fourth bottle contains a neutralizer; the fifth, water. The task is to determine which of the three liquids should be combined to obtain the brown-red color. As a person is presented these tasks, his answers—and more importantly, the reasons for these answers—are solicited. These replies reveal his thought processes, his level of reasoning.

An implementation strategy or system has been devised at Temple University (Stephens & Simpkins, 1975)) that incorporates the three guidelines stated at the outset: activities appropriate for an individual's level of development, an action-oriented environment that emphasizes the ongoing interactive process of learning, and a teacher trained in Piagetian theory and assessment.

The system is being used currently in two remediation projects. One remediation project seeks to promote reasoning in congenitally blind pupils. Findings from a previous project have indicated that when compared with sighted subjects of equivalent IQs, the congenitally blind experienced delays of from 4 to 8 years in the development of reasoning. The other remediation project seeks to promote reasoning in mentally retarded, socially maladjusted pupils. It may be presumptuous to state that our aims are "to promote reasoning." Therefore, a correct phrasing would be that the goals of both of the projects are to promote purposeful interaction with objects and people, and because of Piaget's theoretical work, it is posited that, in turn, this interaction will promote the development of reasoning.

The system is both a teacher-training system and a pupil-remediation system. A step-by-step analysis of this approach would include: teacher training in theory, in assessment of reasoning, and in devising reasoning activities; individual assessment of the reasoning of the experimental and control pupils included in the study; review and profiling of individual pupils' reasoning skills; development or adaptation of individually appropriate activities; conduct of tutorial training periods during which the pupil is provided with reasoning activities; and at the end of a 15-month or 2-year remediation period, readministration of the reasoning assessments. Comparison is made between pre- and postscores (experimental, control, and experimental versus control) to determine if significant development has occurred.

It should be noted that in one project, the tutorial training is planned for a 15-month period, in the other for a 2-year period. If training had been designed to elicit a correct response to a particular situation in a particular area, gains would have been expected in a relatively short time. However, when effort centers, and appropriately so, on extending the structures of operational thought and on facilitating the development of reasoning, a longer period is required.

In a previous study (Stephens & Simpkins, 1974), scores were obtained from 26 Piagetian measures of reasoning and on chronological age (CA) and mental age (MA) and from subtests of the Wechsler verbal scale (WISC) and the Wide Range Achievement Test (WRAT). It was our desire to see what basic abilities were represented. To define the basic abilities, the Kaiser Varimax orthogonal solution was employed, and 10 interpretable factors were extracted from scores for the blind (Stephens & Simpkins, 1974, pp. 50–51):

Factor 1, which represented Piagetian reversibility of thought at the concrete and formal level, was defined by major loadings from seven conservation assessments.

Factor 2 had negative loadings from WISC information, WISC arithmetic, and WRAT arithmetic and positive loadings from CA, MA, and a Piagetian task of hierarchical classification.

Factor 3, which was defined by WRAT reading and WRAT spelling subscores appeared to represent ability in language arts.

Factor 4 was suggestive of combinatory logic; it had major loadings from WISC similarities and chemistry.

Factor 5 had major loadings from seven Piagetian assessments that measured basic or initial ability in concrete reasoning; these tasks involved numerical correspondence, hierarchical classification, subcategorization, memory, and mental imagery.

Factor 6, also a Piagetian factor, represented the ability to dissociate notions of weight and volume and engage in formal or abstract thought.

Factor 7 was defined by Piagetian measures of spatial relationships, hierarchical classification, and WISC measured comprehension; the structure served to suggest analytical reasoning ability.

Factor 8 had major loadings from Piagetian measures assessing thought that was transitory between the concrete and formal levels.

Factor 9, with loadings from a WISC measure that assessed the recall of digits and a Piagetian measure of mental imagery that involved changing perspectives, was suggestive of skill in grouping objects and numbers in situations involving short-term memory.

Factor 10 served to indicate verbal facility because of its two loadings from Wechsler measures of verbal ability, Wechsler vocabulary, and Wechsler verbal IQ.

Of the 10 factors described above, 4 were defined solely by Piagetian measurements, 2 exclusively by Wechsler verbal and WRAT scores, and 4 by combinations of the Wechsler verbal and Piagetian reasoning measures.

A factor analysis of scores for sighted subjects on Piagetian reasoning measures, CA, MA, and scores on the Wechsler scales and the WRAT was also carried out. Eight interpretable factors were derived from the analysis (Stephens & Simpkins, 1974, p. 52):

Factor 1, a Piagetian conservation factor, was defined by loadings from 11 conservation variables, a classificatory variable, and a mental imagery variable and by CA. Flexibility and reversibility of operational thought processes were the basic abilities represented by the factor.

Factor 2 was primarily a WRAT factor; the three WRAT subscores combined with Wechsler arithmetic to suggest an academic performance factor.

Factor 3, a Wechsler factor, had three major loadings: Wechsler comprehension, IQ, and MA.

Factor 4, a factor representative of classificatory and combinatorial logic, had loadings from a Piagetian variable involving hierarchical classification and one involving combinatorial logic at the formal (abstract) level. The major loading for Wechsler similarities also occurred on this factor.

Factor 5 was defined by loadings from variables representative of thought that was in transition from the concrete to the formal level. A task that involved simultaneous classification of two criteria also contributed to the strength of the factor.

Factor 6, a verbal factor, contained loadings from WISC information and WISC vocabulary.

Factor 7 had major contributions from WISC digit span and a Piagetian measure that assessed the ability to anticipate changes in perspective when objects were viewed from different angles.

Factor 8 was characterized by mobility in reformulating mental images that involved spatial relations. Three Piagetian measures of spatial relations and a Piagetian measure of formal thought combined to define the factor.

As an effort was made to promote logical thought in the congenitally blind subjects, a chart or profile was made of a subject's performance on the 10 factors derived from the analysis of scores for the blind. Activities were designed to promote acquisition of these basic abilities. The same procedure was used to devise intervention programs for the mentally retarded, socially maladjusted subjects. In this instance, factors derived from the analysis of sighted subjects' scores were used.

Because a developmental approach implies sequentially designed activities, factor-based modules were devised. A module was defined as a series of sequentially related activities that have a common theme and a common goal and are based on a common factor or basic ability. The key to each module was interaction with objects and people. Overviews of specific modules follow.

The objective of the first module, systems and variables, was to promote the discovery of variables that effect the interaction of a system. The factor labeled *combinatory logic* represents the ability to combine variables systematically as search is made for the particular combination required to produce a desired effect. In one activity, the system, a "whirly-bird," devised by Karplus (1971), consists of a propeller-type device. The propeller contains a series of holes in which rivets can be inserted. A rubber band that is hooked to the base of the propeller stand can be wound around the post that attaches the propeller to the stand. As the rubber band unwinds, the propeller is set in motion. To adapt the "whirly-bird" for use with blind pupils, a straw was attached to the post and a nail to the base. Each rotation of the propeller resulted in a sound as the straw brushed past the nail. In the initial phase, the pupil manipulated the system, that is, wound the rubber band and counted the number of turns the propeller made. In subsequent phases, he inserted rivets in the propeller arm and recorded the number of turns made by the propeller as different combinations and locations of rivets were employed. Through interaction with the object, he discovered whether the number of rivets, the position of the rivets, and the number of twists given the rubber band contributed to the number of times the propeller rotated. Each of the contributing variables were altered systematically and the resulting rotations of the propeller recorded. Histograms were made from these data. In each activity, the pupil learned by doing: he set up the experiment, altered the variables, recorded the data, and constructed the histograms (Wexler, in press).

Another activity within the same module, although geared to a higher interest level, also involved mental manipulation of variables. The Herefordshire Farm Game, devised by Tidswell (Taylor & Walford, 1972), provided a framework in which a child could actively explore patterns of land use and choice of crop. The pupil was provided the following information:

> Mr. Brown is a farmer at Canon Pyon and is going abroad for five years. Imagine that you have been appointed to manage the farm while he is away. He has instructed you to make as much profit for him as possible and you must therefore plan carefully. He also does not wish to change the fruit and hop fields while he is away. Study the plan of the farm together with the details of fields and crops.
>
> 1. The farm is 235 acres in size and is divided into 12 fields.
> 2. Details on the fields are included in the text.
> 3. Each year you may grow any one of the listed six crops in a field labeled "Free Choice," provided that you do not grow the same crop in the same field in two successive years. The crops are: barley, wheat, oats, peas, beans, sugar beets.
>
> *Crop choice:* Assume the fertility of each field is the same, since Mr. Brown is a good farmer and has fed his soils correctly for a long time. The crop yield therefore will depend on the weather for the year, which is called *climate.* You may expect any one of four kinds of weather:
>
> 1. Wet warm
> 2. Dry warm
> 3. Wet cool
> 4. Dry cool
>
> You do not know how often or when each type of weather occurs.
>
> The income per acre from each crop depends upon the weather and can be obtained from the text.
>
> *Example:* If you choose to grow peas in Field 7 and the season is a wet warm one, then your income is
>
> 8 (income per acre) × 20 (number of acres) = 160

Procedure for the game:
1. Choose the crops for your fields and enter them on the worksheet.
2. Check that you have not broken the rules about the crops for each field for each year.
3. Use a die or table or random numbers and determine the weather for each year.
4. Enter the income correctly for each field and add up the total. Enter this total opposite Year 1 in the table on the worksheet.
5. Repeat for five years and find the total income for the whole period.

The child may vary the climatic conditions in order to ascertain the effects of climate on crops. In addition, the teacher may ask a variety of questions, such as:

Why can't you change the hop and fruit field during the five years?
Why is there no income from the woodland?
Why aren't you allowed to grow the same crop in every field?
What else other than weather could affect the yield of your crops?
When did you make your most profit? Why?
When did you make your least profit? Why?
If you knew which kind of weather to expect, how much profit could you make in one year?
What other factors could influence your decision about which crops to grow each year?

This theme could grow into a class project involving a class garden. With today's world food problem, this game could lead the student into a wider study of the variables involved in food production and possible solutions to this greater problem (Simpkins, 1976).

A second module, reproductory imagery, has been developed to promote mental imagery in the blind. Mental imagery is accepted as a key component of the intellectual process, a component that, according to Piaget, develops over a period of time. The blind obviously are limited in the development of mental images. However, research (Stephens & Simpkins, 1974) has indicated a limited presence of the process. Learning activities have been devised in an attempt to promote mental imagery in the blind. The present module, which consists of five sequential activities, deals with reproductory imagery. The pretest assessed the ability to reproduce bead patterns. Following the successful completion of this task the pupil was presented a cardboard on which four objects were placed. Through tactual exploration the pupil located the objects. The teacher then moved one or more objects and requested that the child determine which object was moved and to return it to its original position (Walton, 1974).

Three subsequent activities were adapted from "Mapping: Making Maps and Mapping Games" (ESS, 1971). In one, which involved verbal reproduction, the pupil constructed a design from blocks of different shapes. He then described the design to his partner and in turn the partner reproduced it from the verbal cues. Designs involving either two or three dimensions could be used.

The next activity was a game of tic-tac-toe. In it, the pupil told his partner where to put the mark, and the partner told the pupil where he should put his mark.

Geoboards were used in an activity that required that yarn or rubber bands be used on the boards to indicate paths. After the pupil constructed a path, he explained it to his partner, who then had to reproduce it.

In sighted persons, mental imagery generally is well established prior to the attainment of concrete operations. Initial use of the above module resulted in gains in the imagery skills of the blind pupils. It was hypothesized that this would contribute to a strengthening of the operational abilities basic to concrete operations (Pote, 1976).

A third module, cooking, was designed for socially maladjusted, educable, mentally retarded pupils. These activities maintained motivation and high interest levels, yet avoided being frustratingly difficult. The kitchen provides a perfect laboratory for developing concepts of substance, weight, and volume, plus classificatory skills and understanding of cause and effect. Cooking is an activity that permits questioning and inquiry. However, the teacher did not cook; she questioned. Since the original goal was an inquiring mind, not cooked food, the initial dish was hot chocolate or a simple pudding. Questioning and planning differed from that used in a conventional class as it centered on the classification of procedures in terms of time sequence and responsibilities and the discussion of measurement via use of seriated measuring cups and spoons. Conservation principles led to discussions of concepts of weight versus volume. Questions were asked, such as: "Does a cup of sugar weigh more than a cup of flour?" "What happens to flour when it is sifted, to butter when you melt it, to egg whites when they are beaten?" "How can you tell when something is boiling, why must it boil?" It was the questions and the seeking of answers that were emphasized throughout the cooking activities. As understanding and skill increased simple one- or two-step recipes were replaced by recipies that entailed a multifaceted series of operations. These provided opportunities for classificatory experiences, for in-depth analyses of cause and effect, and for the manipulation of variables (Sower, 1974). Learning proceeded as the pupil interacted with the ingredients.

Throughout the modules, emphasis was on learning that occured through the pupil's own questioning, manipulating, inventing, and solving. The intrinsic curiosity that motivates knowing (Wolff, 1975) was encouraged rather than rote answers, which are provoked through repetitious reinforcers. "To acquire concepts such as seriation, classification and conservation takes time, repetition and practice. Once discovered by change in one context, a new idea must be explored in other contexts, observed from different perspectives and integrated with other schemes of thought, before it is consolidated as a stable tool of thinking" (Wolff, 1975, p. 5).

ACKNOWLEDGMENT

The research reported herein was performed pursuant to a grant with Bureau for Education of the Handicapped, Office of Education, U.S. Department of Health, Education and Welfare. Contractors undertaking such projects under government sponsorship are encouraged to express freely their professional judgment in the conduct of the project.

References

Inhelder, B., *The diagnosis of reasoning in the mentally retarded.* New York: John Day, 1968.

Karplus, R. *Subsystems and variables: The science curriculum improvement study.* Chicago: Rand McNally, 1971.

Mapping: Making maps and mapping games. *Educational Development Center Elementary Science Study.* New York: McGraw-Hill, 1971.

Piaget, J. *The child's conception of number.* New York: Humanities, 1952.

Piaget, J., & Inhelder, B. *La genèse des structures logiques élémentaires: Classification et sériation.* Neuchatel: Delachaux et Niestlé, 1959.

Piaget, J., and Inhelder, B. Les images mentales. *Traité de Psychologie,* 1963, *1,* 65–100.

Piaget, J., & Inhelder, B. *Cognitive assessments.* Personal communication, University of Geneva, 1964.

Pote, J. *Module: Reproductory mental imagery.* (Cognitive Remediation Research Project: Student Activity Manual). Unpublished manuscript, University of Texas at Dallas, 1976.

Simpkins, K. *Module: Formal logic.* (Cognitive Remediation Research Project: Student Activity Manual). Unpublished manuscript, University of Texas at Dallas, 1976.

Sower, R. *Module: Cooking activities.* (Analysis and Training of Reasoning Research Project: Student Activity Guide). Unpublished manuscript, Philadelphia Child Guidance Center, 1974.

Stephens, W. B., & Simpkins, K. *The reasoning, moral judgment, and moral conduct of the congenitally blind* (Final Report, Project No. OEG-0-72-5464). Philadelphia: Temple University, 1974.

Stephens, W. B., & Simpkins, K. *Cognitive remediation in persons congenitally blind* (Project No. OEG-0-74-7445). Philadelphia: Temple University, 1975.

Taylor, J. L., & Walford, R. *Simulation in the classroom.* Baltimore: Penguin Books, 1972.

Walton, J. *Logical–mathematical thinking and the pre-school classroom.* College Park, Md.: Head Start Regional Resource and Training Center, 4321 Hartwick Road, 1974.

Wexler, M. *Module: Combinatory logic.* (Cognitive Remediation Research Project, Student Activity Manual). Unpublished manuscript, University of Texas at Dallas, 1975.

Wolff, P. H. What Piaget did not intend. *Proceedings of the Fourth Interdisciplinary Seminar on Piagetian Theory and Implications for the Helping Professions.* Los Angeles: University of Southern California, 1975.

PART III:
APPLICATION

CHAPTER 11

Some Implications
of Jean Piaget's Theory
for the Education of Young Children

Lois P. Macomber

Temple University, Philadelphia, Pennsylvania

In his studies of the developing intellect throughout the evolution of his model, Piaget has clung to certain principles, many of which reflect his biological interests. His faith in these principles has been substantiated by his own research and that of his Genevan colleagues, most notably that of Barbël Inhelder. The many replications of his work in this country and Canada have also provided substantial support for his position. It is these principles that will be presented, since they are essential to those working with the development of intellectual skills. However, just as the total model cannot be presented within the limits of this paper, neither can all of the principles. Thus, applying the criterion of value to educators of young children, I have selected the following:

1. All development is hierarchical, that is, we must all go through the same stages in the same sequence, moving from the simple to the complex.
2. Early learning is slower than later learning, although the rate at which we progress through a given stage is a function of an interaction between our environment and our genetic endowment. By genetic endowment. Piaget means a healthy organism and not of specific genetic programming, as is the mode today.
3. Development is divided into four general stages or phases, with a gradual transition from one to another. Each of the four stages is characterized by modes of learning and thinking unique to that stage.
4. Because of the hierarchical nature of Piaget's theory, thought and intelli-

gence are rooted in the actions of the sensorimotor period, the first of the four stages of cognitive development. Thus, for Piaget, thought and intelligence are internalized actions.

5. Throughout all of the stages, two "cognitive functions" are present that are invariant. These are organization and adaptation. The former is involved in the categorization of sensory data. The latter is comprised of assimilation, the taking in of new information, and accommodation, the adjusting of the existing knowledge to the new information.

6. The result of the above invariant or unchanging functions is what Piaget refers to as "cognitive structures." The cognitive structures are formed actively by each individual and contain all of the information that he has assimilated and accommodated or is in the process of adapting.

7. The cognitive structures result in behaviors from which the content of the structures can be inferred. Therefore, Piaget refers to such responses as "cognitive content." Since the cognitive structures vary in content from individual to individual according to personal experiences and level of maturation, the behaviors or cognitive content vary accordingly.

8. As a result of the above, Piaget concludes that innate factors, environment, social transmission, and equilibration all play roles in what we know and in how we use our knowledge. For him, equilibration consists of the processes of equilibrium and disequilibrium which are in relative balance at all maturational levels, motivating us not only to assimilate and accommodate within stages but also to move from one stage to another. It is the disequilibrium that motivates us to learn and the return to equilibrium that leaves us at a higher level of learning.

With these principles in mind, the first topic of discussion will be the four major stages of cognitive development identified by Piaget, namely, the sensorimotor period, the preoperational period, the concrete operational period, and the formal operational period. Each stage has been named according to the logical operations or processes that characterize the stage.

Volumes could be written about the characteristics of each stage—and, in fact, have been. Again, there are limitations that allow only the most cursory review of the stages. Yet, each has important implications for the educator, whether he be a classroom teacher, a curriculum specialist, or an administrator.

The first stage, the sensorimotor period, has been mentioned previously in the major principles set forth above. This stage is characterized by action and the beginnings of both affect and cognition, in that order. Near the end of this stage, action is internalized, providing the origins of intelligence as intelligence is usually defined. Simultaneously, imitative action is internalized as the image providing the beginnings of thought processes.

While the sensorimotor period lasts from birth to approximately the age of 2 in most children, it has many implications for practice with children who are retarded, whether from organic defects, from stimulus deprivation, or from some interaction of the two factors. Even when working with more advanced children, should one embark upon a study of the sensorimotor period, one would find some valuable clues for educational practice, clues that may aid some children in the knowing process if not in the learning process. However, one will find that all of the implications that are derived for educational practice from this period are based upon action, not on the part of the teacher but on the part of the child who is attempting to gain understanding.

The fourth period, the formal operations stage, is also applicable to teachers. Piaget refers to this period as "formal operations," since individuals at this stage are able to engage in both inductive and deductive thought. They are also able to engage in abstract and hypothetical thought without dependence upon concrete situations. Piaget is of the opinion that this period commences somewhere between the ages of 11 and 14 in the average individual. However, he is adamant about the fact that just because we are able to engage in formal operations is no guarantee that we will do so consistently. We often find remnants of preoperational thought in the adult that are not unlike the thought processes that characterize the preschooler.

By this time, it is obvious that we have jumped from the first stage to the last stage with no mention of the intervening stages. This has been done by design for two reasons. First, in some of Piaget's work, the preoperational and the concrete operational stages have been combined as one stage under the title of "concrete operations." However, the differences between the children in the second stage and those in the third are so marked that it is more functional to keep the two stages separate, with children in the second stage being referred to as preoperational and those in the third as concrete operational. The second reason for speaking of the intervening stages last is related. By contrasting the middle two stages, we can arrive at a better understanding of the nature of the preoperational child. In addition, the transition between the second and third stage, which Piaget considers as commencing somewhere between the ages of 6 and 8 in normal children, should be noted.

What, then, are the predominant characteristics of a child in the preoperational period, those critical years from 2 to 7? Without the insights provided by Piaget's work, we might not know, since the preoperational period is a period in our lives from which we have few memories. Those that we have retained have been reconstructed as we have matured. In short, our memories from the preoperational period tend to be distorted at best. As a result, we adults have assumed for years that children think and learn as we do, albeit in a more simplistic manner. Piaget's work has pointed out that these assumptions have resulted in a grave misconception of the nature of the preoperational child. Children in the preoperational stage neither learn nor think as we do. Furthermore, they do not even perceive as we do, all of which accounts for the sometimes amusing, sometimes baffling behaviors of the preoperational child. To make matters still more complex, their modes of perception and thought have little in common with those of children in the concrete operational stage.

If the preoperational child neither thinks as does the child in the concrete operational stage nor as the adult does in the formal operational stage, how does he think? As mentioned earlier, the individual in the formal operational stage is able to think both inductively and deductively, although he may resort to more primitive modes of thought from time to time. The child in the concrete operational stage is able to engage in one mode of logical thought, namely, inductive thought. In contrast, the preoperational child is able to think neither inductively nor deductively. This does not mean that the preoperational child uses many modes of thought, none of which are logical in the strictest sense of the word. Piaget describes children in this age range as using transductive thought, a form of prelogical thought that connects one specific to another specific because two observable events have occurred contiguously and the child has associated them as if there were a logical connection between them Sometimes transductive thought results in right answers, and at other times it results in answers that are incorrect. However, if one were to analyze the thought processes without regard to the correctness of the answers, he would discover that the reasoning strategies that the child utilizes in arriving at the answer remain prelogical at this stage.

Let me describe an illustration of transductive thought from my own life. When I was 3, my mother was taken to the hospital to give birth, which raised the inevitable question of where babies come from. My little Dutch grandmother was the recipient of the question, and her response was to take me out to my grandfather's cabbage patch and point out the long rows of red and green cabbages as the source of babies. My brother arrived home from the hospital, and presumably I accepted him as coming from one of the cabbages. However, shortly after, I saw a black baby for the first time. After some brief study, I turned to its mother and asked if her baby came from a red cabbage. I might add that this is neither a memory nor a reconstructed memory on my part but simply information I gained by hearing my mother speak of how logical I was at such a young age. I have never had the heart to disillusion her by pointing out that it was an association characteristic of those found in prelogical, transductive thought.

In addition to transductive thought, the preoperational child engages in egocentric thought. Piaget explains carefully that he is not attaching the negative connotation that we tend to attach to the term *egocentric*. For him *egocentric thought* implies that the child during the preoperational period is completely unaware that anyone could hold another point of view from the one he holds. By the same token, the preoperational child feels that what he knows, the rest of the world knows. A child may come up to you and start speaking of an event that occurred in his home the evening before and be absolutely confident that you know exactly what he is talking about, when you, in fact, have no reference point whatsoever for the conversation. If you question the child about it, he may even respond with a statement such as "You know" or "You remember!"

A third form of thought seen in children of this age is magical thought. The preoperational child often feels that he has magical powers as a result of his confusion of cause and effect. For example, my own daughter thought that she could control traffic lights by simply chanting "Red light, red light, turn green." It was some time before she arrived at the realization that she had no control over the lights whatsoever. Because of the magical-thought process, no amount of explanation would have helped her to arrive at that understanding any earlier than she did. Magical thought also occurs in the young child in other forms. Children at this age find it difficult, if not impossible, to say "I don't know." Instead, when confronted with a question to which they do not know the answer, they are apt to give you fanciful answers. When describing their perceptual processes later, I will illustrate their ingenuity, although I am certain that you have also encountered such examples frequently.

Animistic thought is a fourth mode of thought that exists in the young child, a mode that tends to linger throughout subsequent stages. Animistic thought is simply thought that attributes living properties to inanimate objects. At first, this mode of thought is applied to all inanimate objects, perhaps as an extension of egocentric thought. A young child may insist that his teddy bear is hungry and needs a cookie just as he does. Just as often, it is the child's imaginary playmate, a product of magical thought, who needs the cookie or some other thing that the child himself wants. Animistic thought has been observed in still other forms. If a child's favorite dish breaks, he may talk to it and say something like, "Poor dish. Does it hurt bad?" On the other hand, if he accidently stumbles over a chair, he may turn around and kick the chair saying, "Naughty chair!"

Later on in the preoperational stage, animistic thought is restricted to objects that move under their own power such as windup toys and electric trains. It is this latter aspect that is reflected frequently in adult behavior and language. For example, how many of us use masculine and feminine genders to refer to inanimate objects? More specifically, how many of us have cars or boats to which have been attached names or to which we talk in some fashion?

Before we leave the realm of thought in the young child, two points should be made. First, the modes of thought are not mutually exclusive, and frequently two or more occur in the same incident, as illustrated above in the cases of the imaginary playmate and the traffic light incident. Second, and more important to educational practice, thought in the young child is static and thus irreversible. As adults, we can reverse a thought process at will. For example, one may arrive at a conclusion and return to the starting point. For a young child, this is an impossible task, since he can think in one direction only because of the nature of thought in his prelogical state.

Just as modes of thought interact in the preoperational child, so do perceptions and thought. The young child is handicapped in that his perceptions are not constant, and yet he is bound by what he can perceive. Thus, reality for the young child is what he perceives as reality with no qualifications. As if this does not complicate his life enough, there is another factor that makes the situation even more complex, and that is the child's tenuous grasp of reality. For the young child, fantasy and reality often become confused; fantasy becomes reality for him since he perceives it as reality. Again, you may have seen many examples of this phenomenon. A young child may start out romping with an adult. One moment, reality is firm and the child squeals with delight. A moment later, he may be screaming in terror as reality slips away and the playful adult assumes some menacing role in the child's fantasy. You may see the same phenomenon as well in some children's reactions to the fairy tales that we adults have considered to be classics for children. The witch in "Hansel and Gretel" or the big bad wolf in "Little Red Riding Hood" become terrifying when fantasy replaces reality in the child's perception.

Piaget points out many examples of the interaction of perception and thought, although he separates the two as distinct processes. Because thought in the young child is prelogical and under the influence of perception, causality is unclear to the child as well. Thus, the child attributes causality to what he can observe. One of Piaget's classic examples is one child's response when asked why the wind blows. In essence, the child's response was "Because the trees move," a phenomenon observable to the child.

However, Piaget has gone beyond this point to study the effects of perceptual inconstancy in the young child. Here we find his classic work on conservation, the phenomenon that marks the transition between the preoperational stage and the stage of concrete operations. In many ingenious experiments, Piaget has demonstrated the preoperational child's lack of conservation. In other words, the preoperational child is limited in that he can attend to only one dimension at a time, while conservers can not only attend to but take into consideration two or more dimensions simultaneously. It is the dominant stimulus that the child perceives that governs his thought processes at the preoperational stage. The child makes the discovery only after he is ready to handle two or more perceptual stimuli simultaneously.

The preoperational child who lacks number conservation will conclude that there are more beads of a given color than the total number of beads if the beads are not assorted evenly by color. He will also answer that there are more beads when they are spread out in a long line than when they are grouped together. When he is asked "Why?" we often elicit magical thought with answers such as "You just put it there" or "More fell from the ceiling." The magical thought represents his need to account for the inconsistency he perceives because of limitations in his ability to perceive and comprehend an operation that is carried out in front of him.

The second form of conservation is that of conservation of mass, which the child attains somewhat later than number conservation. Again, the underlying principle remains the same. Mass conservation is attained when the child is able to take into consideration both length and width, or two comparable dimensions. Prior to that time, the dominant stimulus is the one that he perceives and the one to which he responds. On the other hand, Madison Avenue is aware that we adults sometimes act as nonconservers just as we sometimes engage in modes of thought other than formal thought. For example, how often have we purchased the tall package rather than the short package, only to discover that it contains no more and sometimes less because we have failed to consider width as well as height?

One might suspect that weight conservation would follow mass conservation closely in time. For most children, this is not the case. Even after mass conservation has been attained, the child has to work to develop weight conservation. He may be convinced that there is the same amount of material in two objects regardless of their shape, but he may be equally convinced that there is one that weighs more than the other even though both objects are made of the same material. If such is the case, he is a conserver of mass but a nonconserver of weight. On the other hand, when he discovers that equal amounts of the same kind of material weigh the same without regard to their shape, he has become a conserver of weight.

The fourth form of conservation and the last to appear is that of volume. Piaget is of the opinion that most children become conservers of volume around the age of 11, near the end of the concrete operations stage. Yet, on occasion, many individuals in the formal operations period make the same mistake that the child makes and react only to the dominant dimension or stimulus rather than to all of the pertinent dimensions.

By now, it is clear that we are indebted to Piaget for clarifying the nature of the preoperational child, whose learning we are expected to facilitate, not inhibit. To summarize what Piaget has clarified, let us compare the preoperational child with the child in the concrete operational stage. First, the preoperational child differs from the more mature child in the modes of thought used, namely, prelogical, transductive, egocentric, magical, and animistic thought in contrast to the logical, inductive thought characteristic of the child in the concrete operational period. Second, the preoperational child is characterized by lack of reversibility in thought, while the child in the concrete operations period has no such limitation. Third, the preoperational child is dominated by his perceptions, which are inconstant, while the child in the concrete operations stage is freed from perceptual domination and simultaneously develops constancy in perception. Finally, the preoperational child lacks conservation, while the child in the subsequent stage has mastered the early forms of conservation, if not all of them

What does all of this mean to educators of the preoperational child? The implications are many and profound. The most obvious of all appears to be the most devastating; that is, our present educational system is attempting to educate the preoperational child as if he were functioning at the concrete operational level or even above.

While we have shared Piaget's position on the importance of early childhood and the critical nature of this period to future development, we have not shared his insights. Working from our basic assumption that children think, perceive, and learn as we do, even the most child-centered of us have innocently fallen into the trap of expecting children in the preoperational stage to think logically. Thus, we have established educational systems, curricula, and teaching strategies that interfere with rather than facilitate learning in the preoperational child.

What is the answer to this situation, which has serious implications both for the young child and for the early childhood education profession? Piaget has not been explicit on this point, although he has cited examples in which experimental stimulation appears to have facilitated learning. Two opposing views have been advanced to date. Bereiter has removed himself from the field of early childhood education and has taken the position that education before the age of 8 is a waste of both time and money. Furth and Elkind, on the other hand, have called for the abandonment of schools for learning in favor of schools for thinking. A third, more moderate approach can be proposed that incorporates Piaget's implications for education. Schools can and should develop thinking as well as learning. Let us keep our schools for learning and redefine the learning tasks expected of children so that they are consistent with the child's abilities and limitations as pointed out by Piaget. With new insights into the preoperational child, traditional expectations can be discarded in favor of developmental and learning tasks that are more realistic.

There are several reasons for advocating this approach. First, Piaget has emphasized the importance of the slow learning of the early years to all later intellectual achievement. Second, Piaget has stressed that efforts to force children through stages, or efforts to force them to work at levels above their own, result in delaying normal progress through the stage. Thus, patience in the early years is rewarded by more efficient and rapid learning in later years. Third, such an approach demonstrates respect for the child as a thinker and a learner, providing him with the opportunity to experience success in school. The latter, of course, is vital to his healthy emotional development. Fourth, such an approach places the emphasis in education where it belongs, that is, on understanding and not on memorization used as a mechanism to cope with an incomprehensible system. In Piaget's terms, it is emphasizing the cognitive structures that are reflected in the cognitive content, rather than attempting to teach cognitive content or the behavior with the expectation that cognitive structures will follow. Finally, the educational process would provide less frustration and more satisfaction to teachers and parents, as well as to children, than it does at present.

Such an approach would call for changes in curriculum, instructional strategies, facilities, and equipment. Furthermore, it would place demands for change on administrators, teachers, and parents alike. Some of the changes necessary would be minor, but others would be difficult and painful as we develop a program that is in the best interest of the preoperational child. However painful, we must make the effort if we wish to help and not hinder the young child in the learning-to-learn process.

What changes are necessary in curriculum if we are to adjust the curriculum to the thinking and learning modes of the preoperational child? While we cannot cover each area, some desirable changes in the areas of language and arithmetic can be pointed out. In the language area, more time would be allotted to conversation, utilizing an aural–oral approach in an effort to tune the child in to new words and correct grammatical structure. However, emphasis would be placed upon the function and not the structure of the language. Since language is cognitive content or behavior used to express either thoughts or knowledge that exist in the cognitive structures, it would be taught neither for the purpose of inducing thought nor as an end in itself. As Piaget indicates, language is necessary but not a sufficient condition to thought. Thus, there would be less emphasis on early acquisition of reading and more emphasis on building the foundations for comprehension necessary to success when formal reading is introduced.

Arithmetic would also depart from the traditional approach. Time would be spent on the development of number concepts until the child had a firm grasp of those, since the curriculum designer would be cognizant of this as an initial step on the way to number conservation. Then, and only then, would addition be introduced as an arithmetic process, since arithmetic processes have no meaning to the child prior to the development of the number concepts. After the child has developed competency in addition, he would then be introduced to multiplication, a shortcut to addition that does not require the reversal in thought inherent in the subtraction process.

Other curricular changes would involve culling out all instructional materials calling for inductive or deductive reasoning. That would rule out most programmed instruction, since existing programs are largely deductive. In place of these, the teacher would spend more time in helping children develop readiness by providing exposure to varied and sequenced activities on the experience continuum. Within the parameters of safety, much more freedom would be allotted to children to move, explore, and discover than at present. In Piaget's terms, children would be freed to "reinvent knowledge." In educational terms, each child would be developing a large portion of his own curriculum out of the many experiences available to him. While the latter may sound revolutionary, it is not, for in reality that is what actually occurs in every classroom today. No matter what a teacher makes available, a child learns what he is ready to learn and what is of interest to him.

Not only would there be changes in the curriculum but there would be changes in the classroom itself. Classrooms would be comprised of much open space for the movement essential to cognitive development. Experience corners where children could explore with water, sand, and other natural materials would be available. In the era of the open classroom none of the above sounds radical. However, there would be one major departure from the ideal classroom as most of us have visualized it. Because of the child's perceptual inconstancy and his attention to the dominant stimuli, the number of extraneous stimuli would be reduced substantially. There would be few, if any, pictures on the wall. There would be no gaily colored bulletin boards constructed by the teacher to distract the child. These can be placed at eye level in hallways, where they can be enjoyed by children without interfering with the learning process. The colors in the classroom would be subdued and restful, rather than the primary colors in use today. At the same time, the classrooms would be free of unnecessary clutter. In short, classrooms would be organized to facilitate learning in the preoperational child instead of being organized to be aesthetically appealing to adults, who have already achieved perceptual constancy.

There would be changes in the role of the teacher as well as in his knowledge. Instead of reinforcing right answers, he would be asking "Why?" in an attempt to determine the thought processes utilized by the child conversing with him. His role would be that of the facilitating adult and not that of the group leader. In fact, whatever groups exist would be ever changing, comprised of a few children spontaneously drawn together by a mutual interest or activity. However, the teacher would be able to recognize stages of growth by cognitive content and would constantly be diagnosing where a child was and what kinds of activities the child would need in order to progress. Based upon his diagnosis and prescription, the teacher would determine what instructional strategies would be most effective with the child in question. Thus, the teacher's diagnostic, prescriptive, and evaluative skills would enable him to individualize instruction in the true sense and relieve him of our current dilemma of giving lip service and little more to individualization. The teacher's objective would be to help each child to think and to learn as much as he could within the limits imposed upon him by his preoperational state. The teacher would not be bound to a series of behavioral objectives to be applied to all children. Rather, he would have faith in his own ability and the sequential nature of children's development.

Based upon an understanding of the preoperational child, the teacher would make more judicious selections of educational toys and materials. Cognizant of the child's problem in sorting out stimuli, the teacher would order equipment that emphasized the dominant stimulus to be considered by the child. If color is the stimulus to be considered, the size and shape of the objects to be compared would remain constant. If seriation is to be considered, the shape and color of the objects would remain constant. If equipment appealing to adults but of little educational value to children has been provided—for example, a toy in which variations of color and size have been combined—the teacher would not hesitate to repaint it all one color to aid a child in learning about size.

Just as new activities are called for, some of the activities carried out by teachers now would be eliminated because of their increased understanding of the preoperational child. While a teacher would continue to enjoy the humor in a preoperational explanation, he would not attempt to give the child a correct explanation. Rather, he would counter with an appropriate question or puzzle that would help the child to discover the fallacy of his thinking through the development of disequilibrium. The teacher would not spend a lot of time emphasizing the importance of sharing or of trying to get one child to understand another's feelings. He would know that understanding of these concepts is impossible to the preoperational child because of his egocentric thought. The teacher would recognize that, at best, his explanation could only serve to tune the child in to elaborative language. If sharing remained a value at this age level, the teacher would know that he can best accomplish it by providing a model for imitation. Through imitation and eventually through logical thought, the child will learn to share and will understand the meaning of sharing. The teacher would know that labeling a child as selfish accomplishes nothing positive, for the only sharing that occurs at this stage occurs as a result of conditioning rather than as a result of understanding. Once again, the latter emphasized cognitive content at the expense of the development of cognitive structures. The teacher would recognize the nature of magical thought and find no need to label that either. Rather, he would ask a simple, reality-based question in an effort to help the child to think through the situation. Often the question will be to little avail, but the teacher would know that it is the best that he can do to cope with magical thought. Of course, recognizing the child's tenuous hold on reality, the teacher would not engage in fantasy with the child in the preoperational stage. Rather, he would help the child to anchor reality by remaining reality-oriented himself.

However, no matter how skillful a teacher becomes in working with the preoperational child, he can never function independently of the administration and of the parents of the children. Thus, he would have the task of helping administrators understand what he knows about the preoperational child. The teacher and the administrator would then unite in educating parents and the community on the need for change in the educational program. Emphasis would be placed upon the psychological basis for the change, including an understanding of the enigma of the preoperational child. This type of sharing would enable parents, teachers, and administrators to work cooperatively in behalf of the young child, a particularly important point because of the influence of early development on all later development.

There is one place where the administrator, of necessity, would stand alone. If he has recognized the need for an education program for parents on the nature of the preoperational child, he has an advantage. However, he would be in the position of having to do some additional educating if he carries Piaget's theory to its logical conclusion. First of all, he would know that early learning takes time and, further, is reconstructed through time. Thus, to evaluate the achievement or intelligence of the preoperational child in a formal fashion would be in large part a waste of time and money. He would know that learning cannot be measured before it takes place. He also would know that early learning is a slow process, requiring a great deal of time for consolidation. Upon consolidation, learning can finally be expressed as cognitive content, usually measured in the realm of language skills. Standardized tests that look at the product or cognitive content, not the process, provide little valid information during the preoperational period. Thus, it would be the administrator's role to convince his board members to discard formal testing programs as evidence of achievement in young children.

However, the school system would be left with another task, evaluation of the early childhood education program Just as tests of individual children during the preoperational period would reveal little valid information, tests of the children in the program would reveal little that is valid about the program itself. Early childhood education programs cannot be evaluated for effectiveness based upon the performance of its participants in the preoperational stage alone. Thus, longitudinal studies would be necessary, studies that reveal how children reconstruct their preoperational learnings upon becoming operational. Such is the challenge to the administrators and the school system. It is quite a challenge, indeed, when one looks at the contemporary push for statistical results showing immediate gains—before the child's learning can become operational.

In conclusion, what has been reported as some implications of Piaget's theory for education affects each of us, without regard to our specific roles. It is proposed that we recognize the critical nature of early childhood in relationship to later cognitive development and accept the challenges of Piaget in behalf of the preoperational child.

References

Fransworth, P. R. (Ed). *Annual review of psychology*. Palo Alto, Calif.: Annual Reviews, Inc. 1965.

Hapgood, M. The open classroom: Protect it from its friends. *Saturday Review*, September 18, 1971, 66–75.

Piaget, J. Autobiography. In E. G. Boring, (Eds.), *A history of psychology in autobiography*, Vol. 4. Worcester, Mass.: Clarke University Press, 1952. (*a*)

Piaget J. *The origins of intelligence in children*. New York: Norton, 1952. (*b*)

Piaget, J. [*The construction of reality in the child*] (M. Cook,trans.). New York: Basic Books, 1954.

Piaget, J. *The language and thought of the child*. Cleveland and New York: Meridian Books, World Publishing Co., 1955.

Piaget, J. [*Play, dreams, and imitation in childhood*] (C. Cattegno & F. M. Hodgson, trans.). New York: Norton, 1962.

Piaget, J. *The psychology of intelligence*. Patterson, N.J.: Littlefield, Adams, 1963.

Piaget, J. *The child's conception of the world.* Totowa, N.J.: Littlefield, Adams, 1967.

Piaget, J. *Mechanisms of perception.* New York: Basic Books, 1969.

Piaget, J., & Inhelder, B. [*The Psychology of the Child*] (H. Weaver, trans.). New York: Basic Books, 1969.

Piaget, J., & Inhelder, B. *Mental imagery in the child.* New York: Basic Books, 1971.

Ripple, R. E., & Rockcastle, V. N. (Eds.). *Piaget rediscovered.* Ithaca, N.Y.: School of Education, Cornell University Press, 1964.

Also several speeches in 1970–1971 including those of Jean Piaget, Bärbel Inhelder, David Elkind, and Hans Furth at Temple University and Carl Bereiter at Johns Hopkins University.

CHAPTER 12

Piaget's Theory Applied to a Social Studies Curriculum

Barbara Z. Presseisen

Research for Better Schools, Philadelphia, Pennsylvania

Curriculum development, like many areas of education, has undergone several major transformations in the 20th century. Before I get to the main topic of this paper—the application of Piaget's theory to the social studies curriculum—it is important to look first at curriculum development itself. I propose that an examination of the changes and emphases of the development of curriculum during this century will lead to the best understanding of the importance and application of Piaget's theory.

What is curriculum? For years this question was answered simply and directly. Curriculum is the content of learning. Proponents of this view are interested in the *what* of education rather than how it is conveyed. They often focus on the disciplines of knowledge as the central concern of the curriculum. "What knowledge is of most worth?" asked Spencer in 1854 (Spencer, 1963, pp. 21–76). Many educators are still asking that question today, and their response is often the 3 Rs, a curriculum that includes no social studies at all!

There is also a broader and more comprehensive approach to content-centered curriculum than the very limited 3R view. Advocates of *basic skills learning* are closely related to the 3R approach to education, but their delineation of knowledge is more extensive. The basic skills approach can include in the school's program four major areas of subject matter: language arts, mathematics, social studies, and science. Implicit in this view of knowledge is the need for a balanced and more generalized view of the world. And more important is their focus within subject matter on the capabilities necessary to a balanced and generalized view. This approach reminds us of the development of curriculum in ancient times when the *trivium,* including grammar, rhetoric, and dialectic, was joined with the *quadrivium,* consisting of geometry, arithmetic, astronomy, and the theory of music, to form the first basis of higher education (Castle, 1964, p. 59). The essential capabilities of learning in Caesar's world may have been present in this ancient program, but alas, there was still no social studies in that curriculum.

For educators chiefly concerned with children, the content approach to curriculum as the 3Rs, or as basic skills, is obviously inadequate. Almost from the outset of the 20th century, the writings of John Dewey countered the lack of the learner's role in the content conception of schooling. Learning can occur, said Dewey (1938, p. 20), only when the child is actively involved in the process of education. The curriculum is the vehicle of the learning experience; it is a means to a much greater end than mere static knowledge. Content is still important, but in Dewey's view, the real challenge of the school's program is to *stimulate children's active involvement* within their educational experience. Such involvement has both cognitive and affective dimensions.

The battle between the content people and the child-centered curriculum is probably the literature on which many of us were trained. While that battle was being waged, however, some very interesting developments were occurring in education that were bound to influence both curriculum and curriculum makers. First, the emergence of the technology of multimedia instruction revolutionized the availability and dispersal of audio and visual information. One could argue the pros and cons of utilizing television or films or cassette tape in the classroom. Nevertheless, one must admit that the various modern means of conveying imagery and sound today do influence the ways that students think, and these must be considered in decisions about curriculum and instruction.

Secondly, the educatonal world has become increasingly sensitive to the variation of both abilities and the styles of learning that characterize school populations. Once we began to study intelligence, as well as measure it, we had to ask what we were going to do about it in making curricular provisions. We began to raise questions, too, about the arbitrary organization of the school, about how we nailed down learning responses much as we had bolted desks in exact rows and ratios. Furthermore, our instructional designs had to reflect something about how we assess results *en route,* if only to determine if we are doing what we claim to be doing and if we do it consistently.

And thirdly, education has become very self-conscious about its own sociology. What roles do we want students and teachers to fulfill in what types of environment? Do we want alternate systems, and, if so, what classroom management plans are needed to make these alternatives possible? The development of open classrooms made it necessary to train open-classroom teachers; it also created the demand for open-classroom curricula. In many cases, we must first decide what that means before such a curriculum can actually be designed.

What does all this suggest to educators who want to find out about applying Piaget's fertile theory to the social studies area of the school's curriculum? It suggests that there are some key elements in curriculum development that must be accounted for in such an application. These elements, in fact, may become the criteria for evaluating the success of such an application. We will list them briefly:

1. *Content.* What is the significance of information in the curriculum, either as basic subject matter or the more formal disciplines of knowledge?
2. *Process.* What is the significance of the child's learning processes, both cognitive and affective, in the curriculum, and how are these provided for?
3. *Instructional design.* What is the sequence of instructional events in the curriculum and how are concerns such as technology, intelligence, and assessment related to this design?
4. *Management plan.* How is the design to be implemented in the classroom, and of what consequence is this implementation to the behavioral expectations of both teachers and students?
5. *Evaluation.* What can be learned about the effectiveness of this curriculum in terms of validity and reliability of data, on what populations, and under what conditions?

Having considered these questions, we can now more fruitfully turn to Piaget's theory and examine it as a basis for curriculum development in the social studies. One can also examine his particular thoughts on social education *per se,* an area Piaget has only recently begun to write about extensively. Finally, an actual social studies program under development is described that purports to apply Piaget's theory to its overall curricular organization. Included is a description of the application of the program, the constraints placed on the actual testing of the program, and some tentative results of that testing.

It is well known that for a long time Piaget shied away from stating educational principles and suggested that it was the responsibility of professional educators to find out if there were seeds of pedagogical wisdom in his work. Some of the earlier discussions about Piaget, such as Hunt's (1961) and Bruner's (1960), were thus trail blazers in educational theory. More recently, Piaget (1973) has begun to speak on educational topics, and to a certain extent, he has removed the guesswork for the educator and the editor alike.

Every educator should be aware of certain basic assumptions that Piaget suggests as the hallmarks of child development. Four main principles can be cited from the extensive writings of Piaget. These principles are stated in many different ways in different contexts, but they are the foundation of much of the work of the Genevan school.

First, Piaget proposes that the growth of intelligence in all children is essentially the result of the development of *mental structures* that rest on basic skills rather than on inherited abilities. To Piaget (1970*b*), these mental structures develop as the child's mental organization becomes a more complex and more efficient representation of the reality that the child has experienced. Like the progressivists and Dewey, who were mentioned earlier, Piaget has a special understanding of the role of experience in learning. This understanding is tied to his conception of *action* in the building of mental structures. This point brings us to the second basic assumption of Piaget's theory.

According to Piaget (1976), intellectual skills develop as a result of the child's continuous interaction or exchange with his environment. One of Piaget's favored notions is that of *operation,* to act upon the objects one observes and studies. If the goal of education is to encourage creative rather than imitative minds, then the child must operate or act himself. It is only by internalizing such direct operations, says Piaget (1964), that the child learns to think. Knowledge is thus derived both from objects themselves and from actions performed on objects. The roots of thought are in *doing* for Piaget as they were for Dewey. But the structures of thought, according to the Swiss psychologist, develop because the child does certain things at certain significant or critical moments in the sequence of his learning. The individual child learns in terms of his past history or experiences, as well as in terms of his present or current capabilities. This notion serves to introduce the third major assumption of Piaget's genetic theory.

Piaget maintains that the structures of intellect develop or advance through a sequence of related *stages,* which produce *qualitative* changes in the way children think and operate upon their environment. With his well-known collaborator, Bärbel Inhelder, Piaget maintains that the order of the occurrence of these mental stages is fixed and regular. Although children reach a given stage at differing rates, Genevan research (Piaget & Inhelder, 1969, p. 153) suggests that the order of the succession of stages is constant and that the time variation can be used as a factor in cross-cultural or specialized studies. Certainly, Piaget and Inhelder argue that it is the operations underlying the stage that should be studied and not the mere chronological age of the child involved.

One of the more interesting implications of the stage aspect of Piaget's theory is that one becomes more aware of the dynamism in children's thought. A child's mind is not clearly black or explicitly white. Transitional stages are periods of normal disruption, as the child learns new ways to structure his world and to clarify his understanding. A child may not function on the same level or at the same stage across all areas of his intellectual life, perhaps because his experience is more limited in one than in another. He may even vacillate within a given area over a period of time. Piaget (1967, p. 121) encourages us to watch the child's performance over time, to look for the more reversible operations and the growing understanding and complexity of various conservations.

Three main aspects of Piaget's theory have been noted so far—structure, operation, and stage—as important factors of child development. There is one more that seems very significant to his theory and important to education as well. That is the principle of motivation for learning, as Piaget sees it. The important *adaptive* nature of human intellect is what is underlined here. Piaget

(1967, p. 8) sees all mental life as tending progressively to assimilate the surrounding environment. In other words, children are naturally curious: they are inherently motivated to explore and master their surroundings. As they satisfy their inquisitiveness, their activity lessens, they accommodate the new information, and they are momentarily quiescent—that is, until something else taps that curiosity. This built-in drive for learning may be sustained, encouraged, and directed by a responsive environment, or it may be dulled by an unresponsive one. The school may be a critical factor in this exchange. It seems likely that an educational environment that fosters learning motivated by fear or that encourages accomplishment because of external rewards may well stifle the child's natural drive for competence. On analyzing learning *via* Piagetian theory, Elkind (1974, pp. 1–10) goes one step further. He maintains that the child's drive for competence includes fundamental aesthetic propensities; that is, the child has a desire and a talent to express this curiosity in ways that are aesthetically pleasing and gratifying. Certainly, that creative aspect will influence the social organization of the school, if not color the social exchange in all education. It is to Piaget's view on socialization to which we now turn.

To many educators, Piaget's theory of child development is essentially a cognitive theory. He is concerned with logical operations, with teaching children to think. That is, of course, very true. But what of the affective and social sides of human behavior? Piaget and Inhelder (1969 p. 117) accept as commonplace knowledge that cognitive and affective or social development are inseparable and parallel. Piaget shows direct relationships between the preoperational child and precooperative behavior on the part of the 5- to 7-year-old, who often speaks in monologues with himself. The logical development of the child is directly influenced by the relationship between the child and the adult, an exchange that is the source of educational and verbal transmission of cultural elements. His cognitive progression is similarly influenced by social relations with his peers, other children, and playmates with whom a continuous and constructive process of reciprocal socialization parallels the give and take of cognitive interaction.

A case in point, which illustrates the significance of social exchange on child development, is the development of moral reasoning, a topic on which Piaget wrote extensively as early as 1935 (Piaget, 1965). Essentially, he showed that the child's social exchanges in real life—particularly in instances involving rules, such as games, or in family interactions—give rise to a process of structuration that leads from a state of relative lack of coordination to a state of coordination of points of view and cooperation in action and communication. To quote Piaget,

> A child of four or five, for example, is often not aware that he is himself the brother or sister of his brother or sister. This lack of perspective affects the logic of relations as well as the awareness of self. When he reaches the level of operations, he will by that very fact be capable of cooperation—and it is impossible to separate cause from effect in this integrated process. (Piaget & Inhelder, 1969, p. 129)

In other words, according to Piaget, social interactions are the stuff of much of the child's intellectual process-building. One does not think in a vacuum. An operation can be an action *on people* as much as an action on things. With the development of language, the potential of social exchange *via* verbal communication is endless and presents to the child a whole new basis of reality. It is such a reality that is the foundation of the child's moral being as well as his unique intellectual development. Piaget's view of knowledge is also influenced by his position on a single logic underlying the child's cognitive, affective, and social development. Piaget depicts knowledge as a molar entity, synonymous with conceptual wholes. Such a position enables Piaget (1970a) to deal with *interdisciplinary* relationships among various subject matters. The division of compartmentalized subject fields within knowledge is a scholarly convenience, according to Piaget, perhaps a requisite for productive research, but by no means an intellectual necessity. Piaget is impressed more by the parallel structures or patterns that cut across the various disciplines of knowledge than with fragmentary conceptualizations of adult thought (Presseisen, 1971). He seeks to build understanding of the common mechanism of an area of knowledge through general problems of that area that get at basic operations. In particular, he looks for self-regulating devices within a system that permits a researcher to understand the underlying operations or transformations in the total system (Piaget, 1970a).

Piaget can become very philosophical and esoteric as far as educational practitioners are concerned. However, as far as knowledge in the school is concerned, according to Piaget, the social sciences are of particular importance to learning in an interdisciplinary way. The human branches of science, he says, are of special structural value because of their strong linguistic tradition (Piaget, 1973). It is a linguistic tradition akin to that of Lévi-Strauss and Chomsky, in which underlying structures, like behavioral patterns, are acquired by external transmission through what Piaget calls "multiple and differentiated social interactions" (Piaget, 1973, p. 115). But it should be emphasized that what Piaget seeks to teach through interdisciplinary social science is not merely information about social institutions. He sees the social sciences as the focus for the full development of the child's personality and his respect for human rights and fundamental freedoms, as well.

In one of his most recent writings, Piaget (1973, pp. 89–91) charges the school with producing not only a fully operational thinker but a fully responsible human being, too. The social education that the child receives requires not only that he learn the laws of logic but that he voluntarily subject himself to a system of mutual norms that, in effect, subordinate his liberty in respect of others. There is a great similarity here between Piaget's viewpoint and that of John Dewey in *Democracy and Education* and of the progressivist position as a whole, as pointed out in Overton's (1972, pp. 88–115) article on Piaget and progressivism. On the one hand, Piaget stresses that the content of social information must be appropriate to the thought structures of the learner at his stage of development. On the other hand, he also says that the progressivists' emphasis on a curriculum for doing is sound in terms of their assertions about motivation for learning, the self-direction of the student, and freedom in the classroom.

But Piaget goes beyond Dewey in what he expects of the school. The operations involved in the learning of social sciences *demand* collaboration and exchange between the student and his classmates. A real formation of the tools of intellect, says Piaget (1973, p. 93), requires a collective atmosphere of active and experimental investigation, as well as discussion in common. In terms of moral education, Piaget maintains that if a student is intellectually passive, he will also not know how to be free ethically. For the Genevan theorist, the cognitive development of reciprocity and intellect are correlative aspects of the social development of independence and personality.

Thus, in the social studies, Piaget suggests that what is significant is not the particular answer a student gives to a query in the subject matter, but the structure of the question he is striving to answer. And equally important is how the student goes about creating an answer in terms of consultation and collaboration on the topic with his own peers. In social science learning, there is room for mutual stimulation and mutual control, as well as for the exercise of a critical spirit. When social education includes these elements, according to Piaget, we shall be creating men and women "who are capable of doing new things, not simply of repeating what other generations have done—men who are creative, inventive, and discoverers" (Duckworth, 1964, p. 5).

We now turn to a social studies curriculum that is actively trying to put Piaget's theory into practice. The curriculum to be described in the next portion of this discussion is developmental. There is no guarantee that it works. Several prominent experts in Piagetian research serve as consultants to the project, but the overall analysis takes much time and a long evaluation, and we hasten to suggest that the reader be very wary of anyone who offers an instant Piagetian curriculum. Instead, we propose that the key elements of curriculum development that we discussed earlier be brought to bear on such a program.

The social studies program described here is known as SEARCH, an acronym for the *S*ocial *E*ncounter *A*nd *R*esearch *C*urriculum for *H*umanization. The primary goal of the SEARCH curriculum is to individualize the learning of social education: to provide for each child's individual differences while he learns social studies and to give each student a larger measure of individual control over his acquisition of social information. There are several contingencies that follow from this objective. First, providing for different ability levels or competencies requires diagnostic evaluation measures as well as flexible schedules of instruction. Second, to assume control over one's learning implies possibilities of choice and self-correction. Certainly a self-contained classroom or a strictly textbook-bound instructional sequence would poorly serve individualization as described.

What basic assumptions underlie SEARCH? The first two letters of the acronym represent the ideal way a student should meet social phenomena: a *Social Encounter*, a natural relationship neither contrived so much that it has no reality about it nor imposed from such a limited disciplinary point of view that it has no meaning for the learner.

The second SEARCH cornerstone concerns the processes involved in the mastery of social studies knowledge. These processes should be built upon cognitive operations and social perspectives that are appropriate and available to the learner. This aspect of SEARCH strives to make it possible for the student *to operate* upon the material in the Piagetian sense. When the student is so actively involved, he is engaged in a *Research Curriculum*—and two more letters have been added to the SEARCH acronym.

Lastly, the basic characteristics of SEARCH require that the learning be *Humanistically* inspired. The cognitive material must be related to the affective development of the learner, so that he finds in his studies a reflection of the experience of all humankind. This position implies there is no real social learning unless the child can integrate experience of the calssroom into his own social reality. In a larger sense, it means that the gap between explanations of reality resting on the social science disciplines and reality itself must be bridged by a larger human and more personal description of the workings of living social institutions. So much for the meaning of the SEARCH acronym. Now let us examine the curricular structure of the actual program.

SEARCH is conceived as a basic social education program, currently with a K−12 range. With design and development comes a fairly extensive tryout or field test of the material and an evaluation scheme to monitor and assess the effects of the material. SEARCH also claims to be developmental in that it strives to apply Piaget's theory to the organization and the development of the classroom materials. This is achieved in part by the assignment of developmental levels to the 13 years of education. There are four such levels identified in the program, each level parallels the child's chronological advancement.

The primary focus of a SEARCH developmental level is *what children do:* how they operate or perceive a particular set of circumstances on both cognitive and social dimensions. Drawing from Piaget's stage theory, the SEARCH levels are roughly related to the child's age and his grade at school. Level A consists of "kindergarten and first and second grade," but the real concern is the nongraded one, a concern with the preoperational cognitive dimension and the precooperative social orientation of self-action. The material at this level is conceived in terms of how the child sees it; in fact, preoperations is seen as a grand experience in observation development. At Level B, "third grade through sixth," if one is forced to relate to such a distinction, SEARCH material is focused on the child as the concrete operator with the first awareness of both self and others in his social world.

SEARCH DEVELOPMENTAL LEVELS

COGNITIVE OPERATIONS		SOCIAL ORIENTATION
Formal Operations	LEVEL D AGES 15 - 18	Ideational Relations (values, ideas on the human condition)
Transition to early Formal Operations	LEVEL C AGES 12 - 14	Inter-group Relations
Concrete Operations	LEVEL B AGES 8 - 11	Interpersonal Relations (self and group activity)
Pre-operational Thought	LEVEL A AGES 5 - 7	Personal Relations (self action)

FIGURE 1. Cognitive and affective processes in SEARCH.

SEARCH has made a conscious decision to be interdisciplinary in its content. The several disciplines usually associated with social studies—history, geography, economics, political science, anthropology, sociology, and psychology—have to be interrelated in some way if their conceptual organization is to be made available to the student. SEARCH has developed five *functions* to do this task. These five psychosocial functions are the recurring themes of social existence and, at the same time, are both integrating factors and advanced organizers of content. Figure 2 shows how the SEARCH functions are related to general social themes in the world order and to various disciplines of knowledge from which their content can be derived. It should be noted that there is no mutually exclusive relationship between a SEARCH function and the specific disciplines. Specific concepts may appear in various functions' materials but be viewed differently because of the underlying theme served by that function. The interrelated concerns of social existence do not obliterate the unique focus of each of the several functions.

The specific units of study in SEARCH are built around the five psychosocial functions. The content chart of Level A units shows how the material is being developed for the 5- to 7-year-old.

The SEARCH functions, in the column on the left, are expressed in personal terms in Level A material. Two units of study in each function have been selected for each stage, or a year's program of SEARCH. Thus, 10 SEARCH units are considered, on the average, to be a year's program of social education. The average child completes a SEARCH unit in about 4½ hours of classroom activity. Let us look at the units of Stage I to get some feeling for what the kindergartner's experience is in SEARCH.

FUNCTIONS AS ADVANCED ORGANIZERS OF CONTENT		
SEARCH FUNCTIONS	GENERAL THEME	RELATED DISCIPLINES
SELF-REALIZING	Personality	Psychology, Sociology, Anthropology
GOVERNING	Order	Political Science, Ethics, Law
PRODUCING AND CONSUMING GOODS AND SERVICES	Value	Economics, Sociology
UTILIZING ENVIRONMENTS	Cosmos	Geography, Political Science, Economics
INTERPRETING AND GENERATING IDEAS AND EVENTS	Culture	History, Anthropology, Religion, Aesthetics, Psychology

FIGURE 2. The organization of content in SEARCH.

SCOPE AND SEQUENCE OF SEARCH UNITS FOR GRADES K, 1 AND 2

LEVEL A

FUNCTION	STAGE I	STAGE II	STAGE III
SELF-REALIZING (S) Personal Characteristics	(1) I HAVE A BODY (2) I HAVE AN APPEARANCE	(3) I HAVE SENSES (4) I HAVE FEELINGS	(5) I HAVE AN IDENTITY (6) I HAVE A FAMILY
GOVERNING (G) Personal Responsibilities	(1) I CARE FOR MYSELF (2) I CARE FOR MY HOME	(3) I CARE FOR MY CLASSROOM (4) I CARE FOR MY DOG	(5) I FOLLOW RULES (6) I FOLLOW LAWS AND CUSTOMS
PRODUCING AND CONSUMING (P) Personal Economy	(1) I USE MY DAY TO DO THINGS (2) I PRODUCE AND CONSUME	(3) I PRODUCE SERVICES (4) I CONSUME OTHER PEOPLE'S GOODS AND SERVICES	(5) I PAY FOR THINGS (6) I SHOP IN A MARKETPLACE
UTILIZING ENVIRONMENTS (U) Personal Ecology	(1) I HAVE SURROUNDINGS (2) I TRAVEL IN MY SURROUNDINGS	(3) I MEET PEOPLE IN MY SURROUNDINGS (4) I MAP MY SURROUNDINGS	(5) I MAKE MAPS OF MY SURROUNDINGS (6) I USE TOOLS IN MY SURROUNDINGS
INTERPRETING AND GENERATING (I) Personal Awareness And Achievement	(1) I GROW AND CHANGE (2) I SEE THE SEASONS CHANGE	(3) I KNOW SPECIAL DAYS (4) I KNOW SPECIAL PLACES	(5) I KNOW SPECIAL TIMES (6) I KNOW SPECIAL PEOPLE

© Research for Better Schools, Inc., 1975

FIGURE 3. Unit content in primary grades.

The first function developed in SEARCH is "Self-Realizing." "Self-Realizing" or S Units seek to build an understanding of the interactive elements of identity and personality in social organization. They seek to make the child more aware of himself within the larger community. There are specific concepts in every SEARCH unit, each linked with a student objective. These concepts are often drawn from disciplines such as psychology, sociology, or anthropology. But one should remember that these must be seen as the student sees them and can relate to them. So Unit S1 is "I Have a Body," and S2 is "I Have an Appearance," both under the S or "Self-Realizing" function at Level A, "Personal Characteristics."

The second function in SEARCH is "Governing," and it seeks to bring about the recognition and development of the skills and concepts leading toward orderly social interaction. The discipline of political science and related fields such as ethics or law underlie this content organizer. There is a great deal of interest, in the post-Watergate world, in the workings and importance of the law. SEARCH begins the awareness of responsibility from the very basic notion of taking care of oneself as in Unit G1, "I Care for Myself." Keeping both fantasy and reality in the Level A child's world, SEARCH introduces both human and animal characters in the story sequences. Unit G1, "I Care for Myself," stars Mr. Sam Safety and Ms. Debby Dare. In G2, "I Care for My Home," an industrious beaver named Billy tells the story. Level A units are named from the child's point of view; thus all the A units begin with *I*. At Level B, the unit names start with *We*.

The third SEARCH function has to do with "Producing and Consuming," obviously introducing the child to basic economic dimensions and to the world of work. In Unit P1, "I Use My Day to Do Things," Level A children are introduced to the use of time as a valued commodity. The main character is an American Indian named Stanley Crow. This is followed by P2, "I Produce and Consume," a unit in which two young girls named Patty Production and Connie Consumption explain the rudiments of basic economic life and exchange to the students.

Only the Stage I or kindergarten units of Level A have been reviewed here. It is suggested that the units be kept in sequence—that is, 1 should be taught before 2—but *any* of the functions could be studied at any time.

The fourth function, U, is for "Utilizing Environments," those materials in SEARCH that stress ecological and geographical concepts. The main SEARCH character in Unit U1, "I Have Surroundings," is Greta Mae Grasshopper, who introduces to children the basic aspects of the environment around them. Greta Mae is followed by two other SEARCH characters off to learn about various forms of transportation in Unit U2, "I Travel in My Surroundings." These characters are Manuel Ramirez and Charlotte Bronowski. The reader can see that there is more than a *Sesame Street* interest in character generation in SEARCH. Ethnic variety and concerns about racial or sexual bias are necessary elements of a social studies program today: these are imbedded in SEARCH materials and characters, even for kindergarten students.

The fifth and last SEARCH Function is "Interpreting and Generating Ideas and Events," the I Units. These are the cultural units of SEARCH, stemming from history, anthropology, and psychology and concentrating on man's creative achievements. In Unit 1, the main character is an 11-year-old girl, Penelope Jones, who with her time machine tells about "I Grow and Change." Penelope introduces the concepts of time and growth to kindergarteners by comparing herself with her 6-year-old sister. And finally, there is one of SEARCH's favorite characters, Owlice the Owl, in Unit I2, "I See the Seasons Change." I Units introduce the concept of time to students much as U Units introduce the concept of space. These are two important social studies concepts, as well as basic Piagetian building blocks.

SEARCH has been developed as a multimedia program. The child's perceptual needs demand something graphic and stimulating, but we believe that material must come alive for conceptual reasons, too. The manipulative quality of operating on those things that one studies has brought puzzles and games into SEARCH instruction, as well as traditional materials of the primary classroom: paints, clay, crayons, scissors, and paste. Teachers in our training program are encouraged to use multimedia to extend the ideas in the basic content. These materials are also actually employed in our instruction.

There is also the concern that SEARCH serve individualized needs. If the program was to be useful to various students at differing times and to be available at the student's optimum rate, it was necessary to develop an instructional plan for all units of SEARCH.

The SEARCH flowchart of the sequence of instructional events in every unit is called the SEARCH Map. It is one of the first things taught to kindergarten children and they are instructed, without having to read words, to follow the symbols on the instruction chart.

The first thing that happens in a SEARCH unit is that the child is diagnostically tested for the unit, hence the *UD* diamond on the left for "Unit Diagnostic." *O* stands for "Orientation," the circle, and is mainly a motivational or introductory group session, followed by the three main instructional phases of the unit: *E* for "Encounter," *R* for "Research," and *A* for "Action." There are double ERA activities in SEARCH because we premise a choice on the

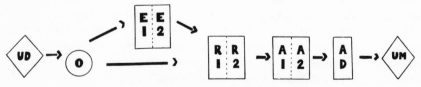

FIGURE 4. The SEARCH map.

student's part between fairly equivalent kinds of lessons. The difference in E activities one and two in Level A units is in alternative media, such as using a book instead of a slide tape presentation. Action is divided, too, between Production and Demonstration, which will be discussed later. Finally, the child is tested again to find out what he has accomplished in the unit and to compare his performance to his record before instruction. In the field test of SEARCH, these tests are used with a control classroom to see how comparable students perform on the instruments without any actual instruction in SEARCH.

Once a child has selected his unit of study—and the teacher determines what units are available—the very first thing he must do is to take a test to find out what he knows about that unit. He therefore takes a Unit Diagnostic. There are three subtests in a Unit Diagnostic. The first test examines the child in terms of his fluency in language, which is an evocative measure. That means the child must show that he has the necessary language for understanding the unit available to him; he does so by performance. The language test of the Unit Diagnostic requires individual administration, and it must be given first so as not to contaminate the second test. The teacher records the student's language responses and limits his or her own intervention or probing during the examination.

The second subtest of the Unit Diagnostic is an Image Test. SEARCH maintains that the child must learn the appropriate imagery of the particular content of a unit in order to work productively with the unit. Therefore, a pretest is given to find out what the child *can show* that he can do with respect to the imagery. Performance is sometimes the test, but more often it is a written choice. Since language must be used to convey our requests to the child, that test is given first, to see that we do not teach with the test itself.

The Language and Image Tests are really pretests for SEARCH Encounter activities, which seek to teach the nessary language and imagery for completing the unit. The third subtest, Research, strives to examine the child in terms of the more manipulative processes of a research activity. The child might be asked to use Encounter information to work out a particular problem. The Image and Research subtests are usually organized to be small-group or individual tests, and the child most often responds to them in a written manner.

Following the Unit Diagnostic on the SEARCH Map is the Orientation session, the circle, which is primarily a motivational lesson for the student. It strives to introduce the child to the unit. The teacher uses material in a larger group setting and the group is composed of children starting a unit that they have just commonly selected. In orientation, a particular piece of motivating material—a poster or a picture—might spur discussion. Language exchange is important, and the child has a chance to express what he knows about the topic before instruction begins.

There is no reading in Level A SEARCH materials. The first- or second-grade nonreader in social studies is not penalized because he cannot read at grade level.

Cassette tapes and graphics are used to carry information to the student. Teachers have often been seen to relate SEARCH materials to their language programs, and they provide key words and ideas in a literal way. This kind of relationship is a natural one to build in Orientation. It often helps us to see what frame of reference the child brings to our program.

After Orientation, the child either goes on to the Encounter or Research activities as his first instructional event. This is determined by the results of the Unit Diagnostic. If the child shows strong enough ability in the Language and Image subtests, he can skip Encounter and go directly to Research. But if his Language and/or Image work needs further development, he studies the Encounter materials.

Encounter activities usually mean working alone and using a tape with graphics or manipulative material. Sometimes a student uses headsets in Encounter so that he can concentrate on the image and language task. We have to make sure the child knows what we are talking about visually and linguistically before going on to the next place on the SEARCH Map, "Research." In both Encounter and Research activities the child has a choice between two equivalent lessons. As mentioned earlier, in Level A units only the media differ in these activities. In the first classroom tryout, large class groups elected to complete activities R1 or R2. When the fully individualized system is implemented, this choice will just be part of the individual student's sequence through the SEARCH Map.

Research activities strive to apply the Encounter concepts in relatively closed problem situations, to make the child apply the information in his quest for a resolution to the problem. Games or puzzles are very common in Research tasks, and they facilitate making the child operate on objects as he thinks about the concepts in question. Research usually involves a partner relationship in the game or puzzle, and the children are consciously encouraged to share and talk about their tasks. Research is also self-correcting: if your puzzle does not work or your game does not have a winner you may not have done the task correctly. In Level A materials, many of the classic card games of preoperations are used: War, Fish, Old Maid. Simplified Monopoly is found to be effective with the 5- to 7-year old. The most important aspect of the Research activity is the child's working with materials as he resolves the problem—grouping, sorting, comparing, contrasting—preferably with every sense that can be employed. Obviously, the more cognitively active we can make the child in his completion of the Research task, the better our chances to influence his mental structure about the problem.

The third major instructional phase of SEARCH is the Action activity. There are actually two subdivisions of Action, "Production" and "Demonstration." In general, Action aims at the child's applying SEARCH's ideas and concepts to *his* world, to the social reality that the child knows and lives. There are two activities that produce something from which he can choose. Again, the choice is made on the basis of alternate media. After producing a picture or a diorama or a clay model, the child demonstrates his application to his peers and talks about it. Then they share their products and compare their several views of the assigned task.

Action Production first requires some planning of what the child has decided to do. Some children work alone here, some work with friends; that is their choice or the teacher's decision. The novelty of media challenges the child to represent the concepts he has studied in ways that relate to what he knows in his world. Piaget might suggest that every child should reinvent the social phenomena he is studying. That is not a terribly practical goal in some learning situations. In SEARCH, we maintain that at least we can have him *reconstruct* the phenomena. A first-grader's first map of his own home may be an appropriate Action product of reconstruction.

The second Action activity is one of demonstrating, in a large group, what the child has learned or made. Action Demonstration is the chance to perform knowledge in a larger social unit, as in having children act out the actual pieces of furniture on their home or school map. One of our outside evaluators suggested that this activity be moved up to the Orientation session because the motivating influence was so effective. This will be considered in our revision of that particular unit.

The final activity on the SEARCH Map is the Unit Measure, the posttest that examines what has been gained in the unit. The three subtests are repeated, except where Encounter Image and Language were judged competent earlier. Students who showed initial competence do not require retesting. Where deficiencies in either Encounter or Research are found, the student can be recycled to the alternate activity, R2 if he has done R1, to help him work further on that particular aspect of the learning.

There are many difficulties in the gathering of information in a developmental classroom. A great deal goes on and it takes several staff people to monitor it adequately. A rather extensive evaluation plan has been devised that will not be elaborated upon here. Rather, let us close with just a reminder of our main objectives in SEARCH:

1. Has the content of social studies been represented so that it is meaningful to the child and so that he can use it?
2. Has the material been developed so that it is appropriate in terms of the processes the child must use to work out the basic social studies concepts?
3. Has an instructional system been developed that organizes the material into an effective program for the individual to follow, with the options and provisions he needs?

If so, then we have a basic social education program that is worthy of being called Piagetian.

To return to the criteria of curriculum development in the first part of this paper, some very general conclusions might be stated about applying Piagetian theory to a social studies curriculum.

First, conceptual knowledge of social studies is important to basic learning but moreso in interdisciplinary ways than as a strict discipline of knowledge. Expression of the concepts must always be paralleled to the child's cognitive organization and the ways he perceives the material conveying these concepts.

Second, the child's learning processes, both cognitive and affective or social, must be integrated with the stages of development that the students in a program currently manifest. There is more to find out in this area—particularly about students in special education or about students with any learning disability—than curriculum developers realize. For example, problems of imagery and language must be tackled. We must find out more about bilingualism and socialization in the schools, as well.

Third, the role of multimedia is a very important area to tackle in curriculum development. It has been found that in K–3 classrooms, it is "the stuff" that students and teachers really want. A real challenge is how to make the manipulative, graphic, and audio material best relate to the cognitive processes and stages, so that the student operates most freely.

Fourth, it has been found that the management plan is about as good as the teacher education program, and that needs to be developed with the teacher's developmental level and attitude about about teaching as a basic consideration. We would like to see different ways of developing teachers' expertise related to SEARCH—and to Piagetian theory—but that goal is far outside our current work scope.

Last, in terms of evaluation, much more extensive data are needed. SEARCH is made in a craft workshop. No matter how good a population the elementary school we use affords our evaluation staff, a much broader-based and larger N is needed if we are to say that any results are valid. It was said that developing a Piaget-based curriculum is an extensive task and a complex one; we would not want to be discouraging, for it is both challenging and rewarding.

ACKNOWLEDGMENT

Originally presented at a conference on the application of Piaget to Curriculum for Exceptional Children (December 1975) and published here with the permission of the Texas Education Agency and Research for Better Schools, Inc.

References

Bruner, J. *The process of education*. New York: Vintage Books, 1960.
Castle, E. B. *Ancient education and today*. Middlesex, England: Penguin, 1964.
Dewey, J. *Experience and education*. London: Collier-Macmillan, 1938.
Dewey, J. *Democracy and education*. New York: Macmillan, 1964.

Duckworth, E. Piaget rediscovered. In R. E. Ripple & V. N. Rockcastle (Eds.), *Piaget rediscovered*. Ithaca, N.Y.: Cornell University Press, 1964.

Elkind, D. Piaget and British primary education. *Educational Psychologist*, 1974, *2*(1), 1–10.

Hunt, J. McV. *Intelligence and experience*. New York: Ronald Press, 1961.

Overton, W. F. Piaget's theory of intellectual development and progressive education. In *A new look at progressive education*. Washington, D.C.: Association for Supervision and Curriculum Development, 1972.

Piaget, J. Development and learning. In R. E. Ripple & V. N. Rockcastle (Eds.), *Piaget rediscovered*. Ithaca, N.Y.: Cornell University Press, 1964.

Piaget, J. *The moral judgment of the child*. New York: The Free Press, 1965.

Piaget, J. *Six psychological studies*. New York: Random House, 1967.

Piaget, J. *Main trends in inter-disciplinary research*. New York: Harper Torchbooks, 1970. (*a*)

Piaget, J. *Structuralism*. New York: Basic Books, 1970. (*b*)

Piaget, J. *To understand is to invent*. New York: Grossman Publishers, 1973.

Piaget, J. *Le role de l'action dans la formation de la pensée*. Philadelphia: The Jean Piaget Society, 1976.

Piaget, J., & Inhelder, B. [*The Psychology of the Child*] (H. Weaver, trans.). New York: Basic Books, 1969.

Presseisen, B. Z. *Piaget's conception of structure: Implications for curriculum*. Unpublished doctoral dissertation, Temple University, Philadelphia, 1971.

Spencer, H. *Education: Intellectual, moral and physical*. Patterson, N.J.: Littlefield, Adams, 1963.

CHAPTER 13

The Application of Piagetian Learning Theory to a Science Curriculum Project

Marilyn H. Appel

Medical College of Pennsylvania, Philadelphia, Pennsylvania

The purpose of this paper is to discuss the application of Piagetian theory to the development of an individualized science program. From this seemingly simple sentence emerge several very complex issues: the nature of science, the nature of science teaching, the nature of individualization, the process of curriculum development, and the nature of Piagetian theory. It is possible in this discussion merely to touch upon these issues and to show how an attempt to resolve the problems has resulted in a Personalized Approach to Science Education (PASE), a K–8 science program based on the developmental theory of Jean Piaget.

In order to provide a framework for a common understanding of efforts in the development of the science curriculum over the past 50 years, Merrill (1971) described three stages in the evolution of science programs. Stage I may be described briefly as fact-centered: characterized by textbooks and teacher lecture/demonstration methods. Stage II has a process-structure focus. This stage is discussed in detail in a later section of this paper. Stage III is difficult to describe, for we are just beginning to enter this stage. In an attempt to offer some parameters for this stage, Merrill suggested that the science curricula of Stage III will be individualized in terms of instruction and interdisciplinary in terms of science content.

Most of us are familiar with Stage I; it is the way many of us learned science. We had textbooks; we read each chapter carefully and answered the questions at the end of each chapter; and if we felt so inclined, we did "extra credit" reports. We had exams regularly, and to study for them we memorized the bits and pieces of information contained in the text. But science educators, along with the American people, were shaken to their roots when the Russians achieved a successful space mission before we did. Suddenly, the public focused its attention on the ways in which science was taught, and the federal government poured funds into programs to improve science education.

This focus on science education over the past 20 years (since Sputnik) has resulted in a number of science programs designed for use by elementary and secondary school children. These programs vary in content, format, teaching strategy, and price. Many programs retain the traditional textbook, the traditional content, and the traditional teacher-oriented approach to instruction. Some have been updated by the addition of a chapter on space travel, computer technology, environmental science, or other "modern" subjects. Many programs take a "new" approach by including some of the more recent advances in scientific knowledge; others incorporate teaching strategies that psychological and educational research have indicated as promising. The latter programs tend to be characterized by the use of equipment kits, stressing the manipulation of concrete materials, the "inquiry" method, and/or the "discovery" approach.

With aid provided by various federal agencies, many new elementary science programs have emerged, which characterize Stage II in the evolution of science instruction. The most notable survivors are "Science—A Process Approach" (SAPA), the "Elementary Science Study" (ESS), and the "Science Curriculum Improvement Study" (SCIS). A discussion of science curricula would not be complete without some comparison of each of these programs, for each has a different philosophical orientation and a different psychological base.

The "Elementary Science Study" (ESS) may be described as a nonsequenced, activity-oriented program developed primarily to provide children with stimuli to explore natural phenomena and to help children develop favorable attitudes toward science (Rogers & Voelker, 1970). ESS units are organized around natural phenomena that have been shown to be of interest to children. Major emphasis is placed upon getting children involved in exploring, not necessarily in order to learn specific concepts in science but rather to encourage them to ask questions and to find their own answers.

The AAAS sponsored program, entitled "Science—A Process Approach" (SAPA), takes off in quite a different direction. In the foreword to the teachers' guide, SAPA is described as emphasizing the development of competence in "skills basic to further learning" (SAPA, 1965). Each of the processes within the program is hierarchically arranged, and behavioral objectives are carefully defined. The processes have become very familiar; they include, among others: observing, recognizing and using number relations, measuring, recognizing and using space—time relations, classifying, communicating, inferring, and predicting.

The third major survivor of the elementary science reform movement of the sixties is the "Science Curriculum Improvement Study" (SCIS), established in 1962 by Robert Karplus, a professor of theoretical physics at the University of California, Berkeley. The major emphasis in ESS is on the exploration of natural phenomena, and the major emphasis in SAPA is on the acquisition of the basic processes of science. The SCIS program is said to stress "the concepts and phenomena, with process learnings an implicit by-product of the children's experimentation, discussion, and analyses" (Karplus & Thier, 1967, p. 8). SCIS has also been described as a laboratory-centered program built around the major goals of understanding science principles, developing inquiry skills, and developing favorable attitudes toward science (Thomson & Voelker, 1970). In order to produce a science program to help develop children's thinking and inquiry skills, the authors of SCIS believe that the two most significant factors that must be attended to are provision for "active physical and mental exploration of reality, and social interaction with parents, teachers, and peers." For those familiar with Piagetian developmental theory, these notions are not new, and indeed, the authors of SCIS were greatly influenced by Piaget. Throughout the program, they attempted to adhere to Piaget's basic notions concerning cognitive development.

Further evidence of the Piagetian influence may be found in what SCIS terms the "instructional cycle" built into the program. Briefly, the cycle is built on three phases, which are entitled "Exploration," "Invention," and "Discovery." In the exploration phase, children are permitted to "act on" the objects in any way they wish. The teacher then "invents" the terminology in the second phase. In the third part of the instructional cycle, the discovery phase, children apply the knowledge gained in exploration and invention to new situations. The point is made that children explore natural phenomena that are "different" from the ones they are familiar with, so that they will have operational meaning. Otherwise, children would merely be learning new names for familiar experiences (Karplus & Thier, 1967, pp. 37–42).

In the discussion thus far, an attempt has been made to provide the reader with some background in terms of where science was (Stage I) and where science is today (Stage II). Stage II was described in terms of the three major science programs, which have, in fact, changed science teaching on the elementary level for a good proportion of schoolchildren. Although each program stems from a different philosophical base—ESS emphasizing natural phenomena, SAPA emphasizing the processes of science, and SCIS emphasizing the conceptual structure of science—they are all similar in that they stress "hands-on" activities. The impetus for this stress on the hands-on nature of these newer programs was due in large measure to the research on learning performed by Piaget and his collaborators in Geneva. The next portion of the discussion focuses directly on Piaget's notions about science teaching and on the application of Piagetian theory to an individualized program in science for the elementary school. This individualized program, based on Piagetian theory, will hopefully be the harbinger for Stage III in the evolution of science programs.

In describing a curriculum development effort, one might focus on at least three elements of a program: the goals of a program, the science content used in the attempt to achieve these goals, and the instructional strategies consistent not only with the goals but also with the content that is to be learned. One may view these three elements in terms of a very simple model (Figure 1): an equilateral triangle with the term *goals* at the vertex angle, *content* at one of the base angles, and *instructional strategies* at the other base angle. One may superimpose Piagetian theory on this model, determine what Piaget has to say about each of these elements, and then apply the design to the development of a science curriculum.

First, let us look at what might be the goals of science instruction. The most popular goal of science teaching to emerge from the curriculum reform movement of the sixties is termed *scientific literacy*. Scientific literacy has been defined in a number of ways, but perhaps it is more easily understood by means of the following explanation. The fact that Russia had won the first round in the effort to explore outer space had shown the American public that for the most part, we had not been prepared to cope with new and unexpected findings. In other words, we were not scientifically literate citizens. Our legislators had not made the judgments that would have allowed us to reach outer space first. The public felt that the problem was the result of an educational deficiency, particularly in the area of science. The problem could therefore be resolved if the curriculum were to provide students with knowledge and experiences so that they might understand, at least to some degree, the scientific work being done by others, even if they themselves did not become scientists. Scientific literacy has also been defined as the ability to look at a situation from the "scientific point of view" or as a "functional understanding of natural phenomena" (Karplus & Thier, 1967, p. 26). Scientifically literate adults would therefore be able to understand to some degree the problems that scientists face in trying to

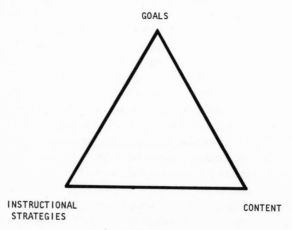

FIGURE 1.

solve the problems of energy and the environment, to evaluate alternatives on the basis of available data, and to make judgments concerning proposed legislation based upon an intelligent appraisal of the specific situation and its long-term ramifications. Piaget has also argued strongly for scientific literacy. He has stated specifically that the major emphasis in science instruction should be the "understanding of certain basic phenomena through the combination of deductive reasoning and the data of experience" (Piaget, 1973, p. 21). Thus, Piaget's notions concerning the major goal of science instruction would appear to be consistent with previous definitions of scientific literacy. He has included not only the knowledge but also the scientific viewpoint.

The developer of a Stage III science program must make certain decisions concerning the elements of the program. One of the decisions would have to be in terms of program goals. There is no doubt that there are any number of goals one might attempt to achieve through science instruction; however, those goals that are chosen reflect the biases, the knowledge, and the value orientation of the developer and are therefore based upon selected criteria. If the criteria were determined by a taking into account of our present knowledge of Stage II science instruction, as well as the teachings of Piaget, there is no question that one of the major thrusts of any Stage III science program would be toward helping children to become scientifically literate adults.

According to the triangular model described previously (Figure 1), once the goal(s) has been chosen, what must now be determined is *what* to teach (content) and *how* to teach it (instructional strategies). It would be foolish, indeed, to assume that there are no alternatives; however, again, the knowledge we have gained from past efforts and the teachings of Piaget may be useful in helping us determine the most appropriate content and instructional strategies.

The present state of knowledge in the area of science is fairly overwhelming. Having children attempt to learn only about the major developments of the past 10 years would provide them with superficial knowledge and a superficial understanding at best. One of the outcomes of the curriculum reform movement of the sixties was the realization that we could not "cover" everything. We could not continue to add chapters to the biology text or to add courses like biochemistry or ecology to the already overloaded rosters of the elementary or secondary school child.

Zaccharias was one of the first developers to attempt to change the focus of the traditional science content. Within the program for which he was responsible, the Physical Science Study Commission (PSSC), a major effort was made to restructure the content of the discipline by reducing the emphasis on facts and placing the emphasis instead on a broader conceptual base. This became the most recognizable characteristic of Stage II science programs: the stress on the structure of the discipline. Both scientists and educators attempted to define the major concepts of science in an effort to determine what content was most appropriate for children to learn. Needless to say, there were almost as many structures to a discipline as there were scientists. However, out of their efforts came the realization that science has not only a substantive structure or structures but a syntactical structure as well (Schwab, 1964, pp. 9–11). In other words, there were broad conceptual schemes that could be defined in a variety of ways, and there was also a methodology to science. In Stage I, this methodology was called the scientific method, and we memorized the steps. In Stage II, the scientific processes were implicit or, as in the case of SAPA, explicit. In the SAPA program, the processes became the content. There is no necessity to belabor the issue. Briefly, we have learned from Stage II that the content of science programs would focus on both structure and process.

Piaget is often reluctant to express his ideas concerning education, but in the case of the content of science instruction, Piaget is very explicit. He points out that: "it is obvious that if the teaching of the sciences is to adapt to the conditions of scientific progress and form creative rather than imitative minds, it should stress structuralism" (Piaget, 1973, p. 28). Piaget goes on to describe structuralism in science for both the physical and the biological sciences as follows: "physical structuralism with its indefinite extension of the attributes of the systems to explanatory models representing the intersection of the objects themselves; biological structuralism with its problems of equilibration or self-regulation" (Piaget, 1973, p. 29). For Piaget, a structuralist approach to choosing the content of science is insufficient for learning. It is also necessary to cultivate the "experimental spirit" (Piaget, 1973). The experimental spirit is essentially providing enough flexibility within the program to allow children to explore and experiment on their own terms, so that they may gain experience and skill in the processes of science.

Thus, Piaget, as well as the Stage II scientists and educators, argues for a process–structure focus for science instruction. In addition, it should be pointed out that for Piaget, process and structure are not separate issues but are interrelated and interacting.

In developing a science program, it is not only necessary to know what to teach, but much consideration must be given to the order in which this content is taught and the level or quality of understanding that is desired. The guiding principle that emerges from Piaget's theory in regard to this aspect of curriculum design is the concept of stage (Inhelder, 1953). According to Piaget, cognitive development is sequential. Each child may develop at his own individual rate, yet all children will pass through a regular sequence of stages in the developmental process, each stage characterized by the nature of the mental operations involved.

To the reader of Piagetian theory, the stages of cognitive development are quite familiar. They have been described in the literature extensively and have been found, through hundreds of research efforts both here and abroad, to be a valid description of the development of thinking. The important issue here, however, is not the stages *per se* but how the knowledge of these stages can be helpful in determing the content hierarchy for science instruction for school-age children.

The first stage of cognitive development, occurring in the first 2 years of a child's life, is characterized by adaptation and the establishment of the concept of object permanence. Object permanence or constancy is essential for later learning. It allows the child to differentiate between himself and the reality that exists externally. Another characteristic of this first stage is the development of a primitive notion of causality and the discovery, through trial-and-error experimentation, that specific actions produce specific results. Furthermore, the child has learned to think symbolically, retaining mental images beyond his immediate perception and anticipating events as well as the results of his actions. The child then enters the preoperational period, characterized by increasing perceptual development, in which he learns to use symbolic substitutes, such as language and mental imagery, for the sensorimotor activities of the previous stage. The behaviors characteristic of the preoperational period are symbolic game-playing and imitation. Response patterns of children during this stage are perceptually centered, and the child believes what he sees rather than what he knows (Pulaski, 1971).

It is not until the child's thought can operate independently of what he sees physically that he enters the period of concrete operations, or the third stage in Piaget's developmental model. Piaget's descriptions of this period of concrete operations have stimulated a great deal of research and are most important to understand in terms of curriculum development. The major idea here is that the child in this stage can now think logically about things he sees and need no longer accept superficial appearances. However, these thought processes are influenced by concrete experiences and direct action. It is the dynamic interaction of the child's actions and the thought processes that are brought to bear on these experiences that help the child to develop and establish the concepts of conservation during this period.

The child is not yet able to deal with abstractions, but as he gains experiences in the concrete stage that reinforce the logical operations and permit him to begin to predict on the basis of this data of experience, he enters the stage of formal operations, or the fourth stage of cognitive development as described by Piaget. The emerging adolescent begins to uncover the general laws and to formulate representational models that can explain his observations.

It is clear that, for Piaget, development is consistent, continuous, and sequential, each stage evolving out of the previous one and contributing to the next. The essence of development is interaction, and the child is an active explorer and discoverer, adjusting to what he perceives and modifying it to meet his needs. The fundamental processes repeat themselves at every stage and within every individual, but a child responds to an event according to his current stage of cognitive development. Piaget explains it this way: "the child must pass through a certain number of stages characterized by ideas which will later be judged erroneous but which appear necessary in order to reach the final correct solution" (Piaget, 1973, p. 21).

The implications of the above statement are far-reaching, not only in terms of curriculum development but also in terms of teacher training. The problems of teacher training are in a subsequent section of this paper.

Thus far, in terms of the triangular model of curriculum design, we have discussed a possible long-range goal and the content of a science program that would be consistent with this goal. In attempts to describe the Piagetian framework and the ways in which it can be related to curriculum design, it becomes clear that in order to help children to become scientifically literate, the curriculum must be structured in such a way as to provide for the development of children's thinking. It is not possible to be scientifically literate, according to the previous definition, at the level of preoperational thought, or even at the level of concrete operations. In order to understand natural phenomena to the degree where judgments can be made concerning the proposed actions of the scientific community, or of the legislature, one should be functioning at the level of formal operations. Thus, not only has Piaget provided us with a basis for choosing science content and the sequencing of it, but also from his theory has evolved another long-range goal: encouraging the development of formal operational thought.

Perhaps it is tautologous to mention cognitive development as a goal, for scientific literacy and formal operational thinking are synergetic: one cannot develop functional understanding of the basic scientific phenomena without the full development of inferential or formal thought processes. It is interesting to note that Piaget and Inhelder point out very clearly the convergence between the understanding of the laws of natural science and hypotheticodeductive thinking (Inhelder & Piaget, 1958).

However, teaching the structure of science, or the laws of natural science, or sequencing the content according to what we know about the stages of cognitive development, will not in themselves build inquiring minds. Here, we are examining the third angle of the model for curriculum design: the instructional strategies that would be most appropriate for the goals and content previously described.

Piaget's general prescription is a familiar one: "to know an object, to know an event, is not simply to look at it and make a mental copy or image of it. To know an object is to act upon it" (Piaget, 1964, p. 177). Piaget goes on to speak specifically of science teaching when he states that major emphasis must be placed on the "use of active methods which gave broad scope to the spontaneous research of the child or adolescent and requires that every new truth to be learned, be rediscovered or at least reconstructed by the student, and not simply imparted to him" (Piaget, 1973, p. 15).

These statements have become the basis for the "discovery methods" or "inquiry approaches" used by Stage II science programs. In addition, the production of kits of science materials along with deemphasizing the textbook method came as the result of the teachings of Piaget and, in this country, Jerome Bruner. Every national and local curriculum development effort from the sixties to the present has placed a major emphasis on the hands-on approach to science instruction. Even textbooks offer suggestions for the use of concrete materials. States that in the past have permitted only textbooks are now beginning to accept programs that have teacher's guides, student workbooklets, and science kits. This is one aspect of the impact of learning theory on program development and teaching.

Although this is a step in the right direction, Piaget warns us that:

> acquisition or construction of fundamental ideas provided data which seem decisively in favor of the active methods, and which require a much more radical reform of intellectual learning than many supporters themselves of the active school image. (Piaget, 1973, pp. 9–10)

It is the contention of this author that individualization of instruction is the instructional strategy most appropriate to the promotion of cognitive development and scientific literacy. Piaget confirms this in a number of ways, but he also points out the danger of individualization when it is thought of merely as "isolation" or "independent study."

Piaget not only stresses individual experience in experimentation but also emphasizes the importance of social interactions and discussions in common. The task of the instructional designer, therefore, is to reconcile individualized instructional strategies and social interaction. It is a difficult but not impossible task, provided that individualization is not viewed in its narrowest sense.

At this point the discussion of each aspect of the model for curriculum design has led us to the following conclusions concerning the elements of a Stage III science program:

1. *Goals.* Scientific literacy—cognitive development.
2. *Content.* Process—structure focus (sequence determined by Piaget's stages of cognitive development).
3. *Instruction.* Individualized while providing social interaction.

A science program containing these elements would appear to fit Merrill's description of a Stage III program. What follows is a description of a science program that not only contains the elements described above but also has its roots in Piagetian theory.

The "Personalized Approach to Science Education" (PASE) is an individualized science program for the primary and middle years that offers a field-tested, uniquely designed product that enables the teacher to provide a personalized program for each child. PASE includes personalized training for the teacher, a classroom management system, lesson activity booklets for the pupil, and keyed science materials designed to make personalized science a reality. In addition, PASE offers increased flexibility, for the program can be used by both students and teachers in a variety of ways.

PASE is a program that has brought together advanced thinking in science curriculum, in learning theory, and in instructional design and management systems. It is the goal of this project to provide a sequential and developmental program for the primary and middle years, organized in a system that facilitates a personalized approach to learning. The system enables the learner to develop and experience science concepts and processes in a completely individualized way. Experience in the PASE program not only allows the learner to understand what scientists face when they try to solve difficult problems of energy and the environment, but it enables them, as citizens, to evaluate alternative solutions on the basis of available data. Eventually, children who have experienced the PASE system will be able to make judgments concerning proposed legislation based upon intelligent appraisal of the specific situation and its long-term ramifications.

Figure 2 illustrates the goals of the program.

The PASE program provides opportunities for children to learn scientific concepts in ways consistent with their own levels of cognitive development and individual learning styles. The recommended individualized system aims to promote the child's self-concept and self-management skills, with the recognition that individualized learning does not mean learning in isolation.

The learner sometimes works alone, at other times works within small groups, and at still other times receives instruction from the teacher in a directed or demonstration lesson. The mode of instruction depends upon the activity the

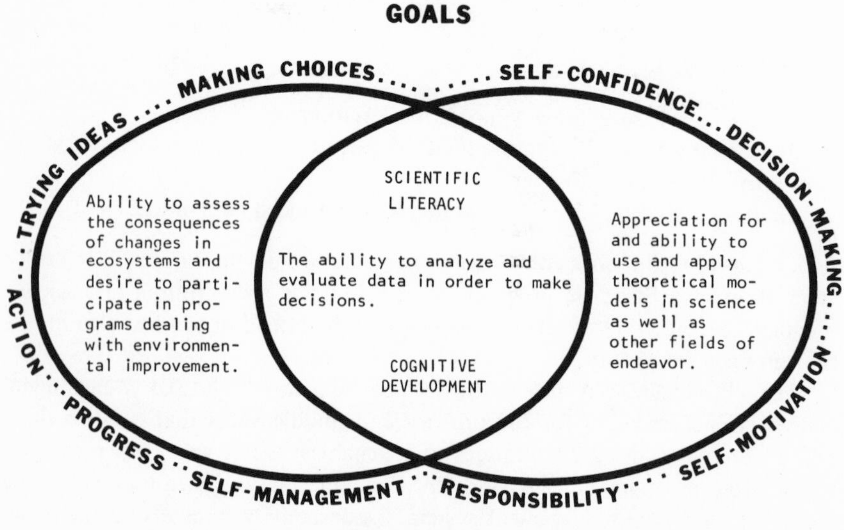

GOALS

FIGURE 2.

child has selected and the concept to be developed. Throughout the program, the learner is offered alternatives for learning involving hands-on activities, recording data, reading, listening to a tape recording, or interacting with peers and/or the teacher.

The variety of ways in which PASE is individualized are described below:

1. Children are placed in the program at a level consistent with their own levels of cognitive development.
2. Children progress at their own rates of speed.
3. Children are evaluated individually by means of a variety of problem-centered activities that they choose to complete.
4. Children choose the lessons they wish to do.
5. Children are rsponsible for picking up and returning all the materials they use.
6. Children use different modes of instruction.
7. Children learn in a variety of social situations.
8. Children keep track of their own progress.

It is expected that science content that has a cognitively logical structure should lead to the desired outcomes described previously. The PASE program develops the concept of "system" in a spiraling fashion from its simplest component—the objects in a system and their attributes—to a more abstract notion of the intersection of a variety of biological and physical systems and their representational models. In the PASE program, the biological and physical sciences are completely integrated.

Figure 3 demonstrates the conceptual framework of PASE along with the appropriate stages of cognitive development and science processes.

A large variety of lessons have been provided to give each child many opportunities to work with and experience a concept in the program. Each child develops an understanding through many experiences with the same concept, using many different activities, instructional media, and instructional techniques. A particular child may do far less, in terms of numbers of lessons or activities, yet gains an understanding of the same concept as the child who may need or want to do many more lessons. The conceptual thrust is thus based upon the acceptance of the individuality of the learner, with many alternatives leading to the same conceptual idea. The paths selected and the amount of time the child utilizes to achieve an understanding of the given concept is a matter of personal choice and teacher guidance.

The variety and the choice built into the PASE program make it necessary to provide the teacher with a way to manage and to keep track of the diversity within a single classroom, so that each child may indeed have a personalized program. The management system has to take into account the children, as individuals, and the materials with which they work. The PASE program provides a management technique through the instructional cycle. Each concept in the program is

CONCEPTUAL FRAMEWORK OF PASE

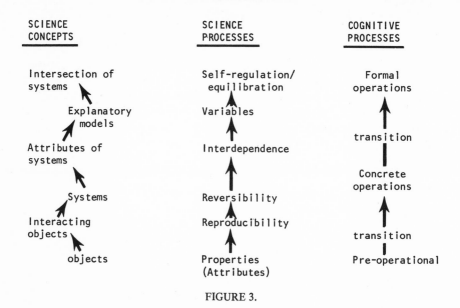

FIGURE 3.

made up of activities that fit into three phases of an instructional cycle. Each child, then, follows the instructional sequence for each of the concepts to be learned at his own level of cognitive functioning.

Upon entering the program at a concept consistent with his level of cognitive development, the child begins with the "exploration" phase of the instructional cycle. He chooses from a variety of exploration lessons according to his own interests and motivation. These preliminary investigations allow the child to become acquainted with the concept to be learned through a variety of concrete, hands-on, open-ended activities. The second phase of the instructional cycle is termed "reflection," in which the child experiences more structured, convergent types of activities based upon a specific concept. Reflection lessons help the child to develop an awareness of scientific phenomena and the language with which to deal with them. The third phase of the instructional cycle is called "investigation," which encompasses divergent, problem-centered activities. Investigation activities are open-ended activities in which a child can apply and extend the knowledge gained in the two previous phases of instruction.

A simple self-management device for each concept in the programs allows the child to keep track of his choices and completed lessons and provides the teacher with the basis for determining where the child is and how he is progressing through the program. A unique feature of the management system is the "self-management" unit for the children new to the program. In this unit, the child learns how to work in the program and the kinds of things for which he is responsible.

Figure 4 shows how a child progresses through the program.

Each unit is accompanied by a set of self-administered pre- and posttests that help the teacher determine the child's need for the unit and/or the need for further work in a particular unit. The management system also includes materials storage, retrieval, and handling. Since the teacher's role is dependent upon continual interactions with the children, it is necessary within a personalized system to direct the teacher's efforts toward the child and to place increased responsibility for care of materials in the hands of the child. For this reason each child is responsible for the acquisition and replacement of the materials as needed.

The hardware of the program is uniquely designed to avoid duplication inherent in other kit programs. This is accomplished through the use of a core kit containing the objects used repeatedly throughout the program to teach several different concepts. Such a kit may serve as a supply center for several teachers. This core kit contains such items as tumblers, vials, terrarium–aquarium containers, bulbs, wires, and other nonconsumables.

Modular kits are also used in conjunction with the core kits and, for the most part, are not used by several teachers at the same time. The modular kits contain the materials used to teach specific subconcepts in the program, for example, food chain–food web and energy transfer.

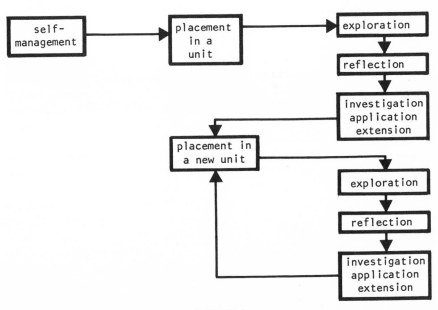

FIGURE 4.

The concepts of the PASE program, while designed to be taught hierarchically, can be taught independently. Thus, a school having a district-designed science curriculum can use those modular kits that teach concepts contained within their own programs.

For each concept in the program, a booklet of lessons is provided. In addition, the lessons are easily identifiable as exploration, reflection, or investigation activities. After placement in a specific concept in the program, the child receives the corresponding booklet of lessons. He then chooses the lessons he wishes to do (beginning with exploration and following the instructional cycle in sequence), removes the chosen lesson from the booklet, gathers the necessary materials, does the experiment, records the results, and places the completed lesson in an individual progress folder. Children progressing through the unit, to reflections and investigations, continue to remove the chosen lessons appropriate to the phase of the instructional cycle and to store completed lessons in the personalized folder as a continuous record of work in that unit. The teacher can pick up an individual child's folder at any time and determine individual progress at a glance.

One of the most important factors heralding the successful implementation of any instructional system is based on how the teacher sees, perceives, and internalizes his or her role within the total framework of the program. Providing a well-organized, realistic, expeditious approach to learning, the program aims to give teachers not only the mind set of success but the skills to ensure it.

In order to adapt to this particular approach to instruction, teachers are provided with a training program that reflects the personalized learning process of PASE. The program has several unique features:

1. It is a separate package.
2. It is self-instructional (i.e., it needs no expert, highly paid consultant to lead expensive workshops).
3. The teacher can choose to work through the program alone or with others in the training.
4. It is self-paced.
5. Teachers experience every aspect of the PASE program that both teacher and student might encounter.

The content of the teacher training package includes the following:

1. Pre- and postassessment activities.
2. The concept of a discussion of personalization.
3. The science content of PASE.
4. Ways to manage a personalized instructional system.
5. The role of the teacher.
6. The use of paraprofessionals when available.
7. The role of the student.

8. Hardware and software: how to set up a personalized learning environment.
9. Follow-up materials: diagnosis of problems before they arise.
10. Care and feeding techniques for living things.

The content and instructional strategies inherent in the teacher training program ensure the successful implementation of the PASE program.

The PASE program, attempting to adhere to the notions of how children learn as proposed by Piaget, has carefully sequenced the science content and has devised the management system necessary to allow teachers to provide for the individual child at his or her level of cognitive development.

ACKNOWLEDGMENT

Originally presented at a conference on the Application of Piaget to Curriculum for Exceptional Children (December 1975) and published here with the permission of the Texas Education Agency.

References

Butts, D. *Teaching science in the elementary school.* New York: The Free Press, 1973.

Capie, W. R. Curriculum reviews: SAPA-II. *Science and Children,* 1975, *12*(4), 28–29.

Inhelder, B. Criteria of stages in mental development. In J. M. Tanner & B. Inhelder (Eds.), *Discussions on child development,* Vol. 1. New York: International University Press, 1953.

Inhelder, B., & Piaget, J. [*The growth of logical thinking from childhood to adolescence: An essay on the construction of formal operational structures*]. (A. Parsons & S. Milgram, trans.). New York: Basic Books, 1958.

Karplus, R., & Thier, H. *A new look at elementary school science.* Chicago: Rand McNally, 1967.

Merrill, R. J. The science curriculum, the science teacher, and NSTA. *The Science Teacher,* 1971, *38*(5), 36–39, 66–67.

Piaget, J. Cognitive development in children: Development and learning. *Journal of Research in Science Teaching,* 1964, *2,* 176–186.

Piaget, J. *To understand is to invent: The future of education.* New York: Grossman, 1973.

Pulaski, M. *Understanding Piaget.* New York: Harper & Row, 1971.

Rogers, R. E., & Voelker, A. M. Programs for improving science instruction in the elementary school: Part I. ESS. *Science and Children,* 1970, *7*(5), 35–43.

Schwab, J. J. Problems, topics, and issues. In *Education and the structure of knowledge.* Chicago: Rand McNally, 1964.

Science—A Process Approach, Foreword. Washington: AAAS, 1965.

Science teaching in elementary and junior high schools. Reprinted from *Science,* 1961, *133*(3469), 2019–2024.

Thomson, B. S., & Voelker, A. M. Programs for improving science instruction in the elementary school: Part II. SCIS. *Science and Children,* 1970, *7*(8), 29–37.

Index